D0765725

THE
SEAFARERS

THE
SEAFARERS
A Journey
Among Birds

Stephen Rutt

Elliott&Thompson

First published 2019 by
Elliott and Thompson Limited
27 John Street, London WC1N 2BX
www.eandtbooks.com

ISBN: 978-1-78396-427-7

Typesetting by Marie Doherty
Printed in the UK by TJ International Ltd

For M.C.

Contents

Introduction: London and Orkney   1

1   Storm Petrels – Shetland   17
2   Skuas – Shetland   37
3   Auks – Northumberland   59
4   Eiders – Northumberland   83
5   Terns – Northumberland   101
6   Gulls – Newcastle   125
7   Manx Shearwaters – Skomer   149
8   Vagrants – Lundy, Fastnet, Sole and Fitzroy   177
9   Gannets – Orkney   197
10 Fulmars – Orkney   221

Epilogue   251

Acknowledgements   255
Bibliography   259
Notes   267
Index   275

Introduction

London and Orkney

The wind is gale-force and has travelled over nothing but sea since Greenland to greet me here. Early March is not an auspicious time to arrive in the northern isles of Scotland. Standing on the airport tarmac at Kirkwall in Orkney, I feel the coldness of it skimming in along the island coast. I feel the insistence of it. The way it isn't stopping at my new coat, but cuts through nylon, fleece, jeans, skin, bone. My flight is to be on the smallest plane I have ever seen. One propeller on each toy wing: two seats wide, four seats long. It is half full, which I'd later learn was busy for the time. Evidently rush hour is different up here. Flying is, too: I give my name without being asked, offer to show my printed ticket, some ID – none of it needed. We walk over the runway, duck under the wing and clamber in.

Engine rumbles. Propellers flicker. Seat shakes. Propellers spin, strobing in the corner of each eye. The judder – the wave of sickness that accompanies sudden motion. We begin to taxi. I run out of options to turn around. I can't go back. I think this might be the most terrifying moment. And then the plane takes off, curving up into the grey above Kirkwall and then it judders and shakes as it hits the wind. I am wrong. I spend the short flight with my fingers crossed, my heart racing, one eye shut and not daring to look, the other wide open, staring at the spindrift racing from the waves. From above, the sea looks dark and frantic, bracketed by tiny green strips of land, the elongated peninsulas and isthmuses of the strangely shaped islands of Orkney. I see white beaches, wide bays, a gannet. Land stretched and warped and frayed. I see the big rocky coast of the island we are landing at. A speck alone, beyond the rest. I see the airstrip, a brown line in a green field, behind a red fence. And I am baffled at why we are coming in sideways.

I see the strata of the rock approaching. I can't take my eye off the rocks, coming close, closer, then the pilot accelerates – the nose spins and the wheels thump into the grass of North Ronaldsay.

I breathe for what feels like the first time.

Some stories have long roots. The roots of this story stretch back over a decade to a teenage me, standing by a bush, at dusk, with my dad. I had said I wanted to go for a walk and he had taken me to Minsmere, the RSPB's site of ornithological pilgrimage on the Suffolk coast. We were listening to a Cetti's warbler, an explosive drumroll of a song, delivered shyly from the deepest undergrowth. This one jumped into a sapling: scrubby and bare, it couldn't hide the small brown bird. Dad, phlegmatic almost all of the time, dissolved in excitement. It was the first he'd seen in a lifetime of birding. I was swept up in all of it – the deep peace of the reedbed rolling away to the horizon, the mud up the back of my calves, unexpected encounters with small, brown, extraordinary birds. From that moment on, I was guided by birds.

Birds were my awakening to the world outside. Birding teaches you to be aware of subtle distinctions that signify differences.

Whether it was the leg colour or a few millimetres' difference in wing length that enabled me to tell two common warblers apart, or the presence of a wing-bar that revealed it to be extremely rare. Whether I was standing in an overgrazed field, a set-aside field or a meadow rich in life that an owl would soon fly over through the thick light of dusk. Whether the wind in October was coming from the north and my day out would be cold and boring, or whether it was coming from the east and it would be cold and rich in potential. It made me pay attention, not just to these things, but to how and when they change. Whether my first swallow of the year was in March or May – and why. Birding forces you to pay attention to the world as it happens around you and gives you a way of decoding it.

Before I became a birder, I was briefly a fisherman. While sitting behind a rod, fruitlessly waiting, I never thought about global warming, the rise in sea levels, or how the algae in the bay of the lake might be caused by the run-off of unpronounceable agro-chemicals with startling side effects. Fishing taught me futility – that things will probably not go your way. Birding taught me to look at and think about the outside world, to engage with the landscape and all it holds.

There is a gentle art to birding. By which I mean there is no correct way to do it. You can go outside for days or just glance out of a window, notice something, and carry on, your day having become slightly wilder, slightly more interesting than it might otherwise have been. It requires no basic equipment other than your own senses and a desire to notice and to know. Birding makes no demands of you other than these. It is gentle because you can't force it. It is more productive not to, better to slow down to the speed of the landscape and blend with it. It is an art because there is no set route, no magic key to finding or knowing a bird. To recognise one requires a myriad of moment-specific considerations. And much of it can be done by intuition – the application of experience – rather than rules. You never stop learning. It can open you up to things either extraordinarily beautiful or extraordinarily depressing.

Being a teenager enabled me to be obsessed without shame. I absorbed the Collins field guide to the birds of Europe. Then Sibley's field guide to American birds. Then the monographs to specific families of birds, then specific species. I absorbed site guides, built a mental map of the world's birds, read blogs, dissected forums. I found a network of others from across Europe and we spent evenings indoors, online, talking about mornings outdoors. We were captivated by the Scottish islands. I had never been but, from the photos I had seen and the books I had read, I constructed my own mythic version of them: quiet, solitary utopias, places where one could not ignore nature, and if one tried then nature would come and find you. Come and rattle at the windowpanes, or land in your garden, or squat on your car bonnet, until you were forced to pay attention again. A place for the inveterately shy.

It is a fifteen-minute flight from the town of Kirkwall, Orkney, to the outer island of North Ronaldsay. I'd come from London, to an island whose population would fit on the top deck of a double-decker bus. It was a sort of decompression therapy – coupled with an urge to satisfy a consuming passion.

I was obsessed with migrant birds. In love with their freedom, their unconstrained border-crossing ability, their bravery at heading out across sea, powered only by small wings. It seemed to me that birds had the power to express untouchable freedoms. If the world we live in can feel entangling, entrapping; birds can transcend that.

I was here to volunteer at the bird observatory, one of the best places to witness migratory birds in Britain. It is no coincidence that the other places that can make that claim – Fair Isle, Portland, Spurn Point, the entirety of the Norfolk coast – are all on the edges of the British Isles. The edges are the first or last land that a small migrating bird finds on its migration over the sea. Last snack or first sleep. These edges are a place for strong winds and tired wings. When the wind is coming from the Continent in migration season, it eases them our way. Bad weather makes them seek shelter in the unlikeliest of places, and on a good day – for which, read, day of hellish wind and rain – there can be a surreal number of birds in odd places. I saw goldcrests in the drystone walls and ditches, woodcocks behind sheds, wrynecks sheltering in the ruined roofs of dilapidated crofts. It's known as a 'fall', for when you are experiencing one, it feels as if birds are falling out of the sky, their onward migration accidentally halted by the need to seek out any sort of solid ground.

Falls are few and far between. On an island roughly 3 miles long and a mile wide, you learn to find pleasure in what you have, not what you want.

When I walked out the morning after I landed, the wind hadn't abated. I crossed two waterlogged fields to the west coast. The sky was dark with impending rain, the coastal rocks white under spume, spindrift blowing about the air like snowflakes in a gale. The air was thick with salt, glazing the landscape. To this day I don't know how I didn't break an ankle there and then on those hidden rocks, white to the eye and slippery as oil. It was an enforced slowdown – all became deliberate, measured, a two-footed crawl. Shedding city speed, one step at a time, while gulls played in the gale around me, starkly white against the sky, light in the heavy weather, free.

I made it to the ramshackle hide by a collapsed drystone wall just as the rain began. It overlooked a loch, instantly churned up by the deluge, while the ducks fled for the meagre shelter of a small muddy bank. The gulls cleared off. The drumming on the roof sounded like applause. And when it stopped, the wind dropped, the clouds dissipated and the sky turned Mediterranean blue. My phone buzzed. A text from Mark, one of the wardens: 'Welcome to Orkney'.

I squelched over the fields back to the main road, and followed it up the high ground to the top of the only hill on the island (although at 20 metres high, 'hill' is perhaps an exaggeration). I could see scattered crofts, some with a waft of smoke from the chimney, others dilapidated and crumbling. I could see the delicate threadwork of the drystone walls, two sandy beaches and a lighthouse. Fair Isle to the north, Westray to the west, Sanday to the south. True horizons again.

⌣

London is no city for an introvert. Or this introvert at least. It should have been the time of my life. I was twenty-one. I had just graduated with a good degree and fallen into a job immediately. I had moved to the capital and lived with friends. We were young and we were free and we had a taste for good booze and bad food. I felt as if I had achieved. I had no idea what was supposed to come next.

I visit it regularly in my mind, trying to walk my memories back to where the rot set in. The front gate in the thin privet hedge, from which every morning a spider would weave its web at face height and catch my housemates unaware. The rosebuds sealed shut, waiting to burst open in the spring sunshine. The curtains still pulled tight. It is a picture of post-war suburban surface bliss. It could be anywhere in the red-brick sprawl of London along the fast roads to the west. Along the street, ambulances hurtle, lights flashing. Busses squeal, cars rev, a Boeing roars along the Heathrow flight path, a sound that reverberates down the road. No birds sing.

From the outside looking in, there appears to be nothing wrong – if you like that kind of place. Slightly staid maybe, possibly slightly stifling, but no warning signs. This was the landscape I lived in – horizons shrunk to the limits of the street. The sodium-orange-stained night sky, which I watched from my bedroom window, waiting for a single star to appear, or for a fox to slink between the parked cars. I would walk around the local park and see more joggers than animals. Here I once startled a snipe one windy morning walk before work and remember vividly the weirdness of it – a bird of the wilder wetlands, flying off towards a horizon of the London Eye and the Shard. It was a small token. Insufficient fuel to maintain the connection to nature, to the world outside.

I had built a mental dependency around space and quietness, the two things that nature gave me that I required to find my peace. Behind the meagre privacy of that privet hedge, starved of nature, I was short-circuiting. Things began making no sense in slow, slow motion.

I was on the London underground. Central line. Saturday evening. Due to meet up with a friend. Unusually, I had a seat, not that that would help. As the journey progressed from the west to the centre of the city, the carriage filled up. Standing room only became no room only, became people squashing on, regardless. Crowds affect my breathing. Crowds make my chest tighten. And the Underground is an airless place anyway, without the crowds; with my breath catching in the back of my throat, my body tensing, sweat spreading from my temples, down my shoulder blades, my vision blurring, the distance over the shoulders of the people was becoming warped, elastic, lightness flooding into my head. I barged out at the next stop, stumbling onto the platform, gripped with fear. Inexplicable fear. I slunk my way, from side street to side street to the rendezvous, very late, dumb with angst.

I knew this to be irrational. Because I had got the Underground before, because I knew there would be coping mechanisms. But I felt like a taxidermy specimen, pinned and mounted, except I was not dead, and the dull weight of anxiety pinning me alive felt impossible to escape from.

I stopped going outside. I stopped answering my phone. I resented speaking, resented breathing fumes and dust instead of air – a fuel rekindling the asthma in my lungs. I took holidays from work to spend lying in bed or on the sofa feeling nerves trembling down my arms, nerves where they hadn't existed before.

Life became policed by the anxieties in my head. The claustrophobia, the primal fear of other people. Anxiety strung me out, made me feel as if I might never again be the person I was. My landscapes, physical and mental, had shrunk from the East Anglia of my childhood, to west London, to the street, to the house, to the days I couldn't leave my room.

Shyness took over. Shyness has always been a part of me, but in the exhaustion, the feeling of permanent defeat, it colonised me like a virus. All-consuming. It silenced me and made me feel burning shame whenever several sets of eyes turned to me and expected an opinion. Silence is a radical approach to a city, to a culture that never shuts up. It was also, for me, futile.

I lasted eighteen months. The bravest thing I did when I was twenty-two was leave. Being young, single and coming to the end of a tenancy agreement is a freedom either glorious or terrifying, but it was a freedom I was unusually determined to make the most of. It was how I ended up on that plane.

$$\smile$$

Flicking through my diaries from that first month on the island, I note a preponderance of words that I would never use now. Elysium, Valhalla, Nirvana: I had found my paradise beyond earthly realms, although it was really just the earth that I had fallen back in love with. These days were a privilege – building stiles, painting the observatory, rewiring the funnel traps[1] for catching birds, tending to the sheep and exploring. I saw a 98 per cent solar eclipse, the Northern Lights, meteors and a lost goshawk flying around in its own raincloud of redshanks. Shorn of the daily stresses of my London life, the daily unpleasantness that people put up with just because it's London, I was attaching significance to everything. The sunset, the stars, the way the wind always whistles over the walls impertinently. The way the sea can be heard from everywhere, unless muffled by a haar or, on the rarest of days, when no wind correlates with no swell and turns the sea into a rippling, velvet-like surface, shining and stilled, and the waves gently kiss the sand. These days become as precious commodities – to be shared but never exchanged.

I have tried to read Thoreau several times and always failed. But I suppose this was my own version of *Walden*, and deliberate living. We were both surrounded by the wild: him only a mile from town, me connecting to people on Twitter and watching *Match of the Day* in the evenings. I don't think this makes the experience less valid. Life is life, anxiety is anxiety – deal with it how you will. Questions of how to live seem the most essential to me. For seven months I chose to live with nature at the foreground of my daily life – noticing the birds, the first flowerings of the marsh orchids, the darkness of the night sky and the lightness of it in midsummer.

I don't think that nature exists as a cure; not properly anyway, not as a replacement for 2,000 years of medical achievement or changing your lifestyle or whatever you do that works for you. I remembered then, away from London, that down the street I lived on, the roots of the plane trees that flanked the road kicked up the paving slabs. And across from my office, the thin summer smoke of buddleia that colonised the top of an old factory chimney and would wave gently in the breeze. I remembered the thunderstorms I used to stop and watch as they cracked open and cleaned out the night sky, and the way that, when I was inside and wouldn't dare to leave the house, spiders would catch my attention, space-walking across the window frame, kicking threads out with their hind legs and weaving them into webs. Somehow I had lost sight of these small comforts. Perhaps they were never enough.

I was still shy on North Ronaldsay. But it no longer felt discordant, as it did in the city. Place and personality rhymed, in a way that nowhere else had, that nowhere else has. Orkney felt like home.

Although the peace felt as if it would last forever, it didn't. The season got busy. I got exhausted. The novelty of weather wore off and it rained all May – and all June – and the grass didn't grow, my wellies wore through and I spent the season with wet socks, waiting for a fall that never arrived. While I waited, I flicked back to pages in the field guide I hadn't looked at for years. London had isolated me from seabirds. There was no prospect of seeing them and they had faded from my mind, other than as memories from holidays to islands and far coastlines. Orkney rekindled an old love.

It was the first tern out of the grey in mid-May. It was the first storm petrel fluttering like a butterfly between the crashing waves, somehow never quite being washed away. The Manx shearwater of spring and the sooty shearwater of autumn, sweeping the Atlantic on stiff wings, in what looks like one perpetual glide. While I once gazed at their pages in guide books on the other side of the country, I was now living among them. Their cold, wet peripheral exoticism was mine too. I lost my heart to the fulmars, the kittiwakes and the black guillemots. I lost my heart to the seabirds.

To understand the appeal of a seabird, it's necessary to explore what a seabird is, and what it isn't. Most birds migrate, most will cross a sea. They are not seabirds, not any more than a seabird becomes a landbird when it sets up residence on a cliff to breed every summer.

A scientist's definition might focus on how they have feathers covering their auditory canal, to prevent water entering their ears when they dive for food, or to prevent flying with muffled hearing, or – more likely – to minimise the effects of pressure. Another scientist's definition might focus on the Procellariiformes: the order that contains the petrel, shearwater and albatross families. They have a tubenose: a prominent bulging nostril above the bill, an adaptation specific to these families, allowing them to smell food on a sea breeze and expel the salt from their exposure to saltwater. But this would be partial definition. It would not include the auks, gannets, gulls, skuas, terns and eiders – all of which are predominantly found, or should be found, on the edge. Some might focus on their power of smell, unusually highly developed in some seabirds, while most other birds cannot smell particularly well. The problem is that all definitions of a seabird are partial. Most would exclude the eider. They might live on the coast, but they feed at sea. It is the sea that defines them and their capacity for coping with it makes them difficult, makes them wild, makes them captivating. The 'should be found' is important here – though some birds always end up lost, things are changing on this front. Some are moving inland.

Seabirds live predominantly out to sea – feed at sea, sleep at sea, and experience a habitat that is simultaneously as vast as the ocean and as small as the gap between two waves. Seabirds are mysterious. Away from islands, they are usually seen from land only when summer storms push across the Atlantic and sweep them towards the ocean's edges. Seabirds love islands, as I love islands: the further out of the way they are, the less disturbance there is, the more perfect they are. All use them to breed – an act of convenience – though the vast majority occupy tiny cliff ledges, several hundred metres above the sea. It's technically land, but I wouldn't want to stand there.

Seabirds are transient, fleeting, remote things – yet they are also moving into towns and cities. When they are written about, they reveal a good deal about the author. As with all animals, they are good subjects on which to project human desire. Seabirds are some of our most loved and hated species. They inspire religious devotion or revolutionary zeal. Hermitic living or the hectic crowd. They are symbols of revolution, pirates and victims. They are bounteous and declining – and, like almost everything symbolic of the remote and wild, they are deeply touched by human activity: pollution, over-fishing, the warming of the seas.

It is 5 a.m. Dawn breaking over the lighthouse. The mucky feeling of being awake and the mind unwilling despite the acrid, too-strong coffee coursing through my body. Rosy dawn, purple clouds, golden light; the sea stilled to a pale-blue mirror. Black guillemots – known by their lovely old island name, 'tystie' – breed here in their hundreds. North Ronaldsay lacks the spectacular cliffs and ledges that most seabirds need to breed. Instead it has a coastline of slippery, sea-slicked rocks and beaches of boulders – ankle-grabbing, unforgiving for the two-legged. Under this geography, lies another – a subterranean labyrinth of nooks and crannies between the rocks. As strange as it may seem, these gaps under rocks are an ideal location for tysties to nest. It complicates keeping track of them, makes the annual census of their breeding population tricky. The best opportunity arises in mid-April, a rare but apparently regular window of calm before the spring storms. In the early morning, the guillemots come out of these gaps – standing proud on the edges of the rocks or surfing the lapping waves. The gentleness of the sea gives them nowhere to hide, enabling the observatory staff to count them. The lack of wind, eerie, making me feel as though I were somewhere else, somewhere other. We all take quarters of the island coast – I count 200 in two hours of walking the rocks. The island's total: 653.

And then, as spring begins in earnest, the guillemots all seem to disappear from the edges. Then guano splashed in the gaps in the rocks, like daubed white paint. Single tysties flying from the sea into the crevices, carrying bouquets of butterfish.

A few weeks later we made our moves, working in pairs, scrambling across the rocks. We'd find these gaps, put our shoulders to the boulders and fish with our hands – stone, shit, stone, fluff. We'd close our hands around the fluff, gently but firmly, and pull them out. The first humans these tystie chicks will have ever seen. They greet us in the same way every time: a nip to the wrist with one end, a dramatic defensive shit from the other, a hosepipe spray of white. The ringing process is quick, to minimise stress. The attaching of a metal ring with a unique code allows us to track the productivity, longevity and dispersal of these birds. We return them to their gaps in the rocks.

We don't have long with each bird – cautious speed, not rushing, but not delaying. By the time we've completed the scramble across one small patch of coastline, the exhaustion is complete. The ache in our arms, the raw beak-pecked flesh at our wrists, our jeans whitened.

The chicks are all in varying stages of development – a symptom of the wet, windy spring, where the usual progression of things was fractured. Some are adult-sized, almost fully feathered, and ready to escape within days. Others are the size of a large pebble, black and fluffy like tumble-dryer lint, with a beak, shiny eyes and full-grown legs.

It was, in spite of the spring, the best year yet for tysties. We found 100 nests and ringed 138 young – more than twice the number of nests and young that there were in 2013. I was not the only one bouncing back. I was not the only one surviving with the weather.

Trapped in the brick sprawl, the labyrinth of suburban streets, I could never imagine becoming so involved with the life of a species as I became with those tysties. A love rooted in empathy begins with getting on hands and knees, prostrate on the rocks, covered in filth. Not quite midwife, not quite impartial observer. Several extended months of low-level anxiety every stormy day, several months of stumbling over rocks, counting beyond my capabilities, and beak-nipped flesh. Several months of hoping on fish swimming unseen in the black Atlantic or azure island bays. It teaches you a species of faith in the resilience of things: in the sea, in small birds, in yourself. At the end of the season, as they decamp from the gaps in the rocks to the sea, they vanish. Numbers dwindle to barely a handful. I wasn't going to be there in winter to see them return, as mostly white, flecked with black feathers – the inverse of their summer plumage. I had faith that they would.

I left Orkney, mostly whole, mostly human again, but with a seabird-shaped hole in my heart. So I travelled again. From Shetland, to the Farnes of Northumberland, down to the Welsh islands off the Pembrokeshire coast, before coming back up to Orkney. I travelled deliberately, to explore the mysteries, paradoxes and histories of this family of birds, the places they reluctantly inhabit and the people who follow them too.

This then is the story of those travels – my love letter, written from the rocks and the edges, for the salt-stained, isolated, and ever-changing lives of seabirds.

1

Storm Petrels – Shetland

There are many shades of darkness. The first is the obsidian sea, glittering towards the last vestige of light on the horizon. Close by, it is absolute black. The sea's motion cannot be seen or felt, only heard in the slap of water on the bows of the boat. The second shade is the sky, solidly overcast, predicting tomorrow's storm. A slighter darkness, the last of the light held in the clouds. There is just enough light to see by without a torch as we disembark onto the jetty at Mousa. It is 10.30 p.m. In an hour it will be dark enough.

To darkness, add silence. Silence and mystery.

We walk along a grass path, in parts worn down to the underlying stone, and cross over the 60-degree-north parallel, marked by a driftwood bench. We pause at a drystone wall that runs across the island, seeing little and hearing nothing. We carry on around a bend and a shape begins to emerge from the dark ground ahead of us.

It is Mousa Broch.

It was built 2,000 years ago, as part of the chain of brochs unique to Iron Age Scotland, found mostly in the highlands and islands. Mousa's is one of the finest remaining examples. It is 13 metres high and shaped like the cooling tower of a power station: circular, wider at the base and gently concaving up to the open top. Built of island stone, it is the same colour as the walls and the stony beaches. In the slowly gathering gloom it looks organic, grown out of the bones of the island. We are unsure why brochs were built and what they might have been used for. The darkness of time: occluded intentions, obscured uses.

We continue towards it. Past a beach of loose rocks. Our ears grasp for sound, but the beach is silent, the stones still holding their nocturnal secrets. And it is thanks to the dry stones of the island – beach, broch and wall – that we are here. Twelve strangers, all compelled to take a late-night boat ride from one of Britain's most remote islands to one of its even smaller neighbours. Drystone structures, without mortar or pooling water, create spaces out of the reach of predators and bad weather. Spaces get colonised. They become shelters for seabirds.

There is a small stone entrance to the broch. We crouch, then shuffle through a 5-metre-long passageway. There is a large step up. We emerge into a circular chamber – a new darkness of stone surroundings, the darkness of a building with no clear purpose. Around this inner chamber and towering above us run two concentric walls – one inner, one outer – their strength drawn from the weight of stones pressing against each other for two millennia. Between these two stone walls – in the darkest of darknesses – rises a staircase. I switch on my head torch, weakly illuminating the steps that curve with the walls as they climb the 13 metres to the top. There is room for only the front half of my boot on each step. I can feel how time has hollowed out the centre of each well-trodden stone. My hands grasp the rocks of each wall for support.

If I can't see birds, then I listen for birds. Here in the silence of the staircase I can rely on another of my senses. I can smell them. The air is thick with the musty scent of storm petrels, the damp, stale smell of old books or older churches. It is similar to the smell of laundry that hasn't dried, a clinging, reluctant dampness, as if the birds themselves can never get dry. It is incongruous, a safely familiar scent, something conservative. It is appropriate that they should smell like an old church, little aired or used: the boatman suggests the origin of the word 'petrel' is found in St Peter, walking on water, given the way the bird's legs dangle over the surface of the sea as it forages between the waves. They were also once imagined to be the souls of drowned sailors and cruel sea captains, trapped in birds that were thought to fly forever.[1]

The truth is more prosaic. Most birds have a poor sense of smell and wouldn't be able to smell a storm petrel. But seabirds are unusual for having and relying on a well-developed sense of smell. In the darkness of the colony at night, in the similarity of the maze of stone gaps, storm petrels can smell each other. And they can smell family. Researchers have discovered that, in the breeding season, storm petrels are more likely to avoid areas marked with the scent of their relatives.[2]

At the top of the staircase a heavy gate of wood and chicken wire seals the space between the walls. I open it with a shove. I step out at the top, the odour of petrels dissipating in a flood of fresh air. I step out at the top onto a narrow ring of stones suspended between the metre-thick walls, a 13-metre fall plunging away each side of me over a low wall, outwards down to the grass and stone surrounding the broch, or inwards down to the inky darkness of the central chamber. From the top, the view of headlands disappearing in the darkness, the hills of Mainland Shetland merging into clouds, the sea as dark as the sky. It takes a moment for place and time to sink in. I stretch my hands out between the walls. Lichens, stiff and wiry after a dry spring, scratch at my fingertips.

Then they begin to sing, from the gaps between the stones, a sound that seems to emerge from below the lichens. The first faintly. Then others. Each storm petrel joining increases the confidence, adding to a quiet choir of birds. Each churrs – hiccups – churrs. It is described by birders as 'like a fairy being sick', a cliché so frequently used as to have its origins lost in a blur of repetition. It is a description that captures the otherworldliness of their song. It is a rhythmical purring, but with the pitch of a Geiger counter, or the tuning of an FM radio through static, or a struggling food blender. The hiccup is a squeak, with a pause, the noise of a cork being twisted in the neck of a glass bottle. To describe it in these ways is to anchor something essentially indescribable in the mundanity of everyday life. But it is essentially unlike these things: it is the sound of the magic of islands.

Darkness creeps; light leaching from the clouds. Storm petrels returning from the sea appear at the edge of vision, firstly as a flicker, an apparition in the dark. Then they jink in on erratic wings, beats too fast to follow, always disappearing. They seem bat-like on the approach to the broch. Their defence in the dark against predators is the utmost agility and unpredictability. There is the darkness of their plumage too. Each erratic wing – only 20 centimetres long – is the colour of the night. A matte but not total black, shaded brown where the stark sun at sea bleaches the feathers. On the underside, a white line where the flight feathers meet the flesh and bone of wing. Then, bizarrely, a white rump that flashes like a beacon in the dark – an advert to predators for which science has no explanation.

At the broch they aim for the walls. Land on the stones, scurry for their gaps, rumps catching the vestigial light. Their feet are tiny, webbed, clawed, and as they scurry they scratch at the desiccated lichens, like mice. Bat-like; mouse-like. Storm petrels are hard to pin down, elusive in the dark; like and unlike other animals. The incubating bird, singing from the broch wall, slips away, out into the darkness of the sea at night.

There are places where time unspools like an old cassette tape reel and cannot be wound back up. There are places where perspective warps and the present and the past are mere touching distance apart. Standing on top of Mousa Broch, senses stimulated by the sight, sound and smell of storm petrels, I look out to the dark mass of Mainland Shetland, where earlier I could see the low, round remains of Burraland Broch. I can see the lighthouse at Sumburgh, blinking rhythmically, where there was once a fort, where once the first fires would have been lit, a message spread from broch to broch giving advance warning of invaders from the south. So one theory goes. But there are other theories too. The mystery doesn't matter, not to me, here, now. In the vanishing light, watching black birds in the night sky and white lights blinking on the horizon, standing where people must have stood, 2,000 years ago, hearing, seeing, feeling the same things.

There are few better places to see storm petrels than Mousa. The island is home to the most easily accessible and perhaps the most famous colony of the birds anywhere in the world. The other colonies are obscure: smaller islands, fewer boats. The birds require the gaps in the rocks but, more pressingly, an absence of rats, cats, stoats or any other land-based mammal that can fish with a clawed paw between the rocks to reach them or their eggs.

This species of storm petrel used to be known, myopically, as British storm petrel. But it is not just British stones they like to nest in; it is not just British-born birds that fly through here. Ringing, the most primitive way of tracking bird movements, has revealed that passing our coastlines at night are storm petrels bred in Portugal and Norway, among other places, on their way to or from waters off South Africa. They are now known as European storm petrel in recognition of the fact that their breeding range extends out beyond our north and western coastline (and that of Ireland) to Norway, Iceland, the Faroes, France, Sardinia, Sicily, the Canaries – even Spain, where they breed on Benidorm Island, fluttering and churring in the darkness just offshore, while the British on holiday party on the dazzlingly lit seafront and in the neon-lit bars, unaware of what shares the night with them.

If you gaze at the broch too long, you begin to feel connections stirring to the deep past, to the Iron Age inhabitants, the master builders and the unbroken line of occupation until the last family left in 1853. Stare deeper at the birds and you go all the way back, back to the deepest past. The marigold-mouthed shag on the rocks hanging its serpentine wings out is beautiful and primitive. It is the connection to the dinosaurs that lurks just beneath the surface of our birds. Mousa is connected to all of this and none of this. Like the storm petrels that slip past in the night, barely there, islands entangle us in a tantalising web of potential connections: flight paths, presences, histories and geographies. All transient.

There is nothing new. There is nowhere new. There is nothing unseen in the large island and small archipelagos that make up Britain. I am following in the footsteps of other watchers, walkers, writers: walking similar islands, watching the same species that they first conjured relationships with, committing my experiences to paper with a like-minded fervour.

I start with the storm petrels as a nod to my forebears. Off the coast of Pembrokeshire, Wales, there lies a small island – an island dreamt about since the time of the Vikings, who saw it from their longboats in its original, mint-green, vegetated condition. They called it Skokholm, meaning 'wooded island' and sailed on. All that remains of that vegetation today are the flowers that survived the Norman farmers, the makers of the island who brought the now ubiquitous rabbits and cleared the land. There is also a farmhouse and a flag of white fabric hoisted high on a driftwood flagpole. On it flutter the images of three storm petrels.

Anyone trying to make a home of an island like Skokholm has to endure the winter. Winter comes with an almost absolute isolation among the crashing waves. It puts a halt to most attempts at staying. To survive these conditions requires more than creating a home. To thrive in these conditions you need to dream.

Ronald Lockley and his first wife, Doris, were the dreamers of this place – the storm petrel flag a result of Doris's handiwork. Ronald Matthias Lockley – or R. M. Lockley as he became known to the world at large – authored fifty-eight books and was a prolific writer of articles, some hugely popular and influential in their day and some still so. Most of his work is inspiring, innovative and the basis for much of what we know – and how we know it – about certain species of bird. His star has sadly been overtaken by figures more grandiose – figures with bigger, better flags.

Lockley was born in Cardiff on 8 November 1903. When he was five, his happy childhood was interrupted by a sudden brush with his own mortality. A freak accident in which an out-of-control horse crushed him against an embankment, leaving him bedbound for a month. In *The Way to an Island* (1941) Lockley remembers reading *The Swiss Family Robinson* during his convalescence. This might be when the desire for an island of his own first lodged in his imagination. It is followed by *Robinson Crusoe*, *The Coral Island* by R. M. Ballantyne, and then works of natural history, including Charles Waterton's *Wanderings in South America* – a book that inspired Charles Darwin and Alfred Russel Wallace as young readers on their way to scientific fame. Lockley's young mind begins to wander through the vastness of imagined space.

The young Lockley was unfamiliar with vast space. He grew up in Whitchurch, at the time a suburb of Cardiff, surrounded by farms and stables that would be subsumed by the city in the 1960s. His universe is the garden and a gap in the wall that leads to the farmer's fields, which would be his surreptitious stomping ground. Lockley feels the lure of the land. The farmer keeps remaking and repairing the drystone wall. The hole keeps reappearing.

When he appeared on *Desert Island Discs* at the age of seventy-six, Lockley was asked how he first became interested in birds. In his answer he pinpoints another period of childhood convalescence, this time sitting still for three months in a chair in the orchard, noticing and keeping a diary of birds and wildflowers.[3] In *The Way to an Island* he recounts how, as a child, he was not allowed to leave the dinner table until he had cleared his plate. He devised a paper-bag-in-pocket system, in which he would stash unwanted food to give to the grateful birds just beyond the hedge. He writes that 'out of this sly practice came the good of intelligent bird-watching'.[4]

Lockley claims with youthful zeal that by the age of ten he 'knew every common bird intimately'.[5] (This is something I would struggle to say even now, after a decade of obsession and with all the benefits of modern equipment and information. I have the *Collins Bird Guide*, a distillation of all Europe's birdlife, with bright images depicting birds drawn from life, and dense text summarising all the potentially useful information. It fits onto an app on my iPhone.) Lockley thought Howard Saunders' breezeblock of a book, *The Manual of British Birds*, was 'indispensable'.[6] The 1927 edition runs to 834 pages. In a knapsack there wouldn't be much space for anything else.

Saunders' book was first published in 1899 and its images are based on taxidermy specimens imaginatively brought back to life by a range of artists, most of whom had not set eyes on the living bird. Most are as stiff as bad waxworks, the subtleties of the warblers lost in the monochrome engravings. The seabirds that Lockley grew up to love are all standing on rocks, not flying as they are almost always seen, and it's like trying to understand an opera from the captions, or a film from the script. Sometimes this disconnect produces impossible images. The artist has the legs of the Manx shearwater far enough back to be anatomically correct, but somehow holding the front of the body up – a stance the birds are physically incapable of holding. They don't walk, they shuffle.

If there is a gap between the images of dead birds and the real living bird, then the text goes some way to closing it, offering alternative names and detailed information on distribution. The description of plumage leaves a lot to the imagination, an indication that identifying living wild birds was still a relatively unusual activity.

Lockley was born at an auspicious time for the study of natural history. The Royal Society for the Protection of Birds had been formed in 1889 by Emily Williamson as part of the first stirrings of concern about conservation in the public imagination. It was a movement with which Lockley was instinctively in tune. In his early teenage years he used to go egg collecting. He watches a spotted flycatcher nesting in the garden and gets drawn into the way the parents come and go, and defend their young from a cat. He names them. A real-life prototype *Springwatch*. It is the first instance of his style of studying: of patient observation, matched with an enquiring, curious mind and a respect for the lives of birds. It is the first hint that his boyish enthusiasm would form the career that would go on to shape the entire field of birdwatching. His time with the spotted flycatcher nest is the moment Lockley gives up egg collecting. It is the summer of 1919, the fifteen-year-old's self-imposed ban coming thirty-five years before egg collecting is officially made illegal.

At around the same time Lockley builds a hut for himself in the woods between two streams and gives it the name 'Moorhen Island'. It's a place where he can store books, write poems and bunk off his education in favour of just being in the woods, being solitary and being with his burgeoning interest in nature that nobody shares. In his recollections it is Eden-like.

Lockley's early life was characterised by islands – fictional and metaphorical. Islands of the mind, islands of obsession, islands of himself. By the age of five he had decided that he would probably spend the rest of his life alone. Looking back in 1969 in *The Island*, he identifies his 'most burning desire' to 'dwell alone and simply upon a small island of my own, to study its wildlife intimately'.[7]

Then there comes a day trip to his first real island: Lundy in the Bristol Channel, 12 miles off the coast of north Devon. He identifies the auks – guillemots and razorbills – and kittiwakes on the cliffs. It is not until the boat back that he finally meets the species he would later become synonymous with, the Manx shearwater, mustering in the sea. Somehow he manages to identify them from the engraving in *The Manual of British Birds*. It is more than likely that shearwaters bred on Lundy then, though Lockley seems unaware of this. He suggests they're heading to Pembrokeshire, to Skokholm and Skomer. His curiosity was caught. It was inevitable that he would follow them there.

Lockley was twenty-four when he arrived at Skokholm. I was just about to turn twenty-three when I washed up in North Ronaldsay. I follow an echo of him throughout my journey.

It was on Skokholm that Lockley came across a storm petrel for the first time. Standing there, among the weird nocturnal orchestra of seabirds, he likened the storm petrel's cry to the mechanical, percussive notes made by grasshoppers. He found the birds nesting in the drystone walls, smelled the same musky odour that I experienced on Mousa. Picking one up, he found it 'a delicate, dainty, almost ethereal creature'.[8] Later, while refurbishing the roof on his farmhouse, he removes a flagstone and finds a fully grown young storm petrel in its cavity nest. He literally lives with them, sharing shelter between old stones, as generations of dwellers in that farmhouse would have done.

Lockley names his little boat after the species. The iconic photo of him as a young man shows him with his hands on the tiller, wearing a waistcoat and shirt, skin ruddy in the sunlight and hair touched by the breeze. The *Storm Petrel* gives him the freedom to run between islands and buy supplies on the mainland. It lets him fish and catch crabs and sell them. It lets his island life take flight.

When Lockley first began his study of storm petrels, little was known about any of Britain's seabirds. The challenges of such study are obvious. They live either in enclosed, invisible places – down burrows or between cracks – or the complete opposite: endless, unbound ocean. Lockley brought what he described as 'perhaps divine awe'[9] to his studies, but divine awe is not an insurance against mistakes. Eagerness can trump sensitivity and the nests he'd marked out to study were abandoned by the birds after a couple of intrusions. The species, he discovered, does not like excessive handling, something he found 'disheartening'.[10] It is his Manx shearwater techniques that let him properly monitor the storm petrel colony: the construction of a little dried-grass gate that the bird knocks out on leaving and in on returning, to monitor the adult's movements. Instead of disturbing the nest, he uses a soft piece of wire, moulded like a sheephook, to coax the petrel into his hand. Six out of ten nests survive the next season.

Lockley begins, with others who would join him on the island, to piece together the riddle of a storm petrel's life. The minimum of a month they spend on the island before laying eggs. The length of time an adult will incubate the egg, without feeding, waiting for the other adult to return. The month and a week and a few days it takes for the parents to incubate the egg until it hatches. We know this now, but there remains much that we don't know. The study of storm petrels continues. I am conscious of following an echo of Lockley during my own small contribution to the cause on North Ronaldsay.

The Pitt Rivers Museum in Oxford has a storm petrel candle in its collection. It is a European storm petrel, with a tarred wick pulled through its body. The terse caption suggests it was used by fishermen visiting the Northern Isles up to the nineteenth century – indeed the object is said to have been collected in 1892. In his book *Birds and People* Mark Cocker explains:

> The birds are so rich in oil that the Faroese would decapitate the young . . . dry them and thread a woollen wick through their bodies. They were then burned as night lights and one tradition . . . was to gather in the farmhouse, tell tales, sing old ballads (and presumably drink alcohol) until the *drunnhviti* had burned through.[11]

It is a scene that speaks of the stranger, darker world of the far north.

In the summer, on the other hand, night in the northern isles does not fall as a true darkness. The northwards tilt of the earth is sufficient for the perpetual Arctic summer to bleed south and colour the northern horizon at night with a lingering sunset. It means that to ring storm petrels, you choose the cloudy nights. The darkest of the light nights. We begin at 10.30 p.m., assembling the speakers, running the cables to the observatory's van battery, unfurling the mist nets, arranging the pockets in the mesh that the birds drop into and nestle in snugly, safely, before being quickly removed. We play their song on repeat. Churr-hiccup-churr, as if we are revellers at some interspecies storm petrel rave. Then we wait. The darker the night, the closer they come to land. Storm petrels don't breed on North Ronaldsay but they do funnel through the firths that thread between the islands, each one a narrow sea path on their night flight. By ringing them we take the pulse of their passing. Some nights a bird is caught here after midnight, then found on Fair Isle, 30 miles northeast, before the end of the next day.

They come close to midnight. Then they nestle in the pockets of our nets, deceived by the fake song of their species. They are put in cloth bags, momentarily calmed in the dark, while they are brought the short distance to the ringing shed. In the dim light of wind-up torches, we take measurements: wing length and weight, scribbling them down with blunt pencils. The storm petrels fit snug in the palm of my hand. Their legs are spindly, their feet over-sized, the bill delicate despite a curving tip and the tubenose; it looks shrunken. One we catch has a white semi-circle of feathers under the eye, a smudgy white line on the nape, ear and throat. We make a special note: aberrant.

Mostly they are placid to hold. After the ring is squeezed shut around the leg, I open my palm and release the bird. It takes one second before springing out and into the darkness, its white rump the last thing the eye can see, jinking into the night. Others take a little longer. We put them on the stone wall and keep an eye on them as they flicker themselves into flight again, like a moth that trembles, then springs off. The darkness; their freedom.

It is 1901. The other end of Europe. Writer Maxim Gorky is dreaming of another kind of freedom. A friend of Lenin and later of Stalin, he writes politically charged poems to foment the slow swelling of rebellion in the long prelude to the Russian Revolution. One of his most famous efforts is the 'The Song of the Stormy Petrel', a poem in which the petrel flies alone over a stormy sea. Around this central protagonist, Gorky arrays other sea birds – penguins, loons (divers) and grebes – and accuses them of cowardice.

Gorky, of course, is not really writing about nature. He uses the image well – the brave petrel performing the apparently imposs-ible feat of overcoming the storm – but his choice of bird also taps into the folkloric heritage of the species. Storm petrels were once referred to colloquially as 'Mother Carey's Chickens', with Mother Carey believed to be a corruption of the Virgin Mary. It is a blas-phemy that reveals something of the profound fear these birds inspired – thanks to the habitual tendency of humans to confuse cause and effect. The fact that petrels appeared at the same time as storms was taken as proof of cause rather than effect. Gorky's petrel is to be feared by rulers and censors. His petrel is not just a petrel but a cipher, a political prophecy. A proletariat petrel mak-ing a point, a small bird struggling against the forces of nature, the ultimate nation state. Gorky, of course, is a propagandist not a birdwatcher, and the metaphorical characteristics he ascribes to the bird do not hold up to scrutiny. They might live in dense colonies, but they are not workers. They don't help each other. Like other tubenoses, they abandon their young instead of introducing them to the world. They are left to survive, not to socialise. But then propa-ganda is not required to be ecologically precise and the potency of Gorky's symbolism is undeniable. It is intriguing though that he chose to write about a species that would be unfamiliar to his Russian audience. Storm petrels are not widely known anywhere.

Mousa is tiny – just 1.5 miles long and about a mile wide – and has been uninhabited since the nineteenth century, but it is nonetheless too big and too easily accessible for the liking of our other species of storm petrel. Leach's storm petrel breeds in the Ramna Stacks, Sule Skerry, St Kilda and North Rona – a litany of the truly remote, the truly inaccessible, the utterly unpopulated. So we don't know how many there are. The last survey suggested 48,000 pairs, though there could be many more than that grunting and churring in the night above fractured skerries and forgotten islands.

Leach's storm petrels are bigger, more capable birds than the European storm petrels. They are almost identically plumaged: although the white bar is on the top of the wing instead of under it and the tail is forked instead of straight-edged. They feed out of eyesight of land, searching out the plankton that lies beyond the coastal shelf. That fuels a stronger flight. Deeper, stronger wing-beats. Leach's does not flutter, does not do things without a purpose.

Neither did William Elford Leach, a great naturalist burned out, dead at the age of forty-five. Officially the cause was cholera; unofficially he overworked until he broke down. It was in 1819, before his breakdown, when he was working with the British Museum's natural history collections, that he purchased at auction a specimen of a petrel shot on St Kilda. The following year the renowned Dutch ornithologist Coenraad Jacob Temminck visited the museum and inspected the specimen, describing it as a species new to science. And such was Leach's own reputation in the fields of taxonomy and marine biology – even at the relatively young age of twenty-nine – that the Dutchman gave the bird the scientific name *Procellaria leachii* in honour of its purchaser.[12] Both men were apparently unaware that the species had been found, described and named three years earlier in France as *Procellaria leucorhoa*. Naming is a race and Leach and Temminck had been beaten to it, but their coinage was the one that stuck, the young Englishman's name immortalised in the vernacular. Leach's storm petrel is his flagbearer, the most high profile of the many species that still bear his name: each one a reminder of his brilliant, brief existence.

I have twice come across a Leach's storm petrel. The first encounter came while I was standing in the teeth of a gale on North Uist's Aird an Runair headland, when a stiff spring north-westerly swept three unusually close to land (as in, visible from land) in the company of migrating skuas. A black shape, powerful for its size, jinking up and down with the gale-whipped waves. The other was at a petrel ringing session in North Ronaldsay. I was on shift to take the bags of caught birds to the ringing shed a short distance away. There were three bags. I handed two to the other ringers. I put my hand in the third bag and felt more bird than anticipated. I manoeuvred it into my palm with every hair standing on end, excitement coursing its way through my nervous system. I pulled the bag away. There was a Leach's storm petrel in my hand. I stopped and stared in disbelief. And was sworn at by the others. It sung a snatch of song in my hand, a song not meant to be heard by British ears. It was literally twice the bird a European storm petrel is. A snug fit in hand. A thicker leg, a ring twice as big. On release it leapt out of my hand and headed purposefully out into the thick darkness and left me feeling, in that moment, that nothing could ever compare, no thrill could ever come close to being hands on with an emissary from an absolutely other, absolutely elusive wilderness.

The elusive wilderness of which Leach's storm petrels are a part periodically makes a storm-blown intrusion on land. There is an irony that the best place to see one in Britain is from the concrete seafronts of Merseyside. North-westerly gales in autumn seem to be the Leach's one weakness. Squeezed in by the narrow Irish Sea, caught out by the north coast of Wales, they get swept towards the Mersey Estuary. In conditions that can be hard to stand up in, most birders see their first Leach's storm petrel whipping along the beach, seeking desperate shelter along the seawall, even being blown between their legs. The petrels still fly, as if they can't do anything else, but their flight is weaker, without the power and purpose it has elsewhere. Some make it back out to sea when the gale slackens. Some get caught by gulls, some perish from exhaustion. A small number end up in the reservoirs of the English Midlands.

A Midlands reservoir would not do for Robert Atkinson, an ornithological adventurer of the 1930s. Neither would anywhere with a lighthouse, or anywhere anyone had been with a camera before. His tastes were specific: 'Barren wildness had to be the attraction of the Scottish islands, or there was nothing.'[13] His search for the sublimely out of the way twinned with a desire for little-known birds. In 1935 he found in the index of a bird book what he describes as 'a true ornithologist's child, cumbrously museum named.'[14] It was the 'Leach's fork-tailed petrel': a name that time has pared back. All other information was lacking other than a list of islands where it was supposed to breed. It was an open invitation to a man such as Atkinson. He chose to mount an expedition to North Rona – isolated by a minimum of 40 miles of sea from the nearest human habitation. Perched northwards, the tip of a triangle between Cape Wrath and the Butt of Lewis, it became his desert island ideal.

In Atkinson's book, *Island Going*, he records this trip and the many that followed, all undertaken with his childhood friend John Ainslie and all in pursuit of the Leach's storm petrel and the remoter islands of Scotland. It opens with the implausible logistics of a young man from Oxford in the 1930s, buying a car from a breaker's yard and driving it several hundred miles to Stornoway on the faith of correspondence by letter with the owner of a company of fish-curers and shipbrokers. When they get there, they find he has arranged a boat for them the next day – something I find, eighty years later, quite miraculous. And when they finally make it to North Rona, Atkinson catches his first glimpse of the Leach's storm petrel, and full of 1930s English reserve says, 'So that was it.'[15]

$$\smile$$

My time in Shetland raised hopes that I might encounter Leach's storm petrel for a third time. In the middle of one night during my stay the wind roused, found the corners of the house and whistled. Rain rattled into the window panes and, in the half-light next morning, the voe was ruffled, agitated out of its usual calm state, the waves turning white in what had been a sheltered inlet of sea.

When the weather turns, when the storm hits, you can either meet it or hide from it. I went to meet it at the tip of Eshaness, a peninsular in Northmavine, Mainland Shetland. Eshaness is an old volcano. The cliff is black. The rocks look cremated, chunks strewn around the clifftop like lumps of coal spat out of a fire. Eshaness feels like a furnace. The wind creeps up to 50 mph. A westerly, driving offshore. I am here in hope rather than expectation, hope that the trajectory of the wind will usher the storm petrels that must be out to sea closer to land – close enough to be seen – as they, theoretically, pass around the top of the archipelago to the calmer seas in the lee of the islands. It is one of those ideas that makes sense in theory. On the clifftop, the tailwind is turbo-charging the puffins flying past. Squalls sting into exposed skin. Wind rattles the tripod.

The scope shakes, the rain douses my binoculars until everything is washed with grey and the focus softened, details blurred. The petrels do not come.

I stick the weather out for as long as I can, but the petrels are tougher than me. I spend the rest of the day in the shelter of Scalloway Museum.

The unpredictability of birds is part of their appeal. The only thing more thrawn than the sea is the creatures that depend on it. And in weather like this, the real awe, the real mastery of the bird is apparent. Strange as it may seem, part of me was pleased not to see any storm petrels. I was pleased they were strong enough to handle winds I could not. That this bird, no more than a couple of centimetres larger than a swallow, has the power and poise to deal with a 50 mph west wind, and squalls and crashing waves and a constantly moving seascape around it, an obscured horizon, and no opportunity to rest or feed.

The volcano at Eshaness is Devonian – that's 300–400 million years old, or back from when Shetland lay at the equator. The sense of age here makes it feel as if we are merely pausing as we pass through, tenants of something older, more elemental than our own human lives. That's true for birds too: seabirds, it is thought, colonised Shetland with the advent of the Atlantic current, back when all the islands in this archipelago were joined as one – a mere 10,000 years ago.

I am no geologist. I find it difficult to picture the lives of rocks. I'm a mere birdwatcher, an observer of signs. And all the signs suggest everything here answers to the rock, to the sea and to the wind. But there is an exception to everything. Some life on Shetland answers to the skuas . . .

2

Skuas – Shetland

The RIB* skims past the southern tip of Bressay. The Isle of Noss rears up in front of us, like a manta ray in sandstone, swimming up. Its mouth is the Noup of Noss, the 181-metre cliff that crowns the eastern end of the island. The boatman holds out a herring, as silver as the sky. A great skua swoops low, twice. On the third swoop it holds its wings up high, out of the way, stoops with its neck and plucks it neatly from his hand. It takes a second herring and flies back to Bressay, pursued by a second skua, clever enough to watch, cautious enough not to try.

Noss is sandstone, the colour of concrete, decorated with strands of white guano like old cobwebs. Its cliffs are not eroded sheer or into chunks of rock like others. It is eroded into a bubbling pattern, almost honeycomb in places. It has the architecture of a wasp's nest, the grey sandstone chewed up like a pulp and moulded into elaborate cells and layers that erosion has peeled back and laid open to the air. Like a wasp's nest, there is a sting, a catch, the potential for pain.

Gannets nest on the honeycomb of the cliff in their thousands. They sit in pairs, pointing to the sky, swaying their heads. They stir. The scent of the boat's herring fills the air. They take off, tessellating in a sky that is suddenly as much bird as light. The great skuas

---

* Rigid-inflatable boat.

lurk. The boatman takes a tube, dips it into the sea and slides the herring down it and into the current, drifting away from the boat. The gannets call, go quiet, and plunge.

Gannets have a 6-foot wingspan. Skuas don't. Gannets have a dagger for each mandible and screw themselves up into darts as they thump into the sea, bill first. En masse they become a hailstorm of birds, churning the water, splashing the boat.

There are two great skuas in the storm. On paper the fight is a ridiculous mismatch. As the gannets surface, clutching fish, the two skuas pounce, bludgeoning through the frenzied flock to get to the gannets surfacing with fish. They mug them with power.

$$\smile$$

There are four species of skua in British waters. Two are resident and two are transient. Three are alike in plumage. All are similar in manners.

The most sought after is the most transient. Long-tailed skua breed on the Arctic tundra, its population tied, like so many species of the far north, to the boom and bust of lemming populations. It is the smallest of the world's skuas. They are all angles: slender wings bent back halfway, and a thin body drawn out into a pencil line of a tail. They are mostly grey, as grey as the waves, but their breast diffusely turns a pale yellow, the colour running up onto the nape and offsetting a black cap. The two outermost wing feathers have bright white shafts, a small flash when they fly. They pass the northwest coasts of Britain every May, having spent the winter lingering in the South Atlantic, as far south as the tips of Africa and America. They pass mostly unnoticed, far out, following the curve of currents skirting the top of Britain, aiming for the north coast of Norway. To see them from Britain takes a specific sort of gale. The correct angle of a north-westerly. One that feels like a spin cycle, like masochism. A 40-mph tailwind makes a speedy bird even quicker. Even the quickest glimpse through rain-sodden binoculars feels like a victory, the stuff of dreams.

These winds bring another species of skua close to British shores. The pomarine skua – abbreviated by the cold-lipped, storm-lashed birder to 'pom' – is a bruiser. Pomarine skuas spend the winter in the northern hemisphere, mostly in the sea off West Africa, but some wander, or some never make it that far, and they are the likeliest of the skuas to be seen from the British coast in winter. Their plumage is cleaner cut. A darker back, a more sharply defined pale belly, a larger white flash of feathers on the tips of the wings. They are bulky – thicker winged, their pot bellies drawn out into a club-ended tail, frequently likened to a spoon. A fully spooned pom skua gets birders very excited. Pomarine skuas are easier to see – they travel up the English Channel every spring as well, often in gentler weather – despite breeding further away than the long-taileds, and they can stream past the coastline, with the elegance and determination of salmon running up Alaskan rivers.

Here on Shetland, in the settled weather of late spring, after their migration, both species are out of the question. Instead we are after great skuas and Arctic skuas, the species that breed here in numbers not found elsewhere in Britain. The Arctic skua is the last of the three that look alike: intermediate in size between long-tailed and pomarine and intermediate in looks. Arctic skuas are still pale underneath and dark grey on top, but the transitions are smoother. They still have a dark cap, but it is less prominent than on a poma-rine. The central tail feathers are drawn out into a needle – a small point, a syringe instead of the rapier tail of a long-tailed skua. The Arctic skua has a more frequent dark morph than the other skuas: a dark chocolate brown, paler around the neck, the black cap still the darkest point.

The great skua is the beast in the family. The only bird I have ever run away from. They are the first skua: the word 'skua' is thought to come from the Faroese island Skúvoy, a place with an infamously large colony of great skuas. On the northern isles they have the evocative name 'bonxie'. To these English ears it sounds suitably bolshie, yet it is from the prosaic Norn* word for a 'dumpy bird'. The biggest skua in the north by a significant margin, it is a muddy brown colour, made up of mottled feathers varying from straw to peaty brown. It is flecked with blond highlights around the head and particularly the neck, where the feathers become shaggier and act as the hackles of a dog. The bill is long, the upper mandible drooping to a wicked hooked tip. The feet are black and clawed and dangle like a boxer's gloves when the bird dives at the heads of passers-by.

There are only a few species that I can remember the exact moment of first seeing them: the where, the when and the feeling. My first great skua is a memory seared indelibly into the birding part of my brain. It was a frigid late-autumn day of the sort that the Norfolk coast seems to specialise in. Golden, low sunlight. Icy winds, as if straight from the Arctic, ploughed straight into the beach. The dull roar of the waves pushing and pulling at the shingle, making and remaking the ground. A dense flock of gulls, reduced to the generic, suddenly splintered, a flurry of noise. They had spotted the danger. It looked bronze in the light. Effortlessly cruising,

---

* A now extinct Norse language spoken on the islands.

catching up with the flock, harrying them: an electric injection of fear, a shiver, synapses flaring. I knew exactly what it was. I had spent long enough staring at the picture in the field guide, puzzling out how to tell the great skua apart from a brown juvenile gull. In the flesh and feather of the moment, it had a charisma that rendered study redundant. The only interruption to their brown colour is the shared family feature: the white shafts on the outermost wing feathers, bigger and brighter in the great skua than in the others. The white flashes in flight in sunlight or against a dark and stormy sea are like a beacon, beckoning the birder to look at the bird.

Fear defines the skuas. It is in everything. It is the fear they strike at the heart of other birds, from auks to gannets. In America they are known as jaegers, the German word for 'hunter', despite skuas not being hunters. They are, in the dulled language of science, kleptoparasites. They are pirates.

It takes the RIB two and a half hours to skim around Noss and Bressay, before it dodges the tankers, ferries and seals in the sound to dock at Lerwick pier. The boat still smells of herring and a territorial grey seal bull heaves itself up out of the water, places its front fins on the stern and looks eagerly about the boat. I am briefly face-to-face with an animal longer than I am tall and more than twice my weight. I shuffle away, feeling not quite fear, but awe, and sensing there is something not quite right about a wild animal looking me in the eye and toothily asking for food.

Lerwick is grey. The buildings and streets are the colour of clouds hanging, threatening rain. The harbour offers shelter for gulls and terns, flocks of fry rippling through the shallows, and moon jellyfish – a lilac four-leaf clover within a transparent frilled circle – gently lapping with the movement of the water. An Arctic skua – all long wings, spike tail and lithe shapes – rips through a waiting tern flock, sparking mass panic. They have no fish to drop.

In the early days of species discovery and naming, the Arctic skua was given the genus name *Stercorarius*, literally 'of shit', as they were seen consuming what was expelled by terrified birds. The obvious, but wrong, conclusion was drawn. It extends to their Scottish dialect name too, the sadly underused 'Skootie Alan'. To skoot is to shit. The Alan part is less clear. In the eighteenth century the Arctic skua was given the name 'parasitick gull', an early, easy misunderstanding between skuas and gulls. They can appear, at first glance, similar. Their basic shape is the same. They both fly power-fully and – in a gull's younger plumages – can be similarly mottled brown. They both use their strength to bully.

The Arctic skua in Lerwick harbour slipped away quickly. The chaos it causes creates a smokescreen for its disappearance. The species is doing the same thing across the archipelago. Shetland has half of Britain's Arctic skua population. The rest is distrib-uted across Orkney, the Hebrides and parts of the Sutherland and Caithness coasts. Shetland's population crashed from 1,912 in 1985 to 1,128 in 2002. The decline has sped up. It is now thought that 81 per cent of the population has vanished from Britain since 1992. This is enough of a decline to make it Britain's fastest-dwindling seabird. This is extinction trajectory. Globally, the picture is dif-ferent: Scotland is the absolute southern limit of the species and they breed throughout the Arctic. Yet any wildlife loss is a cause for worry.

According to a recent study, the rapid decline in Scotland's population of Arctic skuas is down to the simultaneous impact of 'bottom-up and top-down pressures'.[1] From the bottom: the species they steal food from are declining, and the food they are after, sand eels, is also vanishing, victim of a warming sea and fishing fleets. They can't raise enough young any more. At the start of the decline, in 1992, each pair would raise on average 0.91 chicks from each nest. That figure is now 0.29.[2] From the top: great skuas will kill and predate the eggs and young of the Arctic skua, and sometimes even the adult Arctic skua, as well as the auks, terns and small gulls that the Arctic skuas harass. Lerwick harbour – indeed the entire archipelago – would be a calmer place without Arctic skuas, no longer charged with the potential energy of the skua and the sense that any minute now a settled scene could be turned upside down, birds scattered everywhere.

I leave the shelter of the town in the cheapest hire car. Mainland Shetland is massive, too big for buses or walking. We struggle up the hills anyway, the whine of over-worked cylinders instead of over-worked lungs. The modern road south from Lerwick runs parallel to the old road. The old road is a twisted track. The modern road is a wide, smooth, black ribbon between the moors and the fields, fast between Lerwick and the airport at Sumburgh.

Shetland changed when oil was discovered in the North Sea. From 1974 BP's money flooded in as oil flooded out. The terminal built on the shores of Shetland's Sullom Voe in north Mainland was once Europe's largest construction site. The area, previously infamous for being the first place a foreign bomb struck Britain in the Second World War, was changed completely over the six years of construction. It took 6,000 people to build the terminal across 1,000 acres of land. It was built to receive, store and process crude oil and gas before distributing it elsewhere and can handle 1.3 million barrels a day.[3] The figures are darkly awe-inspiring. Through it, modernity and wealth came to the islands. It created a different kind of skilled job, not crofting or fishing, but employment for helicopter pilots, tanker captains, engineers, geologists. It enabled people to stay here instead of leaving for elsewhere.

In 1993 the *Braer* oil disaster happened. A Liberia-registered tanker, with a capacity twice that of the *Exxon Valdez* tanker, lost power in hurricane-force winds south of Shetland. It ran aground, pulled by the currents against the pushing wind into Quendale Bay. The oil spill was massive, but due to the wind, quickly dispersed away from the coastline, preventing an *Exxon Valdez*-style wildlife apocalypse. It is estimated that 1,500 birds died. Fishing was banned for 400 miles around the bay, then lifted for crustaceans in 1994 and scallops in 1995.[4] Due to the way mussels filter water, the contaminants lingered, accumulating, poisoning their flesh. The ban on mussel fishing was not lifted until 2000. It is, I suppose, fortunate it happened in winter, when auks and skuas and terns were either far out to sea or far to the south, at the apogee of their winter migrations. Oil has been a blessing to the functioning of the island, but oil is a curse that hangs over the wildlife – if not as a spillage then in the increasingly changing climate.

The coast of Shetland is characterised by voes, thin inlets of sea running inland like fjords, sheltered by headlands. One of these headlands runs between Quendale Bay, where the *Braer* broke ashore, and Sumburgh Head. It is just back from Sumburgh, along the coast of the voe, that we are heading – in search of a once-lost ancient settlement and in homage to another ornithological forebear. Shetland here is gentler. It is a rolling grassy landscape instead of the highland moors found elsewhere. There are beaches caught in the heads of voes and bays that run into dunes and sandy grass fields. Where there are cliffs, they are lower, less brutally sheer and rocky than elsewhere. It is in this landscape that Jarlshof was found. Or rather, refound – a storm in the nineteenth century revealed a wall in the sand. Archaeology revealed more: a medieval farmstead, a Viking longhouse, Pictish remains, an Iron Age broch and wheelhouse, the burned hearth of a Neolithic dwelling.

I learned about Jarlshof through the work of naturalist James Fisher. He was born in Bristol on 3 September 1912, the son of the headmaster of Oundle School, and given the proper prestigious English education of the time: Eton, then Oxford. He could have run the country if he hadn't studied zoology. The benefit of Fisher's education is that it formed one of the country's best, broadest minds about birds. In a prolific career of books that can now be hard to find, one of his stand-out successes is *The Shell Bird Book*. You have to forgive the corporate greenwash – it was 1966 after all. To begin his mass-market attempt at communicating the wonder and joy of British birdlife, he digresses through 100 million years of history and the lesser-studied topic of paleo-ornithology. He combines a forensic ability to analyse past life with an appreciation for the human lives lived alongside it. The nature of the past points to the future: if it happened once, it can, short of extinction, happen again. Paleo-ornithology is an ornithology of possibility.

The inhabitants of Bronze Age Jarlshof used skuas. Their remains have been found in digs uncovering settlements of that period, alongside the extinct, barely imaginable, great auk. It is not entirely obvious what they would have been used for: food, ritual, or perhaps just killed to prevent the daily harassment. It is the same at the nearby Neolithic village of Old Scatness. The species of skua is not ascertained by the archaeologists, which leaves us a puzzle. *The Birds of Shetland* suggests that the great skua is a recent arrival to the northern hemisphere, as its only relatives are (usually) found deep in the southern hemisphere. The oldest known record of an Arctic skua from the archipelago is from Noss in 1701. Paleo-ornithology, it seems, is still ignored today.

As, sadly, is Fisher. His 1957 *Desert Island Discs* recording is missing from the BBC archive – though from the list of chosen recordings we can see a love of classical music and dusty bar-room jazz. It was recorded before his untimely death in 1970, a car crash cutting short his career, leaving his large family bereft. He was only fifty-eight. In the 1950s and 1960s he was a prominent voice for nature as a TV and radio presenter, making over a thousand broadcasts; an author of guidebooks, travel writing and scientific monographs; and an editor of the prestigious New Naturalist series.[5] He was part of the team that claimed the lonely Atlantic islet of Rockall for Britain in 1955 by cementing the Union Jack to it. He even shaped birding – rather than 'birdwatching' – by coining that snappy contraction himself. Fisher has focused our ideas on birding and nature so successfully that we can see through his eyes. He is like a pair of binoculars: he adds clarity and definition while not impeding our view. And the luxury items he chose for his desert island sojourn? Proper plumbing and binoculars.[6]

They don't make birders like James Fisher any more. Walking around the drystones of Jarlshof, I feel out of place with my binoculars. Unable to imagine either the depth of the past and its accretions or the level of bird hunting that enabled the survival of the people that were here. There are no skuas today – just a Shetland wren sneaking between the gaps of the stones and an old blackbird nest, with one cold egg inside. I'm certain Fisher would be seeing things that I can't.

⌣

Nowhere on Shetland is more than 3 miles from the sea, because of the voes that cut into the heart of the isles and the headlands that splinter outwards. Here you are surrounded by edges. A short drive up the coast takes us to the top end of the Loch of Spiggie, where a pair of bonxies are strafing the surrounding fields, seeking to flush nesting birds from their eggs. The edges are making and remaking themselves. Loch of Spiggie was the sea once, before Scousburgh Sands sealed it off, forming a barrier between loch and sea. Just north lies the tombolo of golden sand that has tied St Ninian's Isle to the mainland since the last Ice Age, being reclaimed by the sea only temporarily on the highest of tides. The sand that some tides take away is replaced by others.

Shetland is young and old. The further up the west side you go, the older the rocks get, until you end up with Lewisian Gneiss. At 3 billion years old, Lewisian Gneiss is the oldest rock in Britain, and older than most life forms on the planet. The ground cloaking it becomes peat, an accumulation of semi-decaying material. Drying out in an apparently exceptionally dry spring, the cuts in the peat bogs – where the peat has been harvested for turf logs to be burned as fuel – makes it seem as if the ground is flaking apart, like dead skin. We take a walk up one gurgling burn into the high peaty moorlands. It feels like the Pennines but unkeepered, unmaintained, and curlews and whimbrels sing through the heather-sided valley. There are skuas just beyond here, just out of reach, as the track dissipates into thick heather and bog and there seems to be no way through. It is a tantalising prospect: skuas on the moors, seabirds away from the sea, but still just out of reach.

It is an unusual sensation, when watching wildlife, to have wildlife watch you back. Skuas are one of the few species who will. To have a bonxie watch you is one thing. To have one fly at you is something else. There is a frisson, a fear that comes from no longer feeling like the most dominant animal in the landscape. I knew a pair of bonxies in a boggy North Ronaldsay field that never managed to raise young. They ignored me all summer, as I walked at a respectful, safe distance past the edge of the field. One day, in late summer, I couldn't see them lurking ominously in the field. I thought it was safe. So I decided to cut through the middle of it, following a natural crease in the land, a ribbon of yellow where the marsh marigolds grew. An unfamiliar route. I was keeping my eyes on both the horizon and the ground underfoot. The first I knew of them was the whistle of wings behind my head. And then the bonxie was banking sharply in front of me, locking eyes, stooping. I felt like a target, as if it was aiming for just behind me and that to get there it would go straight through my skull. It did not. Feet dangling, it pulled out of its stoop a few feet away from my head and, in a blur of brown wings, shot past my ear instead. Sending a message. I stuck my hand above my head – part apology, part deterrent. I never walked that way again.

Fear is not something we usually feel about British nature. Skuas are a correction to that. They demand respect. Arctic skuas are supposed to be even more tenacious than bonxies in defence of their nests and territory. Supposedly they do not whistle past your ear but repeatedly swoop from close range. But – and I am slightly disappointed by this – never on Shetland, Orkney, Sutherland or Handa Island have they targeted me. I have always been too late, too early, never at the right place at the right time. I am torn between wanting to feel the thrill of the attack and respect for the bird, not wanting to disturb it at all.

Skuas are indivisible from Shetland. Through the spring and summer it is the skuas that come, if not to define the coastline here, but to agree with it. There is awe in the edges; of the rocks and waves and wind-scoured clifftops. There is awe in the birds that bully, loaf, stoop at and mug passing gulls for food. It is their right place, their home.

The right place. I am always interested in how people find theirs. Sophie Green, an islander and student who I spoke to, found hers here on Shetland, having visited for a week one September 'to stand at the edge of the world'. And the effect for her and her partner, she says, was that 'we came, we saw, we moved here five months later'. I talk to Green about great skuas, but conversation catches flight and lands inevitably on the landscape.

The sea runs in Green's veins from a childhood on Sheppey. The lure of an unenclosed life is a strong one. The paradox that islands and the sea provides – a hard (wet) border and the space to dream beyond it is powerful. Even though she lives here she dreams of Northmavine: the isthmus of Mavis Grind and the old volcano of Eshaness and a landscape to lose your heart and head to.

Skuas are the seabirds with the power and drama to match the landscape. Great skuas match it for the ridiculous and the sublime. Green's first sighting of a great skua was one taking a ginger nut biscuit from the hand of the Noss boatman. Her second skua was ripping the stomach out of a puffin.

There is a privilege to living here in the post-oil age. Green was recently diagnosed with chronic fatigue syndrome and the precariousness of island life, which hangs over everyone here, can be amplified by living with a chronic illness. But Green feels that if she's struggling, then she is in the best place to cope with it. Breathing in the freshest of Britain's air, listening to the sea and all its birds, she says she feels, momentarily, unbeatable.

Green's favourite place for seeing great skuas is Hermaness. The northernmost headland, the northernmost island of the UK. She promises that there is a part where their territory starts where all you can see for miles are big brown bullets, fighting in puddles, protecting their nests, circling your head.

$\smile$

The irony of great skuas is that they are globally rare, so they are desirable for conservation organisations and the growing ecotourism trade on the archipelago. They are desirable because rare wildlife feels special, because they make the landscape feel unique, different from the rest of the country. Yet they are undesirable for their piracy, which offends our ethical sensibilities, and for the problems they can cause sheep farmers. A further irony: they were initially welcomed by shepherds for their skills at driving away other predators, including white-tailed eagles. But there are no white-tailed eagles left on

Shetland and there haven't been any since 1917: in their absence, 40 per cent of the world's great skua population breeds here.

In the words of Faroese skua expert, Sjúrður Hammer, 'Great skuas have a great talent for finding trouble.' It is this talent that has led to a conflict. One that is reputed to happen on the hush in Shetland, but happens in broad daylight, with full legality, in the Faroe Islands: Faroese farmers shoot both great and Arctic skuas. Great skuas for taking lambs when neither ewes or shepherds are looking. The rationale for shooting Arctic skuas is less clear – it is perhaps a hangover from the days of hunting auks for food, when a skua could flush away a potential meal and leave a family hungry.

Skuas have an unusual cultural life. Their range and their lack of gaudy, easily recognisable plumage mean they're not a commonly known species. But they do have a niche use in the military—industrial complex.

The industry behind the military has a trend of naming its technical creations after wildlife – from de Havilland's moth biplanes in the 1920s and 1930s, to the contemporary harrier jump jet, the F15 eagle, the F16 falcon and the F22 raptor. Things that fly get named after things that fly. It is almost as if the metaphor is a psychological trick that humans want to play on themselves, a belief that human flight is as natural as a bird or moth taking off, that human-on-human aggression is as natural as birds of prey hunting.

The Blackburn Skua was a bomber used by the Allies at the start of the Second World War. It is an inelegant, stubby plane, one that looks as if it was cobbled together from pre-existing pieces that don't quite fit together. The ruins of many minor tragedies with the Skuas

– crash landings, collisions with barrage balloons, fatal stalling – litter Scapa Flow and the seas between Orkney and Shetland.[7] As a plane, it shared something of the skua's etymology. The Skuas were withdrawn in 1941 – replaced with no small irony by the sleeker, faster, more destructive Fairey Fulmar.

But it is not just planes. The Sea Skua is an air-to-surface missile that saw use in the Falklands and the First Gulf War. The Sea Skua is designed to be launched from a helicopter, fly three times faster than the Blackburn Skua, and puncture a hole in the hull of a ship. It then detonates a 30-kilo warhead. Calling it skua makes perverse sense. A skua is an avian air-to-surface missile, a striker of fear and pain into any living thing that strays too close to its territory. Skuas lack malice. They act out of an honest self-defence, the only difference being that they attack instead of retreating or distracting. They tend not to kill. They don't carry warheads, they have mugger-heads; they have no desire to destroy, just an injurious desire for the food of others.

The desire to militarise skuas is not just restricted to military-equipment manufacturers. For Niall Rankin, the metaphor worked both ways. He was a lieutenant colonel in the Scots Guards, as well as a wildlife photographer of international repute. In his 1947 book *The Haunts of British Divers* he records 'a noise like an express train followed by the rush of air similar to the faint blast of a far-off bomb. No part of the bird struck me but the unexpectedness of the thing made me duck instinctively.'[8]

I hate this anthropomorphism. I love skuas, and I am a pacifist. It is a libel, a human imposition on the moral neutrality of the natural world. But this is something of which skuas make a habit: being awkward. Every time a nature documentary shows a skua robbing

a puffin of its fish, the instinct is to question the moral neutrality of nature. Puffins are presented as the hard-working, honest
birds that we innately care about because they're cute. The skuas
are slandered. Social media is outraged. My colleagues hold me
personally responsible for the depravity of skuas. It is wholly untrue.
The narratives we apply to nature reflect our own biases; they are
used to justify our own unrelated morals. It is a flipside of the libel
of naming missiles after skuas. The purpose is not to naturalise our
behaviour, but to elevate ourselves above nature, above other species like skuas.

The day breaks dreich. The valley smothered in drizzle and wispy
clouds. We are heading north, as far as is possible. We are heading
to Unst.

It is not just the lure of our own *Ultima Thule* that draws us
here. Not just our internal magnets that point north, to the furthest
north we can go in the country. Unst is half the distance to Norway
as it is from the English border. It is 640 miles from London and
just 410 miles from the Arctic circle. There is a romance to space
and sheer geographical fact.

On the map Unst looks like a fragment, a chunk of the fraying
northern edge of Shetland floating off further north. It feels that
way too: like an edge and an end of things. The road winds up to the
moors and then heads straight as a spine up the island, past lochans
in gravelly, tundra-like turf. And briefly there is nothing around and
my heart soars for the freedom of it, until we pass Baltasound, the
only thing that resembles a town this far north. Baltasound was once

like a city: in the heyday of the herring industry it had a population of 10,000. It is now a small village. The entire island's population is just 632.

Just beyond Baltasound is the Unst bus shelter: a furnished bus shelter, complete with fridge, microwave and phone line. The decorations change annually and this year there is a large model puffin dressed up as Emmeline Pankhurst with a Woman's Social and Political Union armband around its wing, and flags of purple, white and green. It is part eccentricity, part generosity, and both are the sort of thing that can be cultivated on small islands, where trust holds sway and the prospect of vandalism isn't a concern. The bus shelter is at the corner of a track to the Keen of Hamar. The Keen of Hamar is even weirder: a stony hillside of serpentine, but most of the rocks are sandy brown, with lumps of glossy, glaucous serpentine mixed in. It is a landscape of contradictions: it should look Arctic, but it is too colourful. It looks hard, but the stones are soft underfoot, not yielding like shingle but more like sand. It looks barren, but between the rocks plant life flourishes. I find several groups of Edmondston's chickweed growing among the stones, a plant found nowhere else in the world other than the stony hillsides of Unst. Ten petals of white curve out, around a ring of yellow anthers and an off-white stigma. The flowers look oversized to the rest of the plant that lurks low among the stones. It is appropriate: an endemic, an eccentric, found in the weirdest of habitats on a most unique island.

Unst is the ultimate extremity. As we drive further north, skuas increase their roadside presence. Arctics dashing, always heading over the horizon, eluding a long view. Greats doing the precise opposite, lumbering in lazy flight.

Shetland is a Viking archipelago. It has spent almost as long being ruled by the Norse as it has by the British and even then it was transferred to Britain only as a default on a dowry by a Danish king. The influence is felt in the names, in the old dialect, in the old Scandinavian sagas. Skuas behave like Vikings and the Shetlands are Britain's skua islands. It is almost as if it was meant to be. The Viking heritage on Unst is particularly tangible. By the road is a reconstructed stone longhouse and a wooden longboat that was built in twentieth-century Norway and abandoned in Shetland during an attempt to sail it to North America, following in Leif Erikson's eleventh-century wake. On the headlands of Unst, skuas are raiding and thieving food, stealing territory, behaving aggressively, and are also tenderly feeding their young, raising the next generation. Skuas suffer, like Vikings, from a reputation for spectacular violence and theft – one that is not always deserved.

In Celtic Christianity there is an idea of thin places. Not a literal isthmus, but a metaphysical one, where life stretches and reality wears thin and heaven permeates through. I found one on Unst by the door of a cafe.

On Unst a building can serve multiple purposes. In a steel-framed shed a cafe becomes the village shop, occupying the same lot as a vehicle workshop. Things happen here without airs and graces. Locals take their mid-morning breaks while island-hopping tourists arrive and gaze at the puffin tat and the island souvenirs, made in China. The radio buzzes with the Boys of Summer and I drink my cappuccino, which originated as powder, lumps still floating beneath

The Seafarers

the surface foam. Yet all of this is provisional. All of this is just one life and can be left behind. When you close the cafe door and step out into the breeze you find silence. Then snipe, drumming, and wheatears preening on the fence posts by the road pull you inexorably over the hill and down into the valley. There a flock of great skuas – I counted 187 of them – wash the sea and salt from their feathers in a loch. One more ascent. Park up. Pick up a map from a case weighed down with rocks. Pass through the pearlescent kissing gate. Along the moor boardwalk the celestial flora: tormentil, Spring squill, milkwort, the white stars of dry sphagnum moss and orchids. Heath spotted orchids the size of golf balls on tee-sized stems. Over on the far headland sits the giant golf ball of the Saxa Vord radar installation, a huge white pastiche of the orchids: a newly recommissioned monument to political paranoia. Dark pools stud the moorland. Cotton grass floats cloud-like, fluffy and trembling in the breeze above.

This is what we have come for. This is Hermaness – home to the world's third-largest colony of great skuas, the place that Sophie Green talked so glowingly about. At this time of year they are more interested in each other than in harassing us. Although seemingly omnipresent along the coastline, out of the sea they become something else. They could be raptors, the apex predator of the archipelago. It is to them that all other life here answers.

A pair drifts in. They land on their territory next to the path. Fling their wings back, lean forwards. They call together, to proclaim their bond, a throaty, nagging sound. They are uniquely white speckled down their crown, grizzled, almost old looking.

The further north you go in Shetland the more skuas you see. And the further north you go at Hermaness the more skuas you see, until you reach their zenith on the moor's peak. Skuas cruising, chasing, gliding, patrolling their moor. One swoops low, wings whooshing above our heads, apparently more curious than aggressive, its head turning, tracking, eyes fixed firmly on us. Other birds are noticeably absent. And I still feel a little flutter every time a bonxie flies past. This is true terra skua: land ruled by fear.

Moor becomes grass. The horizon opens up. An edge, then the sea. The cliffs here are almost the end of Britain. Only the skerries of Muckle Flugga and Out Stack lie beyond, between me and the 2,000 miles of open, empty-feeling sea to the North Pole. The cliffs look like the end of land too. In an archipelago of extraordinary walls of rock, where the deepest-possible past comes to bear on our existence, Hermaness is the ruptured end: rock split, folded, forced and thrown. The cliffs look traumatised, slipping their way to the rocks and stacks of the shoreline like smashed teeth. Gannets and auks nest there. A steady supply of skua targets. From the dizzying heights of the cliff edge, they speckle the skerries and stud the sea. The exuberance of life in the Shetland summer.

Crossing back over the moor the same close pair of skuas is still present near the track, but sitting apart. I watch as one, I assume the male, preens, puffs up, waddles over to his partner and, arching his neck, exudes as much tenderness as a skua can. And then, an instant later, he assumes a defence posture, the pair springing back, raising wings, howling. Another male drops in. The new bird grabs the old male. They go beak to beak, the curving machete tip of each bill a whisker away from the other's eyes. The female watches, frozen in her defensive posture. The male's feet kicking, claws scratching at the breast feathers. Wings flapping, frantically. The interloper pins the old male down. For ten minutes they remain locked on the ground in a stasis of equally matched aggression. The interloper tries to press home his advantage, raising his beak to strike. The old male slips out from underneath, takes a step and springs into flight on yet unbroken wings. The interloper closes in after him. The female follows, as a Valkyrie. The old male is ushered on his way.

3

Auks – Northumberland

Before leaving Mainland Shetland, we climb to its southern tip at Sumburgh Head – a narrow point of rock shaped like the prow of a Viking longboat. Standing at the foot of its lighthouse, we bask in a view of sea in three directions and Fair Isle, a whale-backed island in the sea halfway between Shetland and Orkney. A silver sky with high, textured clouds gives the still sea a shimmer, turning grey, silver, blue in stripes. A boat ploughs a small wake through, the only interference. On the thrift-capped cliffs around us crowds of tourists watch in adoration as puffins dive into their burrows, sleep or pose, mere metres from the road.

Like every other member of the auk family, puffins invite anthropomorphism. They stand upright on two legs, familiarly human. Their razorbill cousins look most like Darth Vader in a white smock – sharply black-backed, thick-necked and flat-headed, with a cut-throat razor for a beak and a brilliant white front. Guillemots are similar, but dark chocolate brown instead of black, more slender on the neck and head, a small dagger for a bill. Puffins are – well, everybody knows they are a startling species. In a country where most of the wildlife has been smoothed out, pared down, evolved into the brown and unobtrusive, they are extravagant. Their beak is frippery, the colours bold and saturated, their plumage stark and tuxedo-like. Here at Sumburgh Head, they are busy, always moving, always charismatic – the holy grail for British wildlife, for being not secretive, not brown.

Puffins stand in stark contrast to the Arctic greens and greys of Shetland, and landscapes further north. The scientific name they were given is *Fratercula arctica*: little brother of the Arctic. Their English name is more interesting. 'Puffin' is a word that was applied originally to the young of Manx shearwater that grow larger than adults in their nest burrows.* The definition of that original use of puffin is a bird so fat it is puffed up[1] and the body of a puffin is, as Mark Cocker puts it in *Birds Britannica*, 'sumptuously rotund'.[2] Colloquial names shed another light. In old Shetlandic and Orcadian dialects they are called 'Tammie Nories'. Intriguingly, this is also a term used for the paradoxical character of a person who is 'shy and gauche', which makes sense: they are gaudy and they stand proud, but have that innate distrust of man that marks them as wild.[3] In Faroese-Danish they are 'priest': perhaps due to the pontificating sounds they make.[4] But being portly and noisy cuts both ways. Kenneth Williamson records that a Faroese fishing superstition of not referring to things by their proper names meant 'the parson is mentioned in a mildly libellous fashion as *lundi*, the puffin'.[5] The final twist to this is that the Faroese today still hunt puffins for food, with a net on a 10-foot pole on a clifftop. It is probably safer to be the parson or priest than either the hunter or the puffin.

Sumburgh is Shetland in a microcosm – a place I could happily stay for days on end, where all of the island's species can be seen. But time catches up. Soon we are on a plane curving up and away, its tail to the headland and its nose out to the sea. My mind turns

* More about the Manx shearwater in chapter 7.

to the next destination on my travels – a place almost synonymous with puffins and where I hope to get better views of the other auks too: Northumberland.

This is not one consecutive journey but a series of smaller ones. I have a partner to plot a future with, a cat to stroke, and a job four days of the week to not be fired from. Time off is limited: I had to explore the northeast of England without taking a day off work. And so it is that I find myself on the long haul of a late-night train journey from Essex to Newcastle, followed all too quickly afterwards by a bleary-eyed drive at dawn to my destination on the coast.

Grey sky, grey streets, grey buildings give way to verdant hedge-rows and the deep green lushness of the landscape at England's northeast edge.

Seahouses, 8 a.m. The early grey is burning off in the morning sun. There is no breath of wind and the sea is stilled. The scattered fragments of the Farne Islands are laid out beyond the harbour. Inner Farne is the closest and most prominent of the fifteen small islands, crowned by a whitewashed lighthouse. Binoculars halve the distance and reveal the haywire, fizzing, frantic bird activity – terns and auks buzzing about, heading out and in, mere dots at this distance. Strung out further beyond: Staple, Brownsman and the Longstone lighthouse, little fragmentary lumps of rock that would shape-shift further as the boat ploughed out to meet them.

Seahouses lives for the Farnes. The Farnes lives for its puffins, so Seahouses lives for puffins too, and the high street bears this out. Only the Co-op and the discount clothing store lack puffins in their window displays. Otherwise it's puffin sculptures, puffin bunting, puffin prints, puffin bowls, puffin mugs, puffin coasters, puffin tea towels, puffin scarves, puffin notebooks, puffin erasers. A slogan nestling among this flock reads, '72,000 puffins can't be wrong.' Some are more anatomically correct than others and the most discounted look like sad clowns with the make-up running off their faces. Others look as if the only bird their maker had ever seen was an obese pigeon. The poor razorbills don't get a look in.

By 9.30 a.m. the queue for the boat is over a hundred deep. It gets split between two boats, but people are still wedged in with no room to move. The ropes are untied. 'Howay,' shout the boatmen. A Newcastle United scarf hangs from the front window and shakes with the engine judder, sways with the swell. We are the tourists here. They tell us that it's a southern thing to say 'excuse me'; if anyone is in our way on the islands, we should go with 'get oot the rood'. The boat chuckles at the caricature northerner, hamming up the local for our benefit, reminding us that we're not from around here, we don't really belong, we are all effete and southern and unlike them.

The forecast dictated Staple Island in the morning, Inner Farne in the afternoon, when an increasing westerly wind would make landing at Staple's exposed jetty tricky. The sky fully cleared, the sea blue and choppier than earlier. Sea spray catches me in the face. I wipe it away, lips stinging with salt. I turn back around to stare at the sea. Eiders bob up beside us, terns, gulls, auks overhead. Birds, everywhere. The first puffin flies across, excitement rippling through the crowded boat. The sea here is so fertile that even gannets sweep alongside us, glowing ivory in the sunlight. The nearest they breed is on the Bass Rock, just east of Edinburgh, an old volcanic shard of rock in the sea, white in summer with massed gannet nests. They are border reivers for the abundant fish.

The dark wedge of Staple Island emerges. Scale is tricky. Its cliffs are nothing compared to the vastness of Shetland. The 170 crumbling metres of gneiss at Hermaness dwarfs the Farnes: Staple is barely 250 metres wide at the island's widest point. They are incomparable colonies. But the auks are closer here. More densely packed into a smaller space. Here it feels as if it would be possible to reach out and touch them – though I never would, for their distance feels necessary and vital, and I fear the stab and nip of their beaks.

More impressive than the sight of Staple Island is the smell of it. Bird shit becomes guano when it accumulates and in auk colonies it accumulates as a foul white crust. These islands are formed from dolerite, a cracked, basalt-like volcanic rock, the black, grey and brown of a bruise, except for where the auks nest, where it is painted pale every summer and protected from the rain by the bodies of brooding birds. It has the foul, fermenting smell of canned anchovy brine, seasoned with rotting seaweed. It is the smell of a rich, fish-laden sea. It is the smell of a past, a time before the depredations of industrial fishing. The time in the nineteenth century when the herring wives – women from the east coast of Scotland – would migrate up and down the east coast of Britain, from Shetland to Suffolk, following the fisherman, packing and processing the herring they caught for export. A rich industry until we took too much and an entire nomadic culture collapsed.

The boat pulls up to the slipway. A ranger offers a hand. The boatman an arm. I am bundled on to the island with the upwards motion of the swell, with all the grace of a sentient sack of spuds. The slipway is primitive. Narrow steps kinking across the rocks.

Another ranger checks my ticket, my right to be here among the auks. I'm allowed on. Next to the slipway is a cleft in the coastline, what on the Northern Isles would be called a geo. It is covered in a dense layer of guillemots. Squabbling, murmuring. A gull flies over, looking for loose eggs, rippling the flock – like fur being stroked or a reptile's scales raising and lowering in one sinuous movement.

We make our way across an island that was empty of humans several minutes ago and is now crowded. We muster around the National Trust's shed for an introductory talk from a ranger, while we stare at puffin-decorated tea towels and baseball caps. By the main cliff, pairs of shags sit, serpentine, on nests or next to chicks clad in dense black down that looks like lamb's wool. They are panting already. The gular patch under the bill flared, beak open to the yellow-lined gape, and each mandible moving up and down. It is a long, hot day on the shadeless rocks for their young. The adults can at least go fishing and feel the breeze run through their coiffed head feathers. One adult is wearing a blue ring on its left leg, marked 'AJE'. These are designed to be seen and reported by birders as a way of collecting information on the birds' longevity and distribution. The warden tells me this one was born on the Farnes, has lived on the Farnes, and will likely die here when old and winter storms starve them to death.

Away from the main cliffs, a few razorbill pairs are scattered. One pair stands breast to breast, touch bills and preen each other's heads, nape and clavicle, turning aggressive-looking bills into tools for tenderness. Preening each other (known as allopreening) is an act of courtship, a continual courtship that lasts far longer than the initial meeting and mating. Theirs is a bond that lasts, but needs work, though the bonding seems too pleasurable to be called work. It's hard not to anthropomorphise allopreening – it looks close to affection. Almost human. Razorbills are shyer, more in need of space and quietness than the guillemots. This seems in short supply on Staple, though somehow they manage to find the quiet corners in the bustle to be tender among the stench and the noise and the onlookers.

It is perhaps this shyness that has led to the razorbill being the overlooked auk. It is not just on Staple Island that they exist under the shadow of the guillemot. In ornithology, it is the guillemot's puzzles that are solved. In culture, it is the guillemot with the literary history and the collection of colloquial names. Despite this, the razorbill was the original auk. They were known by the family name until John Ray, a seventeenth-century Essex boy, parson and early ornithologist, gave them the new name and it stuck. The razorbill is saddled on Shetland with 'sea craa' as an old name, suggesting something solitary and dark and not entirely trustworthy. In Orkney they were known as 'coulterneb': literally 'plough beak', for their similarity to the shape of the coulter, a blade that breaks the ground for the plough, but it is also a more imaginative name for the way a diving razorbill's beak carves through water as a plough cuts through earth.[6] That bill – plough or razor – is extraordinary. It is, to my eyes, shaped like a pair of wirecutters. Glossy black, it is marked with vertical ridges, one with a thick white line that is bent at a right angle to one that runs from the back of the top mandible to the eye. There's another white line that runs along the rear of the wing, from the bird's back to where the wing bends. Standing with its back to you and its head at an angle, a razorbill is pure black and three white lines. Their shyness hides their chic.

Binoculars aren't needed on the island. It's possible to see everything without them. Today cameras are commoner than binoculars among the crowds. But binoculars are useful for limiting peripheral vision, for focusing your eyes on just one scene, and searching for others. They cut through the chaos. A slight turn and refocusing to the foreground turns a razorbill pair into a herring gull, dipping its bill into a cracked guillemot egg, yolk dribbling onto hot rock, with the robbed flock in the background blurred and shimmering. Another turn, to focus on the flock: guillemot necks snaking, heads turned towards the gull, eyes focused on the threat. Another half-turn of the focus wheel and puffins appear, flinging themselves into the clifftop, kicking feet out at the last moment, averting painful landings. Some carrying thin, silvery strands of sand eels. It is nature as a kaleidoscope, bright and busy and changing with every turn of the wheel.

Guillemot eggs are a good prize for a gull, as they once were for people. Their yolks are proportionally larger than those of other birds, which makes them richer, more nutritious.[7] South of here, on Yorkshire's 6-mile finger of chalk, Flamborough Head, the colony of guillemots was so vast as to be subject to intensive harvesting. It has been recorded that, 'Up to 140 eggs were taken in a single climb, 1,700 a day and about 130,000 annually by up to four teams.'[8] The sheer number of guillemots nesting, and thriving enough to cope with such losses, is almost unimaginable. As well as the eggs being a delicacy, they had other uses. The Victorian naturalist William Yarrell reports, 'Large numbers of eggs collected at Lundy Island are taken to Bristol, where they are said to be used for clarifying wine; and at Flamborough . . . many were sent to Leeds, the albumen being employed in the preparation of patent leather.'[9]

When not being used, guillemot eggs have been puzzling ornithologists for two centuries. It was in 1831 that William Chapman

Hewitson spun an empty shell and decided that the unique pear shape of a guillemot's egg was best explained as a way to allow an egg to spin instead of being blown or knocked off the narrow cliff ledges the birds nest on. This common-sense explanation entered the canon of popular ornithology and, despite being disproved in the 1980s, it is still commonly regarded as being true. The answer was discovered only in 2017 by Tim Birkhead, a man best described disrespectfully as 'Mr Guillemot' or respectfully as one of Britain's most eminent living ornithologists. His team carried out a complex serious of calculations, demonstrating that the pear-shaped shell of a guillemot egg gives it greater contact with the rough rock surface than a regular-shaped egg, making it much more secure and resistant to the frequent impacts in the dense bustle of the colony.[10] The team's other discovery was that the bulbous, blunt end of the egg was much less likely to be covered in detritus than the other end. This lets the embryo breathe through the porous eggshell, and lessens the likelihood of bacterial infection.[11] This is particularly important as guillemots excrete where they stand, often in the colony. Razorbill eggs provide a nice contrast. They fall between the usual egg shape and the guillemot's egg shape. Their shyness towards colonies means they don't require the same extravagant adaptations for strength and hygiene; they are rarely covered in shit or caught in a crush.

A couple of weeks after the eggs of both species hatch, the young, still only half grown, are led off the cliff. One parent flies down to the sea and calls. The chick jumps. Their primary feathers, the feathers on the very tip of the wing that are essential for flight, haven't grown yet. Instead the chicks glide on stumpy, unfinished wings. The fortunate land in the sea. The less fortunate bounce against rocks on the way down; the impact is said not to affect them, however wince-inducing the collision looks to us.

Once grown, the guillemots develop into a teardrop shape: their bodies wide and stocky, their necks long, their thin heads tapering to a sharp, pointed bill. The further north your guillemot was born, the blacker its back. In England they are a dark brown, mostly all plain. On the Farnes, 6 per cent of the guillemots are not plain, but have a thin white ring of feathers around the eye, extending into a line running towards but not reaching the back of their necks. A figure of 6 per cent does not sound like much. But 6 per cent of a lot is still a lot. Individuals with this line are known as bridled guillemots and they increase in frequency in the north. As yet, we do not know why, although we do know lots about guillemots. We know that their young learn the adult's call in the egg and that a guillemot on a cliff can recognise its partner in flight from over 100 metres away.[12] This acuity wasn't always appreciated. An archaic name for the bird, used even in the Victorian period, was 'foolish guillemot'. 'Guillemot' is an unusual name: it is the diminutive form of the French word for 'William'. It is perhaps partly onomatopoeic, like the bird's American name, 'the murre', for the throaty cacophony that buzzes from the breeding cliffs.

I walk across to the far side of the island, to escape the flock of photographers and rattling shutters. The centre of the island is within a blue rope, the area where we are allowed to wander without fear of trampling nests, though several eider and a great black-backed gull nest are individually marked out or roped off. The dolerite is angular, cracked and uneven as if it has frozen the bubbling heat of the volcano that formed it. It is dappled with sulphurous lichens, tufts of pallid, salty grass and small pools. Staple

Island is a distracting place – it's hard to be around so many birds and still keep an eye on whether your foot is treading on rough rock or into a slimy, algae-slicked puddle. There's an old Norse proverb for being 'as drunk as an auk' based on the unsteady motions of razorbills on land.[13] On Staple Island it's possible to be drunk on auks, blundering about in a daze of birds.

Boats keep arriving. The density of people becomes extraordinary, almost rivalling the density of the guillemots. The only uncrowded part remains the side looking out to Brownsman Island, over a thin gap of sea. My inner razorbill insists I stand there. There are no cliffs here, and there are no puffins, so the people are fewer. Instead, seaweed climbs up the rocks, eiders bob about in the sea, and guillemots arrow overhead, wings quivering, out to sea. The cliffs of Brownsman are, as all cliffs here seem to be, full of guillemots. The side facing us is striped three colours: green from where the strands of seaweed kick up with the tide and try to climb up; dark grey out of the reach of the waves, where only the gulls sit, and ivory where the guillemots nest and wash the rocks with what remains of their digested fish. It is solitude I seek, so I sit there, on the flightpath between those guillemots and the sea. Solitude is an absurd idea here, the busiest island for birds and people.

The boat trips give you several hours on the island. It is not entirely necessary. In that time you can do repeated laps of the roped-in area. You can see every species within a matter of minutes. To do so is to miss the point, spectacularly. Offshore you can see the boat operators mustering, lining up, talking across their sterns until their time to return. To synchronise time with the boatmen you need to sit on a rock and watch the puffins for what they do, which is quite regularly nothing other than standing on the clifftop, stretching, preening, squabbling. They are reminiscent of teenagers sitting in parks, waiting for things to happen. Puffins loiter, in a way that other birds just don't seem to have the time to do.

While they loiter, I loiter. With too much time, I look more closely than I ever have before. I look more closely at the details, I try to see a puffin for its parts, not its whole. I see it for the curving shark's tooth of dark grey–red–grey that surrounds the eye, pointing upwards. I see a dark, indented line that runs back from the eye, like a guillemot's bridle in negative. I see the way that the grey face patch doesn't end at the nape, but carries on in a thin grey line around the back of the neck, joining up with the other side. I see the puffy golden flesh at the gape, bunching up like the folds and bulges of a brain. I see how the grey face patch is smudgey and darker under the gape and behind the eye. And I can still see a puffin only for its head and not its squat body, for its orange-red legs dangling in flight, the last thing you see on a puffin flying directly out to sea. Perhaps it is understandable. The exaggerated features of their faces are comic, naive, and outsized. Cocker suggests, 'We love puffins, it seems, because these funny little birds remind us of our infant selves.'[14]

The largest swathe of grass on the island is a bank in the lee of a fold in the rocks. It is patchy, the vegetation loose and threadbare, the soil riddled with holes. On top of the bank puffins stand, waving their bills around like beacons, waddling on stumpy orange legs that appear too short to support their thick, round bodies in motion. Others fly straight and disappear directly down the holes. They nest there, several feet underground, excavating in the loose soil, turning their flipper-like feet into shovels and their beaks into axes. Once completed, it takes a puffin pair more than a month underground to incubate their solitary egg. More than a month to feed it to the point of fledging. They head far out to sea on those foraging flights, gathering multiple fish. They grasp the fish, bill lined with a multitude of sharp little teeth to keep them in position. Then they face the gull gauntlet, heading back for their burrow, evading the birds trying to bully them out of their fish.

I like puffins, but I like the other auks more. It is, I think, snobbery on my part, the birdwatching equivalent of disliking pop music but listening to it anyway. People are mostly here for the puffins and it is their unique capacity for holding the imagination of people that would otherwise pay no attention that makes them a useful species. They grab headlines and sympathy. They are our public bird, our ambassador for the sea. The town of Amble, halfway to Newcastle from here, holds an annual puffin festival, publicising those that breed on Coquet, Amble's local island, while the town itself fills with crafts, music, talks, walks, surfing and kayaking. Not all of the events have an overt puffin theme. The message is about kindling a love of the locality – the sea and the high street, the environment and the economy. When I passed through, just after the festival had finished, the town was still dressed up in puffins, in a way it would be impossible to imagine had it been a razorbill festival.

There is something almost innocent about Staple Island. It feels unimaginably plentiful and dense and bold and everything modern British nature isn't supposed to be. It feels untouched – untouchable – by humans, yet if you imagine it, you have to imagine something like a zoo. Animals, close, yet out of reach, on display and apparently unbothered by the admiring crowds. Because of it, places like

Staple Island get called seabird cities. It is an easy metaphor, commonly used in promotional materials to convey the sheer, staggering density and diversity of seabird colonies. It contains elements of truth. These colonies are noisy, rambunctious places, home to large populations. But they are also anarchic places far removed from the law and order of a city. There are guillemots covered in the shit of others because they couldn't get out of the way in time. Fights break out. Birds shout over others, steal their fish, pilfer seaweed from their neighbours' nests.

To call Staple Island a city is to draw a false contrast between urban and rural, civilised and wild, natural and unnatural. Places touched by humans and places untouched. I'm not sure that such artificial divisions of the world really apply any more.

There is a school of thought that we are now living in a new epoch – the Anthropocene – defined as the era in which the majority of things on earth have been altered by the actions of humans. The environmentalist Bill McKibben captured its essence well in the title of his 1989 book on global warming, *The End of Nature*. It suggests that the Anthropocene is best regarded as the end of the old normal in nature, the severing of the use of 'natural' and 'normal' as synonyms. In the Anthropocene, nothing quite works as it used to, nothing quite works as it should. The environment is like a train timetable – ecosystems delayed, cancelled, things not arriving, subject to change.

Among those who support the idea of the Anthropocene, there is disagreement on when it should best be said to have started. Some point to the 1950s and the profound shocks of radiation the world received through the first nuclear testing carried out in Nevada. Others go back further, to the invention of the combustion engine and the advent of industrial capitalism in the 1800s, or even as far back as when humans first laid down their spears and sowed crops instead. My view is that the defining moment came with the invention of synthetic plastics at the turn of the twentieth century. By the 1950s the world was already producing 1.7 million tonnes of the stuff, and by 2013 that figure was 299 million tonnes.[15] It is not the sheer amount of plastic that matters so much as its apparent indestructability – its synthetic defiance of the decay and death that all things had hitherto undergone. It was the first invention that truly seemed to sidestep nature and natural processes, which seems to me to be the defining feature of the Anthropocene.

There are many ways that the Anthropocene has denormalised seabirds, though perhaps the most notable, the most disturbing, occurs off the east coast of Greenland. The little auk is an Arctic species, best imagined as a guillemot the size of a starling. The little auks throng the high Arctic cliffs, breeding with a density that is astonishing, in numbers hardly imaginable. They spend the winter in the high north too – a tiny bird tossed about on huge waves, only rarely seen in Britain when they are pushed south by strong northern gales. In a 'normal' state of nature they are some of the wildest, remotest species that exist in the North Atlantic.

But – and this is the Anthropocene, where nature always comes with a but – in two studies, nine years apart, scientists examined the stomachs of some of these auks in east Greenland. A hundred per cent of the little auks tested were found to have ingested the plastics polluting one of the remotest seas in the north.[16] Every single one. The scientists speculate that the prevalence of pale plastics in their stomachs means the auks are confusing them with their food, krill. The same krill that powers the North Atlantic's few remaining blue whales.

The way this works is all gallingly familiar. In 1962 Rachel Carson indicted DDT and other chemicals in *Silent Spring*. In doing so she demonstrated the way that invisible, insidious pollutants can build up in the environment. Derek Ratcliffe built on her work to provide the links between DDT and the thinning of eggshells in peregrine falcons found far away from the original use of the chemicals, eventually succeeding in getting DDT banned in Britain (its ban in the US occurred much earlier). Legislation is slow. We've known for over half a century that potential pollutants will inevitably end up as actual pollutants. That things, once let loose in the environment, travel. In much the same way that DDT sprayed on arable farmland would end up in the eggs of a peregrine's eyrie many miles away, a plastic bag caught in the breeze, a balloon released as a memorial, a dropped water bottle, plastic beads in face scrubs and toothpaste, will inevitably make their way into the water course. They will be washed away, washed into the sea and swept up in ocean currents. American, Icelandic, Faroese plastic washes up on our remotest Atlantic coastlines. Ours gets found on the beaches of the Netherlands, Germany, Scandinavia.

There is a bird that has seen all of this. 'Wisdom' is the oldest wild bird in the world. She is a Laysan albatross, ringed as a nesting adult in 1956, which makes her at least sixty-eight years old. She breeds on Midway Atoll, a tiny volcanic rock and coral island located almost precisely in the middle of the north Pacific Ocean. An American army base since 1903, it was also an albatross colony long before humans knew of its existence. Wisdom has outlived the Nevada nuclear test site; she is older than *Silent Spring*; she has seen cars and plastics become widespread in use, and lived through multiple cycles of economic boom and bust. Through it all she is still raising young. Wisdom is the figurehead of her species, an ambassador for albatrosses. She has seen what is happening to her species.

What is happening is most starkly illustrated in a series of photographs by the artist Chris Jordan.[17] I cannot bear to look at them for very long. They are of the Laysan and black-footed albatross chicks on Midway Atoll. Jordan's photographs bear a poignant resemblance to an anatomical diagram, where half the body's skin has been peeled back to reveal what's inside. Because in these photos it has. His albatross chicks are bone, rotten skin, soiled half-grown feathers. The stomach contents – not rotting – reveal their last meals: lighters, bottle caps, fragments of children's toys. The photographs are not aestheticised. They are all more or less all the same. Taken from directly above, they are close-ups of dead chicks and the plastics spilling out from where their guts should be. These photographs are the direct evidence from the front line of the war plastic is passively waging on our seabirds. Cumulatively, with each photograph, the emotional reaction grows more visceral. My only response is to grieve for birds I have never personally known – to grieve for a species I will probably never get to know.

Other plastics splinter, erode into tiny plastic particles, filaments detectable only under a microscope. They are known as microplastics. These are what were found in the stomachs of the Greenland little auks. Compared with the albatrosses of Midway Atoll, the little auk problem seems less significant. Only forty-four little auks were tested and they appear to be able to survive their dose of microplastics. However, for currently unknown reasons, the population of little auks seems to be decreasing. Often the evidence is not so stark and obvious as it is with the Midway Atoll albatross. A dead auk with microplastics in its gut has not necessarily been killed by them. It is a not quite smoking gun. A recent study by the Scottish Association of Marine Science has found microplastics in species of brittle stars collected from 2 kilometres deep, at the bottom of the Atlantic, dating all the way back to the 1970s. This problem is not new.[18]

⌄

I hope we don't wait for absolute certainty. I hope we don't wait for legislation. We have a culture where I can walk to the supermarket and take home in a tote bag aubergines and cabbages that are individually wrapped in plastic, where I can watch balloons released for celebration or commemoration, and where I can order drinks that come with plastic straws and stirrers that are thrown away after five minutes. This is all frequently unrecyclable. The problem seems out of control. I am guilty. We all are. Disposable plastics are so ingrained in our culture that to go without is almost unimaginable. Yet this is all avoidable.

Solutions are difficult. It is not helped by the fact that the well-informed frequently fail to act. A recent survey of conservationists revealed that their behaviour was on average only marginally better than that of people of other professions. It seems that we aren't as rational – or perhaps as committed? – as we think we are, or perhaps ought to be. A recent research paper by Chelsea Rochman on the impact of marine debris finishes with this ominous warning:

> There is a pressing need for robust, quantitative information to predict ecological impacts to species of wildlife that are considerably contaminated with marine debris. The presence, sizes, frequencies and nature of ecological impacts are

currently largely unknown. There may be large-scale impacts that we are missing simply due to a failure to examine them.[19]

We are not as well informed as we think we might be.

There is one specific warning from the past about this. Only one species of bird that used to breed in modern Britain has gone extinct.

The great auk is hard to imagine. It takes the scientific name *Pinguinus impennis*: the original penguin, or, to translate it cruelly, the fat and flightless. Great auks were large, standing three-quarters of a metre tall. Black-backed, white-fronted, most similar to a razorbill with an additional window of white on the forehead. Like all auks, they were clumsy on land. They nested in an arc across the subarctic North Atlantic, from Orkney to Iceland to Newfoundland. And, as happened to the dodo, they were destroyed by sailors. They would feed hungry sailors, both with their flesh and their eggs, or their oil-rich bodies would fuel fires. The great auk is a species that was pillaged out of existence, aided, in part, by itself. Tame enough, so sailors said, to be ushered on board ships – 200,000 were taken from Funk Island, Newfoundland, alone.

Yarrell's *A History of British Birds* was published forty years after the last great auk was killed. His section on the great auk is included because it 'would be incomplete without a notice of it, albeit "In Memoriam"'.[20] His memorial is a litany of destruction. A series of occasions when the species was killed. It veers from a grudging respect to wanton destruction. For example in Orkney:

> One male . . . had regularly visited Papa Westra [*sic*] for several seasons . . . Mr Bullock had the pleasure of chasing for several hours in a six-oared boat, but without being able to

kill him, for though he frequently got near him, so expert was the bird in its natural element that it appeared impossible to shoot him. The rapidity with which he pursued his course was almost incredible. About a fortnight after Mr Bullock had left Papa Westra, a bird, presumably the same, was obtained and sent to him, and at the sale of his collection was purchased for the British Museum, where it still is.[21]

This should be contrasted with the violence of the British abroad: 'In 1808 the crew of a privateer under British colours remained there [Geirfuglaskér, Iceland*] a whole day, killing many birds and treading down their eggs and young.'[22]

The great auk is so difficult to believe, so the story goes, that the last example of the species in Britain suffered an ignominious end. It was taken while asleep. Its killers tied its legs together and 'took it up to their bothy, kept it alive for three days, and then killed it with a stick, thinking it might be a witch.'[23]

It is hard to imagine the level of destruction, the bloodlust that it takes to eat, burn and collect a species to extinction. Yet it happened to the great auk. It has been going on for thousands of years, and it is still going on today. According to reports published in 2001 by the Conservation of Arctic Flora and Fauna (CAFF), the biodiversity working group of the Arctic Council, the indigenous peoples of Canada have a long history of seabird harvesting dating back thousands of years. European settlers also brought their own tradition of seabird hunting, which has continued for the past

---

* The original Geirfuglaskér was destroyed in a volcanic eruption shortly before the extinction of the species.

500 years.[24] This is not ancient history: the largest recorded seabird hunts took place in the latter decades of the twentieth century in the province of Newfoundland and Labrador. Before 1993 these hunts were estimated to have accounted for between 600,000 and 900,000 birds, a figure that has since been reduced by legislation to 200,000–300,000 birds a year.[25] In the 1990s there were thought to be 10,000 auk hunters in the province, and though a more modern estimate eludes me, it is certain that the practice still happens today. Anecdotally, the shells of shotguns wash across the Atlantic and are found frequently by the beachcombers of Shetland and Orkney.

CAFF's most recent report on the killing of Arctic seabirds sounds an additional warning. Before the twentieth century, 'Hunting was done primarily from non-motorised watercraft and so likely had only a local impact on seabird populations. Since then, human population growth, mechanised transport, and the use of guns has increased the harvest of many species of seabirds.'[26] The threats are obvious and the impact runs in tandem with plastics and climate change. It is likely that auks will always be hunted by the indigenous people of the Arctic and the inhabitants of Newfoundland and Labrador. This is not just a cultural issue, but a deep-seated tradition, one rooted in surviving the long, ice-bound winter. I cannot criticise, even if the echo of the extinction of the great auk leaves me deeply uncomfortable.

The sea and its birds are finite, though they can both look infinite. It wasn't realised how close to extinction that bloodlust had brought the great auks, until they were all stamped out. This was in part because people like Thomas Jefferson, the third president of the United States of America, were of the opinion that nature was too perfect for extinction to happen. With the loss of the great auk we lost more than just the species. There is a link to the exceptionally deep past of the Mesolithic and evidence that they were once more widespread. Cosquer Cave in the south of France has three auk figures daubed on the walls in black pigment. They are plump and flipper-winged, like a child's drawing of a penguin. They look unerringly, uncannily, like great auks. The cave entrance is now, rather appropriately, under water due to the rise in sea level. When we lose wildlife, we lose a part of ourselves and our shared human experience of the world.

We are losing our seabirds. I fear that what we are seeing with plastics is perhaps the beginning of another death spiral. The guillemot is on the amber list of conservation concern. The razorbill is on the amber list of conservation concern. The puffin is on the red list of conservation concern.

I once found a puffin's head on North Ronaldsay's beach. It had been long severed from its neck, more familiar with the salty flow of cold sea around its skull than the warmth of blood. Its golf-ball-sized skull was pitted and eroded. Stained off-white by time. It was defined by the large holes where its absent eyes would have sat. Only the top mandible was still attached: its orange, yellow and blue clown smile faded by death and the sun, like a rictus grin in an old posed photograph. Three grooves down the side of the bill identified it as being a four-year-old bird – dead one year short of becoming a fully breeding adult, a clown in a dinner jacket down a burrow. I have no idea how it died. Gull, skua, otter, misfortune, starvation, pollution – all capable of killing. Some death is natural, some death is necessary. Some death controls numbers, stops puffins from eating all the sand eels, or riddling islands so full of burrows that the soil above the rock collapses and is washed away, as Lockley says happens to the puffins of Grassholm.[27] Some death enables the predator – perhaps a bonxie or a great black-backed gull – to live and rear young. Some die in an oil slick, or tangled in rope. Some die stuffed full of plastics. Some deaths – too many deaths – aren't natural.

In a pub overlooking Seahouses harbour we drain bottles of Farne Island ale. A puffin stares back at us from the label, the Northumbrian flag curling around its neck like a scarf. The beer has no connection to the island beyond the branding. The brewery isn't particularly local either, being sited on an industrial estate west of Newcastle. But sometimes the doe-eyed, bright-coloured puffin branding is hard to resist. Puffins have become more than just a bird. They have transcended themselves. If they went extinct in the next year they would still exist in more than just memories, photographs and taxidermy collections. There is a grim irony to think that the endless plastic-based puffin memorabilia is likely to outlast the species. It's even bleaker to think that it's a symptom of the mindset that will probably cause their extinction – and that of many other species too.

While we have puffins we should celebrate them. Puffins are the bird that everyone knows and loves, even if they can't name any others. And while we still have them in staggering numbers and density, we should make the most of them. Puffins are our public bird, our ambassador for the finite birds and the sea. They can speak for the guillemots and the razorbills and the little auks too. I just hope the tale they tell is not that of the great auk.

4

Eiders – Northumberland

Same day, same boat. Different island. This time Inner Farne, the largest island in the archipelago. It is a greener place than Staple Island, more fertile. In part because it is more sheltered, though that is hard to tell this afternoon: the wind springing unexpectedly as we travel between islands, covering the sun with clouds, and a chill is creeping, threatening rain. The wind rips at dock leaves, nettles and thistles, white clumps of scurvy grass and a few shaking bulbs of sea campion. It is easy to ignore the vegetation between the burrows, to be distracted by the posing puffins and shrieking terns. It isn't the most exciting plantlife – too early in the year for the full display of flowers, too harsh an environment for anything but the hardiest to grow. Those that do, manage to make it in the most marginal of environments. It is easy to underestimate the tenacity of plants that grow here in thin, salty soils, battered by the elements.

Along the boardwalk dock proliferates, hand-sized leaves ruffled by the wind. Under the overhanging privacy of one plant, a black glass-bead eye shines back, feigning sleep. The eider's neck is bent back and her beak tucked under a wing. She looks much neater than I had ever noticed before.

It is human to look at animals and see only yourself. Or rather your limits. I look at eiders, but I really see stoicism. The wind picks up, whipping horizontal rain drops across the island. The drake eiders around the islands head for shelter, curl up on rocks out of the wind and wait it out. The female eider, pretending to sleep in her den of dock and down, broods on, incubating her hidden eggs. She will hardly leave the nest while incubating. Some die of starvation before the eggs hatch.[1]

As the wind ruffles the dock, it reveals more of the eider's plumage. Not plain brown, but browns: a warm chestnut and auburn. There are darker feathers, some almost black on the wing, but all with pale fringes. On her ginger flanks are dark bars spaced out. She is not just brown but spangled and tiger-striped; delicately, cryptically coloured. It is wholly functional camouflage. Nature's beauty is one of the happiest of accidents. It works too. Earlier on Staple Island I had almost stepped on an eider nest, not seeing the female sitting on a platform of grass growing out of a fissure. She blended perfectly with the dappled darkness of grass and dolerite. She could have been a rock formation; she could have taken root and grown from the tattered, salt-bleached grass. Instead she sat, unblinking, unhesitating, devoted to her eggs, centimetres away from the visitors, with only a shin-height cane for her own protection. We were both fortunate I stopped. It would be easy to be auk-blinded and, stumbling across in the whirl and daze of birdlife, not to see her stoically sitting; and not to stop, and to feel the sickening, guilt-making crunch of a breaking egg. I don't know if the risk is worth it. I don't know if it is safer to sit, unseen by egg-snatching gulls, screened by a thicket of legs and tripods, or to be at the mercy of one stray footfall.

Even if the female survives incubation, even if the eggs remain uncrushed by stray feet, the odds are stacked against the next generation. Survival rates for the young in Scotland can be as low as 0.1 per cent.[2] But they are a dogged species. They can live for over thirty years.[3] They get second chances. When winter comes, she will head north to the big east Scottish estuaries, the Forth and the Tay. If she finds a new mate from a different colony, it is he who will move to join her.

The stoicism of the eider on Inner Farne comes as no surprise. I had seen the capability of the species during my stay on North Ronaldsay. It was my second full day and I was retracing the coastal steps I took on the first, familiarising myself with the new territory by blunt repetition. The weather was still pulverising, rattling the glass in the window panes, raindrops sounding like a campfire crackling still thwacking off my hood, still stinging my fingers. Waves curling, crashing. The sea white with the churning of water. In such moments it is impossible to imagine life in the sea, or imagine the sea as anything other than the wild death throes of energy, thrashing. Sound and fury and nothing. It is exhilarating and terrifying. It scrubs the skin like nothing else. Scouring the mind with its elemental otherness and indifference to human endeavour.

Reaching the furthest point of the headland I was about to turn back inland, when in the white horses and clouds of salt spray a pair of eiders flew across the wind, a wingbeat above the crashing surf. A pretty duck bludgeoning its way through the weather. A large duck looking small in its fevered habitat.

Against a storm-ruffled sea, the white drakes stood out starkly. Under their feathers and skin they are fat and muscle. A touch larger than a mallard in every direction but twice as heavy. Their bulk enables them to fly at speeds of at least 70 mph. To find faster you need a swift or a peregrine falcon – birds that would never be seen flying unperturbed in this weather; birds that would not be physically capable of surviving the winter sea in the far north.

There are four species of eider in the world: common, king, spectacled and Steller's. The last three are all Arctic specialists. King and Steller's are rare visitors to British shores. The males are spectacularly adorned with bright colours and elaborate plumage; the females cryptically feathered, camouflaged for their ground. The males of our species, the common eider, are no less spectacular. Unlike the other seaducks, they breed here in good numbers (26,000 pairs at the last count) and spend all year on our coasts. But they are not ours alone. They were spread by the Ice Ages, pushed south to England by the impenetrable ice sheets. As the ice retreated, some stayed south but they spread back north, following the ice edge, to the far north of America, Scandinavia and the far northeast of Russia. They are the global north's seaduck.

They also breed in tiny numbers (between one and five pairs) on Switzerland's inland seas and along the Black Sea coast of Ukraine, where they had been unknown until the 1950s and exceptionally rare until the first successful nest was found in 1975. By the mid-1990s, there were almost a thousand nests.[4] Nobody quite knows why, other than a widespread increase in Europe in the twentieth century.

Our drake eiders are mostly white and black. White back, white thigh, white breast and face. The flanks, rump, lower back and cap are black. Then their plumage gets weirder. On the nape is a sickly pale-green wash, extending around the side of their face. It bisects the black cap and is in turn bisected by a white stripe on the cheek.

The breast is flushed peach in the breeding season. They are built sturdily – or in the words of writer Louis J. Halle, 'too heavily built to be graceful. Of all our ducks it is the most stalwart and powerful, broad in the beam like a seagoing tugboat.'[5] The bill is big and droops at the tip and is lined with teeth-like ridges for the grasping of wet crustacea. Behind the bill runs a small duct to a pair of glands above the eyes. These are the supra-orbital salt glands that clean the bloodstream of salt from a lifetime of seawater. The bill and legs are a dull mustard colour here, although the bill changes colour across the world. The common eiders of the Pacific have a bill varying from marigold to carrot in bright richness.

Across Britain they vary in size. Those I saw flying past the North Ronaldsay headland in a gale are a unique form shared by Orkney, Shetland and the Faroes. Despite the harshness of their surroundings, they are smaller and the females are darker than those found on the British mainland.

Under their surface you begin to understand what makes an eider. The scientific name for their genus is *Somateria*, a portmanteau of the Greek for body and wool. The binomial, the species-specific part of the scientific name is *mollissima*, from the Latin for soft. Eider down is unique. The small fluffy feathers close to the skin on a female eider's breast are plucked and they line their nests with them, a second layer of insulation for keeping eggs and young warm in the short, unpredictable northern summer. It is thought to be one of the best insulating materials in the world and has a use in Arctic clothing: 1.5 kilos of synthetic down supplies insulation to −7°C; 1.5 kilos of eider down insulates to −35°C.[6] Eider down also has a use in luxury duvets. Its French name, *eider à duvet*, rather makes the point.

In 2016 a kilo of eider down (the contents of 60–80 nests) cost about £1,500 at export.[7] The Icelandic Eider Association says an average of 3,000 kilos of down is harvested a year. It makes the eider unusual among seabirds in being actively useful for humans beyond being a source of food. Despite this, eiders are also on the amber list of conservation concern in Britain. Globally they are 'near threatened' and according to Birdlife, eiders 'almost meet the requirements for listing as threatened.'[8] Being economically useful is apparently not enough.

Eiders have never been regularly hunted for food. Erik Pontoppidan, writing in mid-eighteenth-century Norway, records that 'the flesh tastes fishy; so that none of these birds are eat, except by the poor, that sacrifice taste to necessity.'[9] He goes on to gloss the ways that this can be counteracted. It finds a counterpoint, 200 years later, when Margaret B. Stout, wrote her book of recipes for Shetlanders, *Cookery for Northern Wives*. Stout shares Pontoppidan's disdain for the taste of eider meat. Whereas he recommended a marinade of vinegar before roasting, Stout stews hers and serves with lemon. Neither seems particularly appetising.

Erik Pontoppidan is little known nowadays in British natural history. There is perhaps little reason why an eighteenth-century Norwegian bishop would be, after all. Like many early naturalists that we know of, such as John Ray or Gilbert White, he was a religious figure. These were people who had the time to investigate the world around them, which they saw as being full of the wonder of God, and who were educated enough to write and communicate about it. This was, of course, before Charles Darwin challenged a world view that had hitherto seamlessly seen nature as evidence of divine work.

Pontoppidan begins his work *The Natural History of Norway* with a theological justification:

> I am therefore inclined to think, that neither I nor my bretheren transgress the bounds of our ministerial office, by investigating and exhibiting natural truths concerning the works of God ... I am rather of opinion, that a supercilious neglect of such truths, in this critical age, is one of the causes of that contempt, with which the Freethinkers, as they arrogantly title themselves, look on the ministerial function.[10]

Historical irony can be a wonderful thing. A century later and Darwin turns this on its head: studying nature leads to freethinking, agnosticism and atheism, not the neglect of it.

Perhaps unexpectedly Pontoppidan's work is full of good descriptions of birdlife, and a certain charm – helped by being eccentrically inconsistent about names. On the eider (or as he also knew it: the edder, ædder or wild duck), he describes it as 'in shape and size it keeps a medium betwixt the Goose and the Duck, so that one may, with equal reason, call it a small Wild Goose or a large Wild Duck.'[11] His own taxonomic confusion aside, he accurately records its use to the people of northern Scandinavia: 'The feathers of its breast, which are known far and near by the name of Eider-dun, make annually a good livelihood to people in many places.'[12]

Pontoppidan gives this as a reason why eiders tend not to be killed. Yet in Finland's Åland archipelago, spring hunting of eiders falls between local and continental legislation. The local government permits it. In 2001, the estimate was 7,000 males killed. A female eider in a pair does not breed in the same season as being widowed[13] and perhaps because of this the breeding population in the Baltic Sea declined by 40 per cent in 15 years.[14] It is illegal under European law to allow spring hunting in the breeding season and the European Commission has taken the Finnish government to court over it – something that could have been avoided if the Finnish people had taken Pontoppidan's advice.

Intriguingly Pontoppidan suggests eider down was not a universally appreciated substance: 'That this edder-down is unwholesome, and particularly, that it gives the epileptic sickness, is contradicted by Th. Bartholin . . .'[15] The idea that eider down can lead to epilepsy is interesting, in part for being so bizarre. An instance of blaming the blameless and defenceless bird. Eiders have a habit of ending up as the subject of human ideas. They seem to attract the religious as well.

The day after my trip to Inner Farne, I journey further north. The weather is completely different. It is the final day of May. The sky is cloudless, the air breathless. T-shirt and shorts.

The map for here is drawn at low tide. Tucked behind the Holy Island of Lindisfarne lies an islet too small and insignificant for anything more than two lines and a dot on the map inside the speckled foreshore. St Cuthbert's Island is a tidal island – a reluctant island, a twice-a-day island – that this sunny afternoon was just a splash across the rock-strewn, barnacle-studded sea path. Beyond the slippery rocks it is a low grassy mound, speckled with pink thrift and yellow trefoils trembling in the breeze. A thin wooden crucifix stands on top. Off the muddy edges, two female eiders lie sleeping, necks crooked back, beaks under wing.

Eiders don't regularly breed on Holy Island – you won't hear their cooing here – but they can regularly be seen throughout the year, in the shallow water, rooting around the mud and sand for crabs and mussels. But I'm not here for eider – at least not directly. I'm here to look back into the past.

We are 2 miles off the mainland. The Cheviot Hills crown the dark horizon. Tiny villages nestle on the shoreline, obscured by the glare of unrelenting sunlight on sandy beaches, a searing gold band even at this distance. The dunes south point at the distant Farne Islands with an exaggerated rolling wave of sand. To the north, the expanse in between the island and the mainland begins to repeat itself to the horizon, stripes of sandy brown, interrupted by magnesium-white lines, trembling to the end of . . . nothing. Not sea, not land, but something debatable, something uncertain, untrustworthy. The mirage-strewn land of neither. The final temptation for the pilgrims, their own short miles of desert.

The name, Holy Island, and the cross are burdens borne on the land by its human history. It is not just birds that will flock and seek shelter in numbers, out here, on the edge of things.

It is hard on days like this to walk the past back into life. It is hard when the weather saps the atmosphere of a place to rekindle the cold lives of the distant past. Heat induces lethargy, hazes the details, saps the effort.

It doesn't help that nothing visible remains from the depth of past that I want to reach but the physical geography, the broad low sweep of the sandy island and the rocky islet. The red stone of the ruined twelfth-century priory glows like Mars in the sunlight, the impressive vaulting arch somehow still standing in the way of the wind. Underneath the priory remain a few foundations from the original Anglo-Saxon monastery. The associated museum has a few of its carvings: the sun and moon, supple knots and stark crosses crafted out of stone, hard evidence of the people that lived and died and feared the Viking raids here. I have to erase the rest – priory, castle, harbours, houses, car park, tea shop, church – from my mind. But not the eiders.

Northumbria was an Anglo-Saxon kingdom stretching from the Borders to the city of York, and east to the Humber estuary. Its king, Oswald, was Christian but its people were mostly pagan. Oswald invited the Irish monk (and later saint) Aidan over to begin a new monastery here on Lindisfarne, and to begin the conversion of the north to the new religion. Life was hard in seventh-century Northumbria – between the Roman occupation and the Vikings' merciless raids on eastern Britain, which began with the sacking of the Lindisfarne monastery in 793.

Cuthbert, born in 630 and a shepherd in the Cheviots before becoming a monk, was in charge of Lindisfarne Priory. Burned out by the squabbling of different doctrines and interpretations, he was driven to seek the isolation that liberates the mind. He was driven to the life of a hermit.

He began his ascetic existence on the small rocky islet that became known as St Cuthbert's Island. From his time on the island, only the vegetation is likely to have stayed the same. The crumbling remains of an old wall was added later. The cross is a reminder that people like to mark and remember things, a beacon for the pilgrims.

Cuthbert, subject to the evergreen addiction of islands, the search for the ever more remote, left for Inner Farne and a decade of hermitic study, loneliness and theology. The French travel writer, Sylvain Tesson, writing of his own experience of six months alone in the Siberian taiga, writes that 'the luxury of a hermit is beauty. Wherever you look, there is absolute glory.'[16] For Cuthbert there was this beauty, but there were also the seabirds. *Reginaldi Monachi Dunelmensis Libellus de Admirandis*, written by the monk Reginald of Durham in the twelfth century, records:

> In the Island of Farne there are certain creatures which since the days of blessed Cuthbert have been hand-tame . . . birds have been named after the blessed Cuthbert himself . . . They are so tame that they nest inside dwelling houses, where they come to the table, and construct their nests under your bed, yes, and even under bed coverings.

I found this quotation, in its suspiciously informal translation, in a pamphlet about eiders in Lindisfarne's church. The description of eider behaviour seems exaggerated, though they do have a habit of nesting in unusual places, such as behind gas bottles on the Farnes,[17] or under the steps of a well-used stile on the isle of May,[18] a habit that led to stone nest shelters being created in tenth-century Iceland, to help the Vikings collect the down from their nests.

It's the legend that Cuthbert was the first conservationist and eiders the first protected species that has brought me here. It would have taken the restraint of a saint not to hunt these fat, tame ducks, their eggs and down heaven-sent relief for cold, hungry islanders and coastal villagers. Their colonies could have easily been destroyed in a glut of wrung necks and boiled eggs.

Halle records seeing an eider wounded by two men on a boat. Catching it alive, 'they beat it to death with their oars.'[19] Indigenous cultures in northern Canada – particularly the Cree and the Inuit

– hunt eider out of necessity, for food and clothing. Eider are one of the few animals capable of surviving the far northern winter, where they keep patches of Hudson Bay open and unfrozen throughout the winter with the heat and motion of their bodies.*

The use of the name 'St Cuthbert's duck' – or, more colloquially, 'Cuddy's duck' – to refer to eiders still persists in the northeast of England, though it is not in birders' common usage. As a name it is nicer than 'dunter', the colloquial term for eider on the northern isles that derives from its habit as 'one who bobs up and down'.[20] Resident of Lindisfarne, Ian Kerr, argues in his book *The Birds of Holy Island* that the name is a Victorian invention, a faux-timeless tradition with no earlier use, despite Reginald's alleged twelfth-century report. James Fisher, in *The Shell Bird Book*, suggests it 'is a medieval refinement of his history'.[21] He also mentions fossil records from the Viking settlers of Shetland (between the ninth and eleventh centuries) showing that eiders were exploited for food. If 'Cuddy's duck' is a medieval refinement, it makes sense as a lie that those who seek Anglo-Saxon heritage tell themselves, to bolster their own sense of civilisation, against the supposed heathen invaders who eat the blessed ducks.

I don't think it necessarily matters where and when the legend came from or how commonly it remains in use. It preserves a connection, a tradition, between a hermit and his wild animal neighbours. It roots the eiders in the area, as proudly local as the saint. They are ducks with a divine right to life.

---

* I recommend watching the documentary *People of a Feather* (Arctic Eider Society, 2012) for further information about the Inuit and Cree, eiders and changing weather and ice in the Arctic winter.

But is the legend real? In a study of the origins of the association between Cuthbert and eiders, folklorist Antone Minard has identified the earliest reference to the islands as being protected by a law from Cuthbert as recently as 1962, in a work by Northumbrian naturalist and Farne Island specialist Grace Hickling.[22] Her source was Reginald of Durham. Minard identifies this as being an example of folklorismus: the misuse of folklore for commercial ends. Reginald was writing in a guide to the newly opened tomb of St Cuthbert in Durham Cathedral, an embellishment to pull in the pilgrims, that had the ring of potential truth about it. Religious hermits, Minard says, are usually credited with special relationships with animals. So here was Cuthbert's.

The afterlife of Reginald's early marketing fiction was that it has been repeated uncritically since the 1960s and lost to obscurity before. It is a story that speaks to the modern desire for enlightened, empathetic approaches to wild animals, an organic origin for conservation, when, as Minard says, 'What is clearly uppermost in Reginald's mind is the Christian notion of sanctuary and its accompanying protection; there is no hint that the ducks as a species need protection.'[23] The legend is robust; eiders more so. The violence that the legend threatens against eiders never seems to have materialised.

In the grounds of Lindisfarne priory there is a large bronze statue. *Cuthbert of Farne* by Fenwick Lawson depicts a gaunt-faced St Cuthbert, his hands clasped, verdigris robes rippling. He is the picture of stoicism, of quiet devotion, the textures of his robe and craggy face casting him in moody shadows when the stark afternoon sunlight suggests this should be impossible. And taking shelter at his feet? Another stoic. St Cuthbert's duck. The eider.

The lure of alone. It appealed to St Cuthbert. It appeals to me. And it is what brought R. M. Lockley to Skokholm. In fact, Lockley was not alone when he first discovered the island, but on holiday with an older man, an artist and island fanatic that he knew as 'Admiral'.[24] It is love at first, distant, sight: the sandstone island with its 'garland of surf' seen through binoculars from the mainland, where no fisherman would take him due to the weather.[25] His early descriptions are charmingly romantic, laced with possibilities and awe for the future he wants on the island. It is not his first real island, not the first one he had made himself either. His trips with Admiral have taken him to the nearby Skomer and Ramsey islands, both now nature reserves, but then populated. Lockley feels envy.

His desire for isolation does not come twinned with misanthropy, but an earnest, eager love for the lives of animals instead. The first half of the first sentence in the first chapter of Lockley's book, *Dream Island* runs: 'To dwell alone with birds'.[26] He is staking out his ambition, early. *Dream Island* is his first book. It is first published in 1930, the year he turns twenty-seven. His young years spent looking at maps, memorising the names of the remote islands, north and south, reminds me of mine. Dreaming of alone.

Only – and this is to become a recurring theme with Lockley's plans – it doesn't work out like that. Admiral was a dentist but lived on a farm. While he worked in Cardiff, he left the running of it to his daughter, Doris, who had been falling in love with Lockley by letter, while ostensibly exchanging nature notes. His description of this begins with 'More complication was to arise', suggesting that his island Romantic soul probably found human romance not to be his forte.[27] However, he gives up on his vow of celibacy. They wed the next summer, a year after he takes over the island lease, in the church by the beach at the appropriately named St Brides Haven. The hermit becomes a couple. The couple becomes family in the year of *Dream Island*'s publication. Ronald, Doris and Ann Lockley.

Starting a family is not very hermit-like. Saints-to-be did not tend to indulge in such behaviour. But then the Lockleys are not saints: they are not of heaven but of earth. Life in the farmhouse as recorded by Ronald is at the mercy of the elements. Like St Cuthbert, like the eiders. But the elements that strike Skokholm give as well as take. They both make life hard and wreck ships he can salvage. The farmhouse that the Lockleys – and some storm petrels – live in is renovated with timber from a wrecked schooner that was also carrying enough coal to keep their fires lit for several years. It is the sea that provides them with fish and lobsters for sustenance. Their comfort and discomfort on Skokholm is controlled by the sea. Life there, for the Lockleys, is a dialogue between sea and land. Their drive is not to spiritual satisfaction – there is nothing metaphysical about their island life, but something more scientific. The word 'metaphysics' finds its origin in the Greek for 'beyond nature'. For the Lockleys there is no beyond nature, just nature itself. Nothing to transcend.

The world we live in is increasingly urban, increasingly crowded. In Britain, an area the size of the county of Rutland – roughly 147 square miles – is being taken out of natural or agricultural use and built on every decade.[28] The British population is forecast to increase by 5.5 per cent between 2016 and 2026.[29] We have more people, but less natural space to seek shelter in, fewer places to be outside, to feel the full positive effects that science is discovering nature has on our mental and physical health. Fewer places to breathe air without lung-clogging particulate matter and where the buzz in our ears is the sound of our own thrumming blood, or the rolling of waves and the whistling of wind through leaves, not traffic. The problem is not more people, but the loss of space.

And as our natural spaces dwindle, so they also come at a premium. A trip to the Farne Islands costs a lot. Lindisfarne is exclusive. These places are almost all middle class and white. It is also unusual to see a woman outside alone – the hermit you imagine is as male and white and as well insulated from the world as a drake eider. The birder is commonly identifiable from the fieldmarks of a beard and bald-patch. It should not be this way. Nature should not be the preserve of the affluent.

When I first left for Orkney I had only a small amount of savings – but it was enough to be my down against the world. I also had the luxury of youth – of having no ties to bind me to London beyond my employment. For all that I had an overactive flight tendency that at the time drove me to run from my problems rather than to tackle them, I'm also aware that I had the privilege to choose to do so. I had the luxury of indulging my headstrong desire to move very far away. To consider birds as good a map through life as any other.

The birds, my guides then, showed me in seven months on North Ronaldsay things that I now find hard to believe: killer whales, the Northern Lights, meteors and a night sky so bright with stars it looked fake, islands 50 miles off in the absolute clarity of dawn, brilliantly blazing sunsets, the energy coursing through the legs of a newborn lamb leaping and the blood-flaring intent of diving peregrine falcons. I revelled in the exquisite tangible taste of the earth.

In politics and economics, that taste of the environment is regarded as a luxury, secondary to the essential business of making money, a marketing hook for the leisured classes. There's something of that in the story of St Cuthbert too. Before he died, he expressed the desire to be buried in the isolation of Inner Farne, in the place that came to define who he was. Bede, writing in his eighth-century work, *The Ecclesiastical History of the English People*, says that he was, essentially, talked out of it, and into a grave at Lindisfarne Church. A shrine was born. A shrine is a marketing opportunity, a shrine encourages pilgrims and miracles, legends and donations. Later, Cuthbert's remains were taken by the Christians fleeing further Viking invasions to Durham where first a church, then a magnificent cathedral was built to keep his shrine. The simplicity and isolation of the hermit's life gave way to an eternity spent amid the trappings of the city.

Coastal Northumberland is still trading itself on the ideas of Northumbria, the same isolation and solitude that Cuthbert experienced, 1,400 years ago. Time might not have changed the physical geography that much, but finding the same kind of isolation is now a much trickier prospect. Lindisfarne cannily models itself on connections to the past: it has a winery producing mead, gift shops selling ale horns and Celtic designs. Just as St Cuthbert's grave became a commodity, something to experience, so has the island. It is hard to walk out from the village to the coast on a day like today and find a moment's rest, a relief from the tourists, pilgrims, people like me, seeking out the past, feeling conflicted.

5

Terns – Northumberland

They screech like a thing being torn in two. Jump up from the floor to a metre above head height. Swoop, swoop, swoop once more until satisfied the intruder has moved on. They float back down to earth. Rest on their eggs. Look up. See another visitor walking up the path. Jump up. Screech. Repeat.

It's not easy being a tern. It's not so gentle walking in a tern colony.

It is a cold summer's afternoon on Inner Farne. A matt grey sky is fraying at the edges into squalls. A keen breeze nips at the dock and nettles growing, somehow, on the weathered salty rock. Typical island weather for an atypical island. A queue of fifty people waiting for the boat back to the mainland forms the backdrop, as fifty more are disgorged and meet the Arctic terns for the first time.

The slipway is narrow. The terns are hidden by the queue of people waiting to return and the unwary have yet to put on their hats or hold up their arms. They come suddenly, hidden against the grey sky. Translucent wings frantically beating, fierce thin heads wielding beaks as weapons. I want to look but can't for shielding myself. Hat, hands, arm, hiding my soft eyes, soft flesh from their assault. I look down instead, their shrieks passing within a foot of each ear. The slipway becomes boardwalk, fenced off from the rocks by thin blue twine. Under that rope, tern nests. Three brown eggs, smooth as pebbles, property of the tern harassing me. There are so many terns and so many nests here that the transition between terns is almost seamless, as if I was being passed along as a plaything.

There is no running water on Inner Farne. The toilets don't flush. The National Trust runs a basic gift shop for the island essentials: tea towels, fudge, biscuits, postcards you can't post until you get the boat back. All of these emblazoned with puffins. Opposite the compound, the old chapel dedicated to St Cuthbert is built on the site of his old hermitage, a musty, mildewy building with elaborate dark-wooden carvings and tiny windows. It dates back to the fourteenth century but its only use now is to shelter – either terns nesting in its lee, or watchers from the rain – while it elegantly moulders.

Away from the Inner Farne chapel the boardwalk runs to the lighthouse. There is a brief gap in the bombardment before the terns begin again. Their harassment keeps us circulating around the boardwalk, each peck a heartbeat in the vascular flow of tourists. The pace is frenetic. Things go wrong otherwise. People stepping off the boardwalk to pass others. Or people purposefully standing next to tern nests to incite an attack, then standing there while the tern exhausts itself, its eggs exposed to the afternoon chill, with a grin and a thumbs up for the ideal selfie.

The noise is piercing, the action head-spinning, the density and the abundance of birdlife and visitors bewildering. It's like a Hieronymus Bosch painting – a carnival of animals and people unlike anything I have ever experienced. In one way it is heartening that so many people want to spend their Tuesday afternoon in late May experiencing British birdlife. On the other, I feel uneasy about being part of it. The colony is not a fragile place. Rock is not easily damaged. The terns' food supply is not affected by us being here.

The birds are more tolerant – Arctic terns aside – of our presence here than they would be elsewhere. Yet it still feels too much. It's hard to square the National Trust's insistence that it limits visitor numbers to avoid undue disturbance with the 50,000 people that are allowed to come every year.

Terns are not dissimilar to gulls. The basic pattern is the same: thin white body, long white and grey wings, black heads in summer. Enough to confuse me in bright sunlight, when anything white turns dazzling. This is where the similarities end. Terns are thinner, lighter and quicker, capable of speed and sudden turns, diving from height and staggering migrations. They move like mercury and burn as bright as magnesium, when gulls can seem as dynamic as chalk. Terns are innately charismatic, the sort of bird that always seems to be doing something, always seems to be worth watching. They have a habit of nesting on some of our busiest beaches – little terns among the candyfloss and deckchairs of Great Yarmouth; Sandwich terns among the buckets and spades of Blakeney.

Of the five British breeding species of tern, four are true sea-birds, and the fifth is frequently, though not exclusively, found by the coast too. This is the common tern, familiar throughout England as it will breed and feed in reasonably sized lakes or rivers. It is the stand-ard tern. White and grey wings, pale white-grey body, black head, red bill and black tip. All deviate from it, though some hardly at all.

At the opposite ends of the spectrum are the Sandwich tern and the little tern – the former the size of a small gull, the latter with the length of each wing stretching from the thumb to the little finger of my hand spread wide. They are the outliers in size. Both have a black and yellow bill. Little has a white forehead to its black head and Sandwich has a shaggy crest, like a bird with bed head. Sandwich terns are the hardiest of the family.

In the middle of the tern spectrum, there are the near-identical Arctic and roseate terns. Both of them can lay claim to being the most elegant bird. The Arctic in its buoyant, long-winged flight. The roseate's wings are too short to be as elegant in flight, but its tail is long and flicks up, following the sweep of its wing. Its body is pure bright white. Its back a pale shade of grey. Both species are superficially almost impossible to tell apart from the common, except for their wildly differing spirits. Common is the average. The tiny incremental details add up to something other, something greater. Arctic tern, as the name suggests, is at the southern end of its breeding range in Britain. Roseate tern is at the extreme north of a distribution that takes in islands across the Atlantic: from Rockabill off the east coast of Ireland to the Azores and the Caribbean, as well as tropical latitudes in the Indian and Pacific oceans as well. They are an oddity, out of their range, but clinging on. For now.

It was 20 March. I was walking down the broad sandy sweep of Nouster Bay at dusk, before the first Arctic tern had come, before almost anything else had returned to North Ronaldsay after a winter away. I heard a squealing, ripping sound behind me. The field guide I use likens this to a filling, 'like pressing amalgam into tooth'.[1] I remember another field guide description of it as being like a ripping tarpaulin. James Fisher went for a more practical but less memorable 'kirrick'.[2] In that moment, that unpleasant noise was joyous to me. I spun on the spot as a Sandwich tern flew past me, along the tideline, on bouncing wing beats. I was frozen – it promised thaw.

⌄

Terns need help. Terns need hands-on help perhaps more than any other seabird. Down the coast from Seahouses is Long Nanny, a burn and a bay, half a mile south of Beadnell, a pretty, old fishing village nestling among the dunes of Northumberland. The sky is brilliantly blue, the sea too. The beach is smooth golden sand and quiet in the morning, though the return walk will require us to navigate our way through the flocks of sunbathers, kite-flyers and joggers. Strands of black sand – coal dust from the seafloor that washes up with strands of bladderwrack – is a reminder of the industry that once powered the hinterland up here. Ringed plovers move among the strands – stop–sprint–stop–sprint – breathlessly. When they stop and stand they disappear, sand on sand, betrayed only by short orange legs, a short orange bill, a glistening underbelly, as white as the surf, and a coal-black breast band.

The beach curves inland to the burn. The path kinks into the marram grass of the dunes, where a small bridge takes you over the clear, cold water of the burn into the dunes just back from the colony. Up the burn a few terns gather on the bank, some standing in the water, guiding the flow over their feathers. Old plastic crates sit half submerged in sand, blue, yellow and grey, looking like litter fenced off from the beach by a thick blue twine. There is an electric fence and numerous signposts warning off walkers, asking politely for dogs to be on leads.

At the top of the dunes is a hut and a screen, behind which you can view the colony without disturbing the birds. At the bottom, five green tents nestle in the slack. For the nesting season this is the home of five wardens and additional volunteers, people whose love for terns has become a commitment, day and night, to helping give them the best chance of hatching and nursing their young through to the fledging stage. When I visited in 2012 they were dashing over dunes to chase the crows away. In 2017 it was the stoats mounting raids at dawn and dusk, snatching eggs and young, that vexed the wardens. Next year it'll be a different foe – hands-on conservation is not such a gentle art, but an act of utmost dedication. The week before I visited, they were contending with a fish kill from an upstream agricultural pollution incident. The weekend before I visited, the colony was devastated by the most fickle foe: an unusually high tide swept up the beach, flooded the colony and spared only three little tern nests. Only 900 Arctic terns remain scattered over the beach when there should be several thousand.

Several metres from the viewing screen an Arctic tern perches on a post. It is an opportunity actually to look at one, calmly. No ducking required, no hands held out as shields. The red bill shines vividly in the sunlight, the colour of the blood it can draw if you stray too close. It shuffles, droops its wings and holds its tail up, cocked at a 45-degree angle. It calls – then shoots off to see off an intruder. Intruder is a relative term: intruder in the mind of the tern is not the same as intruder to my eye. My eye sees only chaos. Several hundred hyperactive, hyper-aggressive, identical birds. Some perched, some flying or fishing, some sitting flush to their marram grass nests, brooding. They are all intruders or none of them are. It is the same chaos as on Farnes, but their behaviour as it should be: they are attacking each other and not us. There is not the lingering sense nagging away, as I found on the Farnes, that we shouldn't be here, shouldn't be intruding on their territory, distracting them from bombarding each other by bombarding us.

The tide from three days previously seems impossible to imagine on a day such as this. A dark joke on a day when the sun turns skin scarlet, blurs the air and bakes the sand until its hot to touch. In a crate one of the remaining little terns can be seen swimming in the heat haze lifting off the sun-parched sand. The crates are there for the birds to nest in, a last-ditch, last-line of defence from water and footfall, a minor impediment to predation. If there ever was a prize for the unluckiest British bird, the little terns would win it – and then probably lose it again.

In the month of my visit to the colony there are three other high-profile news stories involving little terns: a fox snuck in past the fence at Gronant, North Wales, resulting in the loss of 160 eggs.[3] South of here at Crimdon, Durham, people entered the colony with dogs and destroyed fifty nests.[4] At Kessingland, Suffolk, thieves took ten eggs.[5] The fox is unfortunate. Foxes, stoats, crows, kestrels and gulls will all opportunistically prey on tern chicks and eggs. The human destruction is unforgivable, senseless cruelty. In the month of June 2017, the number of young lost would have been the equivalent of about 10 per cent of the British little tern population had they all fledged.

There is another, closer little tern perched on the beach just beyond the bulk of Arctics. Half the size, as pale above and below, but with proportionally a longer, yellow bill, and a wedge of white extending onto the forehead from above the bill. The familial similarity is still present. Of all the British breeding terns, the little is the odd one out. The only one without a purely black head, the only one with a mostly yellow bill. In the rest of Europe they can breed up large river valleys, but they are resolutely coastal in Britain, as if irresistibly drawn to our busiest beaches.

Working with terns is tricky. They are prone to disaster. Fickle, fluctuating, unpredictable. The perils are many and mainly extremely difficult to defend them from. Sheila, a retired volunteer, is in the middle of her ninth season standing on the viewing platform watching the terns. She points at a pair of terns, ascending close together, high above the dunes, both calling. Nobody knows why they do that. Maybe they're reinforcing their pair bonds. She loves how you can be here for nine long, hot seasons and still see new things. Scurrilously she then says that she's been around the world and seen twelve species of penguin, but this is where she keeps coming back to. She loves the place and the birds.

I understand this.

An interest in birds is rarely just about the birds.

There is an Orcadian lore that Arctic terns return in the first mist of May. Like all lore, it's a whisper through time, lost from its origins through frequent repetition. It is even vague enough to be sometimes true. It was that way for me.

Growing up in the south of England I had become familiar – over-familiar – with common terns. I'd forgotten how different Arctic are, despite being near doppelgängers. The differences, frozen in a field-guide depiction, are a black tip to the bill of a common, a shorter tail, diffuser black to the wing tips and a greyer feather set back from the wing tip. In reality, the difference is the same as the difference between a tern and a gull, or like all close relatives – alike in features but utterly different in spirit. Arctics are more buoyant, elegant, as if they are lighter in flight, brighter than air. Commons always look stiffer, more hurried in contrast. Rather than necessarily seeing or knowing what exactly is different, this is a visual feel – much of birding is done this way – a hard-to-explain seeming difference. We call this feeling jizz – unfortunately.

It takes a certain amount of experience with both species to master birding by feel. In the early days of ornithology, when people would shoot species and describe them for the scientific record, confusion was almost constant, even with the bird dead and in front of you and not flying away. The common tern, the obvious, inland tern, has been known to science since the seventeenth century. The Arctic tern became official in mid-eighteenth-century Denmark, when Morten Thrane Brünnich* described it for science, though this was a year after Erik Pontoppidan published an excellent description of its plumage and distinguishing features, which he then marred by an account of their behaviour:

> Their food is insects and small fish . . . they do not take them with their bill, but with their wings . . . they do it in this manner: they fly several fathoms high, and draw their wings together, and then drop suddenly on this fish like a stone; then they grasp their prey with their wings, and carry them away prisoner.[6]

He neglects to explain how they are supposed to fly away with wings full of fish.

Describing it and making people aware of it are two different things. Henry Seebohm, a Victorian amateur naturalist that the

---

* He is immortalised in the name of the Brünnich's guillemot, a tribute for his pioneering work on Arctic seabirds.

Spectator's obituary[7] described as 'the most original figure since the days of MacGillivray',* thought it had not been described until 1819.[8] Such a mistake from an otherwise authoritative figure is striking. This is not the most egregious example of confusion between the two species. Carl Linnaeus, the great describer and organiser of the natural world, was also confused. When he compiled his tenth edition of the *Systema Naturae*, as R. A. Hume points out, it 'is likely that the bird he described under the name *Sterna hirundo hirundo* was actually a specimen of Arctic, not a common tern'.[9]

It is all a bit of a mess. The finer features of the wing tips – which are actually the easiest way to tell them apart from a distance – were not known about in specialist circles until the 1960s, making an appearance in a widely used field guide only in 1977.[10] And with that, a species that had been known scientifically for over 200 years – but known to the people of northern coastlines a lot longer – was finally properly known and understood.

It was Arctics that were bounding through the air before me, early one grey May morning on North Ronaldsay. They don't nest on the two beaches here. They are the last seabirds arriving to breed and they congregate in the unused spaces: the boggy fields around the loch, up the stony west coast and the rocky northern headland where they are out of the range of fulmars, walkers, and the sheep that will think nothing of decapitating a chick for a quick calcium snack. They see a different geography down on the rocks where people don't walk. The rocks here look shattered, bent and twisted, as if scrunched by time like balls of waste paper. The little cracks and

---

* William MacGillivray, 1796–1852, a Scottish naturalist and ornithologist. This claim is high praise indeed. Seebohm lived and died about forty years after MacGillivray.

ledges give them space enough, funnelling stray tide or rainwater down, away from their eggs.

Averages are unhelpful with terns. They are boom and bust – sometimes in the same season. It took them a week from when they arrived to settle down into their colonies. It took until July for summer to arrive. In the intervening two months of rain, the nests in the bog by the loch were washed out, eggs got cold, the vegetation didn't grow and didn't hide their eggs from the skuas. I watched what looked like teamwork, or perhaps just bold opportunism, as one skua emptied the colony of adults, before a second skua would drift over the unprotected colony, eggs presented like a platter, a small snack fit for the maw of a marauding skua.

No nests from the first attempt survived. Numbers dwindled, then rose again in July in line with the weather. The advantage of being an island in an archipelago studded with tern colonies is that when the conditions are right the terns will find you. July was redemption. Thirty-one days of azure skies, warm seas; the fish that were here, then not here, returned. There were no storms. July was to be the only month on Orkney when I did not need to wear my winter coat at least once. The island became fit for the scientific name of the Arctic tern. *Sterna paradisea*: tern of paradise.

The coast became noisy again. The walk across the rocks to view the colonies were no longer solitary but attended by flashing bills, flickering wings and the heart-wrenching screech of their calls. Even through a hat they still felt like a pinprick. Even when I was aware, anticipating the screech and blow, they still made me slip and spin and fall into rock pools.

When we enter the colonies our heads hang low, eyes fervently scanning the ground for eggs. Nobody wants to be the one to stand on a nest, and nobody does. This shouldn't need to be the case, but this season is out of kilter. Usually the entire colony is at the same stage together, but not this summer. Eggs alongside chicks alongside fully fledged young from other islands, seeking shelter in the mass of birds on North Ronaldsay. The flocking instinct is what powers and protects tern colonies. Their aggression lasts most of the season, even for those who have bred or aren't breeding. Theirs is a colony that lives and dies together.

Before we enter the colonies we watch and wait to pick the ideal day after they've hatched: warm with no wind and no chance of rain, so they do not get cold or caught out in bad weather with us preventing the adults from returning. The perfect day arrives. The perfect mid-afternoon, shirt weather, blue all around the northern headland.

We step out onto the rocks. There is no aerial frenzy, no bombardment. The quiet is jarring, unnerving. The rocks are warm and dry and almost entirely empty. From a count of 150 pairs a few weeks ago, we only find three fledged young and many abandoned eggs, as cold as wet rock to the touch. It is mystifying – this colony was a third bigger than the one next to it and should be better defended. It feels like failure, as if we've somehow failed the birds.

It is not until we leave that we stumble across the reason why. Stashed in a hollow by the drystone dyke, half hidden by the long grass, we find a few loose tern feathers. Then a wing, a tail, legs. Half a chick, feather shafts half grown from its downy wings. The hallmarks of cat predation. A colony without life is a haunting place. Instead of the screeching of adults, all you can hear are waves gently rolling into the shore. The conspicuousness of absence. The wrongness of it is unbearable. And that feels like a disaster.

Elsewhere the blizzard of terns has worked. By the lighthouse we count 95 terns sitting flush on the rocks, immobile and impervious to the thousands more bustling around them. On a fine day a week or so later we enter the colony to a shower of excrement. On the rocks we find chicks. I find one chick hiding with its head tucked into a crevice in the rock. It is downy soft, stone brown, speckled darker. They can vanish from above, but at eye level they look ludicrous, with adult-thick orange legs and a stubby carrot of a beak. Born two days ago, I reckon, though I can't tell for certain. I turn it onto its back, my fingers either side cradling it. I pull out a ring and gently plier it shut, checking to make sure it fits as a perfect circle around its leg. I place it down, back where I found it, to resume its life on the hard rocks.

The ring has a unique code on it and back at the observatory it will be put into the national database. When the bird next gets trapped, the ring code will be read and logged on the database. It's a simple method but it's how we know that Arctic terns can live for a quarter of a century. It's how we know that one tern ringed as a chick in Northumberland was found in Australia four months later.[11]

I walk towards another chick I can see, looking like a stone shuffling over stones. This one is older – it has feathers instead of down, an adult-sized bill and wings that aren't fluffy stumps. I reach down. It jumps up, flaps its wings and takes off. First flight. Its wings are not quite fully grown, its feathers not quite the sharp-tipped tools that will take it to Antarctica. They are stumpy and half formed, but good enough. It flaps deep wingbeats and flies off down the other end of the rocks, gracefully dropping down. I guess some things just come naturally.

I notice one egg tremble, cracks spreading throughout its shell.

An egg tooth – the hard knob on the tip of a chick's bill – breaks through, as the impulse to life drives the chick inside to break the warm wall of its embryonic state and change its world forever. It's a complicated experience. I don't hang around to watch it happen, despite a compulsion, the nagging sense that it will be the most extraordinary, privileged event to witness. By the same token it feels like an intrusion, a transgression of some necessary boundary. It doesn't feel right. I am merely happy enough that there are tern chicks still hatching. It means the world to me.

From the successful colony we counted 95 pairs nesting, and we ringed 59 fully fledged young. Across the island we counted 95 fledged chicks, from the 579 pairs among the 4,000 strong flock. This doesn't sound like a lot – a productivity rate of 0.16 sounds abysmal, actually – but this is a boom summer wrestled out of a washed-away bust of a spring. Each fledged chick feels like a victory, defiance against the wind and the rain, the tides and the skuas, the sheep and the cats. The tenacity of terns.

I once found a dead tern: severed in two, crimson fresh, glassy eyed. Soft to touch – pre-rigor mortis. I'd pulled it out of the long grass under the wind turbine. An Arctic tern with one wing, its chest torn apart. Its heart, as thick as my thumb but half as long, glistened, still damp with blood. With that small organ pumping life around its body, it flies from here to the southern oceans and back to this small island. A distance of 20,000 miles as it chases summer from the north to the south. I saw the length of the world in its heart, a map in its gristle, flyways in its sinews.

The dry statistics are impressive. Scientists are discovering a truth that should seem obvious. Terns don't migrate as the crow flies.[12] Dr Richard Bevan and Dr Chris Redfern from Newcastle University satellite-tagged twenty-eight of the Arctic terns breeding on Inner Farne, recovering twenty-one the next year. The data revealed that having flown down the west coast of Africa, instead of carrying on south, they turned into the Indian Ocean. From there they turned south again to the coast of Antarctica, then west into the Weddell Sea, a huge inlet in the pack ice, closer to South America than Africa. They spend four months in the planet's deepest south, then head back faithfully, as if programmed, to the same island as last summer. The round trip is roughly 60,000 miles. To me, the most impressive thing in all of these statistics is the speed. From leaving the Farne Islands to being off the Cape of Good Hope, South Africa, it took exactly one month of flying. For the return leg from South Africa to the Farnes, it took exactly one month as well.

Arctic terns are on the amber list of UK conservation concern – the same level of worry as little terns, despite outnumbering their smaller relatives by many thousand. Declines are concerning, no matter what the starting population.

And if they go? The world loses a global species – a tie that binds the north and south, the polar bear and penguin. I'm reminded of the great Victorian poet Alfred, Lord Tennyson's struggle to understand how nature changed around him. In the 1850s, while grief-stricken, he wrote of nature: 'So careful of the type she seems, / So careless of the single life.'[13] We have swung almost completely around from Tennyson's concerns. We're now so concerned with the single life that we forget to be careful of the type.

A single dead tern under a turbine is upsetting – evidence for those who don't want to adapt of the inadmissible cost of even a single wind turbine. Global warming driving the species ever further north and south is even worse. At 59 degrees north, Orkney is at the southern end of their breeding range, a range that extends as far north as Cape Morris Jesup, the northernmost tip of mainland Greenland. They spend the winter at the southern edge of the sea. For the great travellers, there's not much more room for them to go. For them, the future planet will start seeming extremely small.

$\smile$

I find birds easier to read than people. When a bird is anxious, it is obvious. The dread of terns is writ large in a swirling cascade of birds. R. M. Lockley and James Fisher were both writing in the shadow of war, but you have to dig deeper to uncover their natural fears and anxieties.

The most interesting island Lockley visits is the island the British exchanged for control of Zanzibar: the newly German North Sea island of Heligoland. In October 1936, Lockley describes an astonishing fall of migrants: '[outdoing] anything I have witnessed at a British ringing station . . . the total of birds ringed that day was . . . a twelfth of the total for the whole year'.[14] Heligoland in the 1930s was strewn with swastikas, propaganda posters, films – Lockley goes to the cinema and sees more propaganda. It reminds him of an ants' nest.

When the Second World War comes he is forced from Skokholm and settles at Inland Farm on the Dinas Head, a part of coastal Pembrokeshire that looks away from Skokholm and Skomer, rather than towards it. James Fisher spent the war conducting rook surveys for the government, at a time when walking countryside lanes, in the sober clothing of a birder, with binoculars, must have been a risky undertaking.* Both continued to write. Fisher was publishing his most important, but not his finest, work: *Watching Birds*. Lockley was writing his finest, but not his most remembered, work: *Letters from Skokholm*. Both are books marked by war.

Watching Birds was published in 1940. Fisher's preface stakes a claim for its lasting importance: 'Some people might consider an apology necessary for the appearance of a book about birds at a time when Britain is fighting for its own and many other lives. I make no such apology. Birds are part of the heritage we are fighting for.'[15] He adds a hopeful vision of the future, a time of increased leisure, where ornithology can be 'for these men and women, and not for the privileged few to whom ornithology has been an indulgence.'[16] Time has proved him right. By 1997 the RSPB had a membership of a million.[17]

Stephen Moss, the birder and writer, links the popularity of *Watching Birds* to the election of Clement Attlee five years later. He suggests, 'The British were tired of privilege and the rigid social class system, and wanted to enjoy the freedom for which they had fought for so long. They were eager for learning and would get it . . . cheap paperbacks like *Watching Birds* . . . would enable the post-war generation to learn more about natural history.'[18]

Fisher's vision survives the twenty-first century better than his book, the product of a different, drier, time. In *Watching Birds* facts trump experience. Moss describes Fisher's educated guesswork – on topics such as how many birds there are in the world – as

* Attracting the attentions of police is an occupational hazard of birding.

coming from 'an overweening self-confidence'.[19] Fisher was a committee man – serving on committees and councils for the British Trust for Ornithology, the Royal Society for the Protection of Birds, the International Union for the Conservation of Nature and the National Parks Commission, among others – and his preface reflects that. It reads like an excerpt of a politician's speech, promising vague things – a better time, more rest and leisure – that he can't deliver.

Letters from Skokholm gathers together Lockley's letters to John Buxton, his brother-in-law, captured in Norway in 1940 and held at Eichstätt prisoner-of-war camp. Lockley's letters are little parcels of Welsh wilderness, a taste of elemental freedom for the prisoner. Buxton was to become an ornithologist of repute, while forging a career as a poet and lecturer in English literature at Oxford. At Eichstätt he observes 'a family of redstarts, unconcerned in the affairs of our skeletal multitude'.[20] These observations were to become his monograph on the species, *The Redstart*, a book that, perhaps more than any other, demonstrates the hope that birds can inspire in ultimate human adversity.

There are plenty of relics of war in the northern isles – particularly around Scapa Flow and Sumburgh Head: the abandoned concrete shells of gun batteries, lookout posts, radar stations, the rusting hulls of sunken boats. And wherever you come across them, there always seems to be a colony of terns nearby. Birds and the military seem to like the same thing about landscapes: the open, the exposed and the coastal. I like to think that serving soldiers, vigilant but bored, saw the vigour with which terns defended their territories and drew their own obvious metaphors.

A forty-minute drive south from Seahouses – a journey much quicker when taken by a tern's wing – lies Coquet Island. Coquet is a dark smudge, a submarine-shaped island. The bulk of it, its rock hull, is low and flat, each side of the higher ground, where there is a handful of scattered old buildings with a lighthouse sailing above like a periscope. It is staffed every spring by an RSPB warden but is otherwise uninhabited, and boat trips are not permitted to land, only to loop around the island. This is because of roseate terns.

Roseates are by far the rarest British tern, the hardest to see and the most stunningly beautiful. In a family of dazzling white feathers, roseates manage to be the whitest, the most freshly laundered on the wings and back and, outside the breeding season, the breast too. Inside the breeding season, a delicate blush flushes across its body from breast to the base of the bill, as if it is embarrassed to be engaged in something so mundane as sitting, brooding its precious eggs. Because these eggs are precious. Recently, there have been fewer than a hundred pairs breeding in Britain, mostly out there on Coquet Island, some on Anglesey, and possibly a tiny handful in Scotland, if they haven't already gone extinct there. The decline from 1970, when a survey found just under a thousand pairs, is, of all the vanishings, possibly the most alarming. If they slipped away, their extinction would pass unnoticed by all except the keenest birders. Their migration is half the distance of an Arctic tern's. They look similar enough to pass as any one of the commoner terns. They hold no particular cultural meaning, despite their beauty and rarity.

Coquet looks inky black against the dark sea. The early-morning sky is a heavy grey, hanging ominously. Male eiders bob and dive, slowly disappearing into the depths of the clear harbour water, while several females herd a crèche along the breakwater rocks. A female goosander tags along with them, choosing to flock with the clos-est thing it can find to itself. Through a telescope Coquet buzzes with terns, indistinct for the distance – like a swarm of flies about a roadkill corpse. Almost certainly – perhaps – roseates. Guessing isn't good enough.

Later I go online. Hidden away on the RSPB's webpage for Coquet is a webcam.[21] It is grainy and the distortion makes the lighthouse lean like the Tower of Pisa. But the sound is unmis-takable. The chatter and screech of terns. Between the nestboxes, daubed with numbers 81, 91, 135, like some random avian bingo, roseate terns perch, screech, fly off. Elegant even when pixelated. Refreshingly, the puffins standing on rocks in the background aren't the main event but simply the *mise-en-scène* of Northumberland.

Over the summer I check back, frequently. I watch as the chicks appear one day, tiny walking balls of fluff, then suddenly larger, feathered. The young share the basic pale grey, fringed with ginger-gold feather edges. They beg fish until they're fully winged, flapping stumpy wings and taking off. Then they beg for fish off camera.

I have once seen a roseate tern in the field. It was distant, but I was spellbound. There is rightly an *omertà* surrounding locations of rare breeding birds – terns are vulnerable enough without egg collectors having access to their location. Which means no identify-ing description. It was a great evocative experience: the tern starkly white and elegant and ill-suited to its backdrop.

The webcam gives you the story arc of a nature documentary in real time, and you supply your own narration, your own sweeping violin music. This is the modern nature experience: visual, aural, and without getting wet, cold or pecked. This is a good thing: bringing the roseate terns into people's lives without disturbing the birds.

This is a bad thing because getting wet and cold seems an essential part of experiencing nature. But something has to give and sometimes believing, not seeing, is the best way to experience the creatures too shy, too evasive to meet us halfway. For the roseate terns, the webcam seems to be working.

Coquet is also home to Sandwich terns. The few terns that sweep close enough to the harbour wall to be identified are all definitely this species. The largest, bulkiest British tern: as grey as the sky and sea on this lightless morning. I saw a few from the muddy edge of Holy Island too, darting in and out of the glare, the sun's white trail across the sea. They have the family habit of being almost completely colourless. They become monotone, slipping from silhouette black to bright white, and all the silver-greys in between. A colour-shifter, a shape-shifter: sometimes elegant and frail, other times powerful, almost gull-like. It makes them a hard species to pin down. In a charismatic family, they are unusual in being more normal than the others. It makes them easier to overlook. Brutally, it makes it harder to find them interesting. The unusual name does not help. The Sandwich tern would seem to be most notable for being one of a number of birds named after places in Kent, but that no longer breed there.* Their names memorialise a time when Kent was the corner, not the garden of England, when it still had the spaces, the heaths and beaches for wildlife, instead of man's hand everywhere.

It's also not really true any more. They are, after all, a tern and would not be so simple. Movement is in their DNA. Sandwich terns

---

* Along with the Dartford warbler, disappeared under concrete, and the Kentish plover, which used to breed on beaches in the southeast, until we discovered seaside tourism.

now prefer Norfolk to Kent – some years Norfolk hosts 40 per cent of the British population; roughly 5 per cent of the European population.[22] They are not so rare, highly strung and temperamentally unlucky but they are picky: 'some [Sandwich tern colonies are] occupied for years and then suddenly deserted, and others in full swing in the early spring only to empty overnight as the birds move elsewhere.'[23] This, suggests Rob Hume, author of bird books and tern expert, is to maximise the success of the colony, which makes sense. But one also gets the sense with terns that they just enjoy being as annoying to us as we are to them.

The differences between the dune-haloed coasts of Northumberland and East Anglia are as subtle as the differences between tern species. One is slightly flatter and has fewer islands, but the essential bones – the beaches, dunes and shallow seas – are the same. They are both perfect for Sandwich terns. But if the roseate terns of Northumberland are benefiting from modern nature, then the Sandwich terns of Norfolk are not.

One of our ways of combating global warming, and the shrinking of the world for Arctic terns, is renewable energy, primarily windfarms. There were thirty-six offshore windfarms, comprising 1,762 individual turbines, by the end of 2017, supplying 6.2 per cent of Britain's electricity demand.[24] They are increasingly being built off the East Anglian coast, where they are sometimes out of sight and usually out of mind. A single dead Arctic tern under a turbine is upsetting. More than a few dead terns under a turbine is to make the case that they should never have been constructed there in the first place. As the most visible seabird off the East Anglian coast, Sandwich terns are not just an indicator of the state of our marine environment but also our energy policy; how our government goes about securing 20 per cent of the UK's energy from renewables by 2020, or how the Scottish government goes about achieving its more appropriate target of 100 per cent.[25]

Sandwich terns forage from height. They aren't as dainty as the other tern species, so when they spot a fish they flip in the air and fly head first at the water. They don't stop, hover, gently reach down and pluck their food from the water's surface. Instead, a couple of metres above the sea, they fold their wings back and they plunge into the water, head first, with their body and wings the shape of a closed pair of scissors. Looking for fish from height involves looking down. Recent research is revealing another facet of tern life that seems so startlingly obvious. Terns – as with most other birds that forage from height – are looking down, not forwards.[26] Flying, as they do, at height, looking for food and not obstacles looming out of the sea where they shouldn't be makes Sandwich terns extremely vulnerable to being split in half by spinning turbine blades.

There is a very modern problem looming. Wind turbines kill terns, but we don't know how many are being killed. We don't know the effect on their food – if fish are attracted or repelled by wind-farms. We don't know the collateral damage in the fight against the global warming that is holding all of the world hostage. This ignorance does not mean we should not carry on fighting against our changing climate. But Sandwich terns are amber-listed for conservation concern. They are as worthy of our concern as the Arctics.

Autumn in Northumberland. For the tern rangers at Long Nanny, heartbreak and joy. Only four little terns fledged out of thirty-eight nests. They started again, in defiance of high tides, only to be struck by the bad luck that follows them around as a species – gulls this time responsible for predating the young. Sometimes the rangers are powerless to prevent losses. The hands-on protection afforded to terns does work. That season there were at least 479 young Arctic terns hatched, but it could have been up to a thousand.[27] In 2018 there were 118 pairs of roseate terns on Coquet: a record count.[28]

Autumn on North Ronaldsay. Absence again. All headlands, bays, lochs and bogs in silence. Wind and rain. The occasional tern still hurries past, southbound, but suddenly they seem out of place. They are no longer starkly white against a blue sky, but grey and flimsy, too light for the weather we are experiencing. They should be halfway south by now – a month and a half after fledging – the birds breeding north of the Arctic circle experiencing night properly for the first time around the equator. In another month or so, as we slip into winter, they'll be back in the season they chase from one end of the earth to the other, at home, in perpetual daylight on the pack ice of the Antarctic summer.

For me, leaving North Ronaldsay was one of the hardest things I have done emotionally. I'm sure it is the same for others: the rangers of the Farnes, the volunteers of Long Nanny, the warden of Coquet. It is different for the terns – no sentiment, just urgency and a pair of wings to take them to the equator, or beyond. They are vulnerable perfectionists – driven to search for just the right location at just the right time, poorly equipped to deal with anything less. Their biology is a deal with the world: turning perfect conditions into the perfection of more terns.

6

Gulls – Newcastle

Nobody knows why the kittiwakes first started coming up the Tyne. The record books show the colonies at the mouth of the river had filled up by the 1960s, which perhaps explains why they went looking elsewhere. Some didn't fly up or down the coast for new cliffs but followed the upstream flow of the river. Instead they found brick walls, iron girders, the Guildhall. We don't know which one was the first bird or how it transmitted the idea to others, that impulse to explore against the norms of their species. But by 1962 their first nest in Gateshead had been made.

Fast forward fifty-five years. It feels as if we are floating.

Standing in Gateshead, it feels as if Newcastle is laid out on a gentle slope just for us: castle turrets, church spires, clock towers, flat-topped office blocks and the metal exoskeleton of the football stadium. There are cranes scraping at the sky, as if lifting the city up and reaching ever higher. Newcastle is not an ordinary city, neither is this an ordinary June day. Heat hazes the horizon. Distorts the edges. Sunlight glints off of glass. The city shimmers. There are bridges – five that I can see on this short stretch of the River Tyne – ruler straight or hooped and floating high over the river, funnelling cars in straight lines. People crawling, tiny as mites. Newcastle and Gateshead rumble around us like the contented purring of a cat. Between the buildings, roads tangle, snarled even late in the morning with traffic.

We are not floating. Gravity anchors us to decking, suspended somehow – I'd really rather not think about how – high above the south bank of the Tyne. We are an appendage to the Baltic Centre for Contemporary Art, penned in by toughened glass and steel beams, held back by sweaty palms, the slight blur of vertigo settling on the brown, lapping river, far below.

The Baltic is not a delicate building. Part of an old flour mill, what remains is the silo building, where the wheat was stored before milling. The main face of the building is a vast wall, an elaboration on the subject of red brick with slightly larger brick columns on each corner. It has no windows. Its only decorative feature is the large 'BALTIC FLOUR MILLS' lettering, embossed between two ledges, that stands proud of the wall by the length of a gull's body. Finished in 1950, it saw thirty-one years of commercial use, before lying derelict, until its late 1990s conversion into a gallery. Beside us: space. Buildings stand apart, spaced out, when they were once built up, tight as a wall of brick, hiding the river. Now they are chrome and Trespa and stand back from the Baltic, as if in respect of this cenotaph of industry. This is the Baltic's human history in a paragraph. Its natural history is wholly more extraordinary.

'Ki ki waaaaaah-k'.

From the two Baltic ledges the kittiwakes cry their name, 'Ki ki waaaaah-k', with the rubbery squeak of someone polishing out a particularly obstinate mark. The kittiwakes sit on top of small nests, studiously out of beak range of each other. The nests are made from sun-dried seaweed and other vegetation, scooped up into a rudimentary cup, moulded with mud and baked by the sun. Periodically one stands up, turns around and, before sitting down again, flashes a glimpse of a pair of blotchy buff eggs. Their backs are pale grey, their bodies white and spaced out like a line of pearls on the urban grit.

I have two confessions.

First, I am apathetic towards gulls. This is, I realise, the avian equivalent of being ambivalent towards Marmite or indifferent to test cricket. I remember my first skua. I remember my first storm petrels, auks and Arctic terns. I can't remember my first gulls. They blend into the background. They are present in all those memories of first encounters, but as scenery, never as specifics. Gulls seem almost innately divisive. For the fervent: trips to the landfill to stare through a fence, as bulldozers plough up garbage and shuffle the packs of gulls. For birder believers, the puzzle of changing plumages, no two examples the same, exciting species hiding in plain sight if you can solve the riddle of their feather patterns. The unbelieving birders turn away, swear, call them all seagulls and look for something more exciting. Local authorities put up pest-control spikes, apply for animal-control licences. The general public wishes they would shut up and stop calling down their chimney pots. I feel none of these reactions, the familiarity breeding not contempt but almost total indifference. But for everything there is always an exception.

Second, narrative is neat; nature is messy. I had of course seen – and will see – kittiwakes throughout this journey, perched on stone lips cut into cliff faces, just large enough to perch sideways on. I had seen kittiwakes on North Ronaldsay, where they do not breed but funnel their way past in midsummer, the adults skimming the coastal rocks in flocks like long strings, dodging skuas. I had seen the young take the direct route, the shortcut straight over the middle of the island. Before the young moult into the adult's soft white and grey with the buttercup-bright bill, they go through a teenage plumage with a black W stamped across the back of their wings, a black nape and a black bill – smart, not scruffy.

They were enjoyable there. A seabird always is. But it was not without a bitter-sweetness. Kittiwakes shouldn't have been flying past in such numbers so soon in the summer. But we were relieved that there were young with them at all. In recent years, kittiwakes have had a torrid time. They were moved onto the red list of conservation concern in 2015[1] (at the same time as puffin, which took the headlines). The most recent British population figures come from 2002 – a count of 378,847 pairs,[2] a decline of 25 per cent in the fourteen years since the previous census. In the subsequent fifteen years all the warning signs remain red: all the graphs are trending downwards. Another recent survey based on the Tyne population points the finger at their inability to raise enough young.[3] Each of those black-stamped juveniles carries the future of the British kittiwake with them. Each one we later found dead, crumpled and washed up on the rocks, or starved in the middle of a muddy field, far from the sea, is another victim, another symptom of a hard-to-diagnose problem.

But – they are gulls. And they are the commonest British breeding gull species too, despite their sudden vanishing. The adults sit on cliffs unobtrusively, but aloof. Away from the auks on Staple Island. They don't nest with the density, noise or squabbles of the guillemots. I had, rudely, thought of them as skua-bait: a bird that attracts the attention of the more dramatic birds. It wasn't until here, hanging above the Tyne, among these outlying pearls, that my interest was hooked.

You could try close-reading the scene, as if it were a work of art. The delicately plumaged kittiwakes – with softer, fluffier, denser-looking feathers than any other gull – pushed up flush to the unforgiving face of the wall. The sheer brick wall as cliff, the smooth concrete ledge as a lip of rock – architecture as geology, habitat as metaphor. The river, tidal here, literally the sea, though you wouldn't see it that way, enclosed as it is by concrete banks with handrailings. Increment by increment, detail by detail, the presence of seabirds in the city makes sense – even if at first reading it seems completely wrong. This isn't science. But nobody really knows precisely what made the kittiwakes travel up the Tyne in the first place and in the absence of that knowledge, metaphor seems as useful as anything else. It might help us imagine places as seen through the kittiwake's eye.

The effect is even better over the river, beyond the fake beach set up for summer, sand spilling over the concrete lip of its enclosure and sprawling over the path, reaching back to the river. Beyond the chain bars and hotels of the riverfront to the Tyne bridge – the emblem of the city. Above me the sky is hidden by four lanes of traffic, droning. Under the bridge, a lattice of ironwork. The girders, struts and stanchions, the ribs and vertebrae of human endeavour. Riveted in place, riveting to walk under, marvelling at the finesse we are capable of with unwieldy, unyielding chunks of iron. Kittiwakes perch on the girders. Nest on the granite tower rising at the back of the bridge, and thread their way through the lattice to fly out and in. Their calls reverberate off the metal and stone wall, cutting through the city drone with the freshness of nature. They decorate the blunt, hard structure. They turn it to their own ends. It is an almost surreal rereading of their landscape.

A kittiwake sped upriver, swung up towards and then past us, kicked out its legs and landed between two nests in a cackle of calls. Changeover. The leaving bird departs downriver. The art of satellite telemetry has tracked kittiwakes from the Tyne Bridge colony to the Farne Deeps – a patch of the North Sea beyond the Farne Islands that heaves with marine life. It's a magnet for fishermen, a hotspot for minke whales, white-beaked dolphins and all the birds of the Farnes. It is an hour's drive from here to the coast near there – or, to put it another way, over 100 miles there and back, on thin wings, when they could just have easily nested in the auk bustle of that archipelago. If they did, they would be dwindling, despite their proximity to the Deeps. The Tyne population is one of the few managing to persist. In 2017, 1,308 apparently occupied nests* were counted.[4] In 2009 that figure had been 465.[5] And nobody really knows why this is happening, why the Tyne is the only place in the world they nest so far inland and why they're bucking the trend of declines.

Urban development is almost always bad for wildlife, and humans can often go out of their way to deter the encroachment of the natural world. In 2011, the now defunct local regeneration company 1NG wrote a report for Newcastle City Council suggesting that kittiwakes were 'not compatible' with the contemporary urban riverside they were trying to achieve. And in 2015 a hotel next to the Tyne bridge attempted to install spikes and netting to deter them, similar to the futile attempts made by buildings across

---

* An apparently occupied nest is defined as a nest capable of keeping young, with an adult in the vicinity.

the country to deter gulls and pigeons. The hotel was denied permission, and the report by 1NG seems to have vanished with the demise of the company.[6] The kittiwakes remain. More than that, they are celebrated. Leaflets are printed and notice boards erected to advertise their continued presence.

Even more remarkable is the kittiwake tower, constructed on the banks of the Tyne as a temporary replacement home for the birds while the Baltic was being redeveloped. It proved similarly popular with birds and people alike, and has stayed, still used, even though the work on the Baltic is now done. In the heat it shimmers from the other side of the river, in a small green space, the closest to the city centre, between the river and a band of trees. A giant tripod with a large, flat rectangular top, fixed with shelves for the birds to nest on. It looks not unlike a football stadium's floodlights, but with bulbs that would periodically screech and fly off. It is a surreal, inspired bit of primitive architecture, wholly in the service of nature. No metaphor needed here.

Maybe the same welcome would have been extended to any other species, but I doubt it. Almost every other urban population of gulls (typically herring or lesser black-backed) in the country (inland or coastal) is hounded, sworn at or banned from being fed. But the Tyne kittiwakes just co-exist, magnificently wild, unobtrusive beyond the 2-metre band of shit underneath the colony. Maybe it's because they don't share our bad habits, or worse, exploit them, which is the mistake that other gulls, foxes, pigeons and squirrels make. They do not dive into bins and upset our sensibilities, or spread litter across pavements while searching for the irresistible animal stench of chicken bones in black rubbish sacks. They are clean.

Under the Baltic, the trapped air between buildings is broiled by the sharp sunlight. It is stifling. On the concrete banks of the river, where a faint breeze gives no relief from the heat, I walk. I watch a herring gull, the bigger, swaggering seagull of stereotype, wrestle with a flounder fished from the river. It threw its head back, opened its bill wide and attempted to force the flat fish down, and then threw its head forwards and chucked the fish on the ground, when the diamond shape got stuck in its gape. It repeated the routine with a brute enthusiasm for eating something that wouldn't physically fit inside it for at least five minutes, before the heat forced me away, back into shade. It stayed, drawing a crowd of amused passers-by. It is hard not to anthropomorphise, watching this gluttonous herring gull and thinking that a kittiwake, which has an elegance that other gulls lack, would never be so uncouth.

Maybe it boils down to this: they eat fish, not chips. Young cod, pollock and anchovies all make up the diet of kittiwakes, as well as the sand eels, herrings and sprats that almost all seabirds seem to exist on. They pluck them daintily from the surface of the sea, or dip their heads under. They don't swoop at us as we sit outside the takeaway.

Nature in the city is often seen as Gothic, chaotic, anarchic, out of place – or out of control. Think of the way buddleia, bindweed and alkanet grow with utmost indifference to human wishes in the neglected corners of our towns and cities. Think of how Richard Jefferies, in his 1885 novel *After London*, decided to evoke the post-apocalyptic city by having it run rife with animals. The animals people like in cities and those they don't seems arbitrary. City dwellers are rightly proud of their peregrine falcons, but generally detest the pigeons that sustain them. Urban parakeets are loved and loathed in equal measure, by those who think they are brash, noisy invaders and those who don't see anything wrong with that. Kittiwakes seem to have passed this mysterious acceptability test with flying colours.

There might be a deeper reason why Newcastle is fond of its kittiwakes. Studies have repeatedly demonstrated the positive connections between nature and mental health, as well as the negative connections between urban environments and mental health. A team of biologists have recently fused these two links together, studying the effects of nature and natural surroundings in urban places on mental health. This is particularly important as, by 2050, more than two-thirds of the world's population is expected to live in an urban environment, which will expose people to 'a higher risk of a range of mental health issues, including depression, generalised anxiety disorders, psychosis and addictive disorders.' The evidence here is so strong that it is an established causal relationship, not a mere association.[7] By designing a smartphone app that asked users a series of questions about their surroundings and mental well-being, the scientists were able to track their participants' exposure to nature and how they felt. What they empirically proved is that exposure to hearing birds singing and seeing the sky provide a benefit to people's mental health, whereas they recorded no consistent benefit for being near water. Even more pertinently, they discovered that the mental benefits of a short-term exposure to nature could still be observed several hours after the interaction, when the subject could be inside, with no immediate access to nature.

All of this seems to me to be absolutely dependent on the person. But it seems plausible to me that the popularity of Newcastle's kittiwakes might be linked in some way to the fact that birds generally make people feel better, and feel better for longer, than they otherwise would in their city-centre environment. That, in their concrete, granite and iron city, they soften the hardness and perhaps make people feel less alone. That connection to nature was what I missed when I lived in the brick labyrinth of London, when I slumped into myself, when I couldn't even bear to walk to the park two streets away or to the nearest duckpond.

This study offers something vital, something that had been lacking. As the authors state, 'Decisions on urban planning and design aimed at improving the mental health of the general population tend to be based upon "conventional wisdom" because of the lack of robust scientific data.'[8] It is far too soon to say whether this report will have any impact on councils and their planners. But we can hope. It's impossible to know for certain, but I think 1NG wouldn't have been so quick to say that the kittiwakes were incompatible with a modern environment if this research had been done before 2011.

$$\smile$$

There is no right way to be a birder: no right place to live and work. James Fisher lived in London, though he escaped most weekends to his native Northamptonshire. R. M. Lockley hated London, although a broadcasting career beckoned:

How far out of touch we were with the normal life of the mainland, country and town, I realised acutely when – hesitatingly, be it said – I answered an invitation to broadcast. I went to London. It was a shock to be among the jaded-looking, pale faces of the men and women, to cram and crush in stuffy tubes and buses, to breathe the fumes of burned oil with which the streets stink, to feel dizzy with the roar of traffic. The feeble flicker of herd excitement in me soon vanished, succeeded by a feeling of despair that the control of nation and wealth should be centred in and dependent on these people. It seemed to me that they were living hopeless, meaningless lives.[9]

Lockley is echoing one of Henry David Thoreau's famous moments of misanthropy, one of the few bits of *Walden* that ever spoke to me in my misery:

The mass of men lead lives of quiet desperation. What is called resignation is confirmed desperation. From the desperate city you go into the desperate country, and have to console yourself with the bravery of mink and muskrats.[10]

Mink and muskrat are both animals used for fur. Their bravery becomes a way for people to survive by dulling the harshness of nature. Thoreau's cynicism is extreme, but it lives for Lockley, a century later.

Lockley has a blind spot towards gulls. He feels no guilt or responsibility towards them on Skokholm. He has a jar of many – at least three figures – of their eggs in pickle, which would sustain his family for 'a few weeks at least'.[11] To last a year he thinks he needs over a thousand. He states, 'There are strict orders as to egg collecting on the island. I allowed only the taking of the eggs of gulls.'[12] He glosses elsewhere that 'I had no qualms either when I saw how cruelly the black-backed gulls would attack and kill a puffin or a young rabbit, or rob a guillemot of its eggs'.[13] This was twenty-four years before egg collecting was banned nationally and eleven years after Lockley stopped collecting the eggs of other species.

The collection of gulls' eggs for food still continues today. One of the species that Lockley would have been eating – herring gulls – are still collected for sustenance in Arctic Norway. Others, such as black-headed gulls, are still legally collected under licence in small numbers to provide a luxury item in delicatessens and restaurants. A single black-headed gull egg for sale online cost £7.65 in 2018.

This is complicated by the spread of the Mediterranean gull. They are a birder's bird: exceptionally similar to the black-headed gull as adults and eggs, which has led to them breeding in black-headed gull colonies in the south of England. It is illegal for them to be disturbed. However, a black-headed gull colony in Poole Harbour, Dorset, was robbed en masse of its eggs illegally in 2016: presumably to supply a black-market desire for black-headed gull eggs. In the raid, Mediterranean gull eggs were taken. Nobody knows if it's a species that is edible, let alone palatable.[14]

Kittiwakes are true seabirds in the way that the other British species of gulls are perhaps not, not strictly anyway. If you've ever been on the receiving end of an irate birder (or just a plain pedant) telling you that there is no such thing as a seagull, they may be technically correct – but the Tyne kittiwakes are as far inland as that species ever gets, anywhere in the world. They leave to spend their winters completely at sea. Somehow, this deceptively gentle-looking thing, with thin, rounded, fragile-looking wings, spends its winters surfing gales across the Atlantic, as far as Greenland – a true and proper seagull.

There are other true seagulls, for whose life Britain is peripheral. The most regular is Sabine's gull, a bird I have apparently seen. When I was a child, one lost Sabine's gull spent the summer in Lowestoft. My dad did not twitch much when I was young, but he made an exception for this bird. I went because what eleven-year-old kid does not want a trip to the seaside? I remember the ice-cream bribe – thick and chocolatey – to stand there by the harbour wall that I could hardly see over and stare at gulls. I remember seeing lots of gulls. I have no recollection of being shown the Sabine's, though my dad swears he did. If I had, my memory would be of a gull smaller than the flock, tail forked like the letter V, dark head with a thick black collar and a yellow-tipped black bill. There are photographs, blurry scans of film prints, of this bird online, and I can see details I would never have noticed at the time: its wings are ragged all along the back. Only the outer primary feathers remain. I'm surprised it could fly. Perhaps its condition kept it there, for that summer of 2003.

Joseph Sabine was a naturalist working in the early Victorian period. He was the younger brother of a naturalist held in higher regard. Edward Sabine accompanied Admiral John Ross on an expedition in 1818. It was an attempt to find the northwest passage that failed when the Arctic light made a mirage of mountains where there was only open sea. Edward Sabine shot a gull and, not recognising it, sent it to his brother. Joseph identified it as a new species. An unusual species too: one that looks cobbled together from other species. Wings of kittiwake, body and head of black-headed gull, tail of swallow-tailed gull (an exotic from the Galapagos). It is a monotype: as the only species of its genus, it is in a family of one. Joseph named it the 'Sabine's gull' – a tribute to his elder brother and not himself, though you could be forgiven for thinking otherwise.

The Sabine's gull breeds in the high Arctic: Greenland, Siberia, and a handful of pairs in the northernmost parts of Svalbard. It nests out on the tundra, a kindred spirit of the Arctic terns. They spend the winter out at sea, mostly on the Pacific coast of South America, though those that pass through the Atlantic stay around the southwest coast of Africa. Small numbers funnel down both coasts of Britain each year, usually ushered on their way by strong gales. It requires a certain luck – luck I've not yet had – to see one.

The southwards migration of the Sabine's gull is impressive. But there are two more impressive species still further north. Edward Sabine and John Ross did not have a good working relationship. John Ross was, on return to Britain, outflanked politically by his crew, who all blamed him for their inability to find the northwest passage. This did not stop Sabine from cultivating a friendship with a younger sailor: James Clark Ross.

James Clark Ross was the nephew of John Ross and a member of that 1818 expedition. He was to excel at the family business of polar exploration by ship, surpassing his uncle's reputation. On another attempt to find the northwest passage in 1823 he shot the first example of a dainty gull, with a soft-pink breast, a black ring around its neck and a diamond-shaped tail. William MacGillivray, one of the eminent naturalists of the day, described it for science, naming it after James Clark Ross, though really the name enshrines the entire Ross dynasty of explorers.* It is appropriate really. Both Rosses –

---

* There is also a seal, a sea and a crater on the moon named after him. The Ross's goose, despite nesting in the high Arctic, is named after an unrelated Ross.

human and gull – have a love of Arctic cold. Satellite-tagged Ross's gulls have revealed that after they have nested on the furthest reaches of the tundra, they fly north to the edge of the pack ice, coming back south to the edge of the tundra again only when the long night of the Arctic winter sets in.[15] Another study from the north coast of Alaska in 2014 has revealed a strong north-easterly movement of the species in October, but where they are heading to, and why, remains unknown. This is essentially all we know about the species. In the words of the report's authors, 'The breeding range and distribution of Ross's gull remains largely speculative.'[16] What isn't speculative is that every few years a Ross's gull turns up along the British coastline, most recently in the decidedly un-Arctic surroundings of Weymouth, Dorset.

The final species stretches the definition of a seabird. It doesn't quite live on the sea, but not quite on the land either. Ivory gulls are species of the ice floe, scavengers of polar bear kills, savaged seals and dead whales. They are a dream of what a gull should be, their plumage a dazzling, pure white, as bright as the sunlit ice they rest on. There are only some 20–30,000 of them left in the world, all restricted in range to the Arctic ice. Their nose for rotting whale, seal or porpoise flesh will carry them occasionally down to Britain and Ireland. It is typically the young that turn up: a duller white, splattered with spots as dark as the Arctic Ocean. Each wandering individual is a surprise, even though we know it happens, we know they're capable of it. Each one is a reminder of what might be lost with the melting of the Arctic. The vast majority sits tight on the edges of the Arctic ice floes, next to the water kept open by winds and currents. Somewhere between sea and land.

If these species are the outliers, then the typical 'seagulls' – herring, lesser black-backed and great black-backed – are all variations on the same thing. They are bulky, big-billed and sturdy-legged. Their calls are a cross between a yap and a yodel and they reverberate through the coastal air at dawn. Though the coast no longer contains them. Of the three species, only great black-backed gulls are now predominantly found by the seaside. Their backs are coal black, their eyes ringed with red. They are dominant among the others and patrol harbours with a brute swagger. Lesser black-backed gulls are smaller, some surprisingly dainty and gentle-looking. Their backs are slate grey, turning progressively darker, eastwards to Finland, where they are known by the pseudonym 'Baltic gull' and look like small great black-backeds. The herring gull is silvery-blue backed, bubblegum-legged and the archetypal gull of British seaside towns.

This description is partial. Like a field guide, it foregrounds the adults in breeding plumage, bright with hormones, in their most distinctive plumages. All three species when born are brown, mottled, feathers individually marked – brown notches, blotches, shafts, anchor shapes, each feather cryptic, together comprising a riddle of a plumage, no two examples ever quite the same, each species separated only by the fine detailing. They go through three years of shifting plumages to arrive at white and the right shade of grey (or black).

These species behave differently to the delicate kittiwakes. Kittiwakes, as a small gull, are milder mannered. The larger species are infamously protective of their nests. And they can be terrifying, skua-like in belligerence and apparent intent. I was harassed on North Ronaldsay for a month by a pair of great black-backed gulls that would take turns calling, then diving on me from behind.

As they reached their apex, they spun back around and dived at me front on. Each dive felt inches away from the tips of my ear, the rush of air from their passing body rippling my hair. The great black-backed is the biggest gull in the world – with 1.5-metre-wide wings, a weight of almost 2 kilos and a thick-tipped machete of a bill. I was relieved they never connected, whether through lack of conviction or the knowledge that it would hurt them as much as me. I was relieved not to have been clobbered on the head on a stony beach within the sea's tidal range.

After the first time I walked at the edge of the sea, or of a field inland. I walked with a hand above my head, avoiding them as much as possible, though they would still come for me. Discretion is the better part of valour when confronted with an animal defending its young. A reminder that we share the planet with creatures who have an equal right to be here. It was a curiosity that they seemed to take aim only at me and none of the other volunteers. As if I'd once strayed too near to their nest by accident and I was then a marked man and no one else was. Research has proved that crow species can remember faces. I would not be surprised if the same were true of the intelligent and resourceful gulls too.

Herring gulls call harshly. At dawn it sounds as if they are trying to hack down the darkness, each 'ack ack ack' an axe swinging against the night. They deliver it with full-bodied enthusiasm, bowing low, then swinging their heads up as they shriek. It is not the most pleasant sound. But it is evocative. For the last seventy-five years herring gulls have been calling over the crashing waves and sentimental strings of the *Desert Island Discs* theme tune. The association with the sea, islands and isolation is so strong that this very British coastal bird, not found outside the northern hemisphere, can be used to evoke in the mind of radio listeners the siren song of being marooned somewhere far off and impossibly remote.

Herring gulls first began nesting on rooftops in the 1920s and lesser black-backed gulls in the 1940s.[17] Their urban populations have grown significantly, but their increased visibility is a mirage, obscuring the truth of their populations. Herring gulls have been red-listed for a decade, and amber-listed for a decade before that. Lesser black-backed gulls have been amber-listed for twenty years with no improvement. All but one of our British breeding gulls (the Mediterranean gull, a new colonist) is declining. We are seeing them more than ever, at a time when there are fewer of them than before. The move inland is a symptom of the sea and the state of our fisheries and the yo-yoing of our fish stocks. Unlike the rest of our seabirds, gulls have the adaptability and the resourcefulness to survive, to move inland, to change diet. The 'seagull' is hardly a seabird any more, in reality if not culture, where the association still clings on in more than just the name.

There lies an irony in being named after your food source. It plants an expectation, puts you in a pigeonhole that's hard, if not impossible, to shake off. Herring gull and seagull – it sounds as if they don't belong in towns. It sounds unnatural. A study from the Hebridean island of Canna has revealed a link between falling catches of fish and rapidly dwindling numbers of gulls. In 1988, there were 1,525 pairs of herring gull on Canna. By 2014 that had fallen to 95 pairs. Concurrently, at the nearby port of Mallaig, the average fish catch had fallen from 13,726 tonnes to 4,456 tonnes.[18]

It is just a link. Circumstantial and uncorroborated. But it fits with declines elsewhere and the general turn towards towns and new food sources.

This adaptability comes with side-effects. The modern diet is comprised of what's available and what's available might not be any good. It affects how the birds breed and live. A study of a colony in the Netherlands revealed that most still feed on a relatively natural diet of mussels and other bivalves. It also found that those with that diet, which is energy poor, tend to have smaller and fewer fledglings than those that feed on high-energy fishery discards and human rubbish.[19] The scientists hypothesise two factors: that mussels are reliably found and our waste is not (or perhaps is not always edible), and that the stresses of breeding might actually lower life expectancy. It did not consider the Welsh herring gull that, infamously, fell into a vat of curry sauce while trying to scavenge at a food factory and turned the colour of a tikka masala.[20] Gulls offer an interesting contrast to the story of auks. Where our waste is polluting the stomachs of auks, it sustains gulls and improves their breeding, in the short term.

Being adaptable does not guarantee you a warm welcome. In 1968 Louis J. Halle could write, 'Gulls . . . in addition to having the ability to accept our civilisation, have also had the indispensable good fortune to be accepted by it.'[21] In Aberdeen, this adaptability is no longer accepted but has crystallised into conflict between humans and gulls. Examples range from the herring gull that became an internet sensation when it was filmed walking into an Aberdeen shop and repeatedly stealing packets of tangy cheese Doritos[22] (another one was recently filmed going after barbecue-flavour crisps[23]), to gulls that are frequently alleged to steal food out of people's hands and attack pets. A fireman once told me that he felt intimidated by a 'gull the size of a small person' in Aberdeen – and this is a man who is prepared to enter a burning building. It seems as though the gulls of Aberdeen are becoming almost a mythical, crypto-zoological beast, a sasquatch for the true believers, the true feelers of fear of gulls. This is not just limited to Aberdeen. Local news reports repeat similar stories the length and breadth of the country. They have replaced feral pigeons as natural enemy number one.

Herring gulls are guilty of everything that the kittiwake, an actual genuine seagull, is not. I feel somehow complicit in this. Or at least not as innocent as I would like to think I am. I don't quite love all birds the way that I know I should. I love kittiwakes despite them being gulls, not because of it. I love them for their delicacy, their flimsiness, and that somehow they can still survive the harshest of winter gales at sea. I don't love herring gulls and frequently wish they'd stop being noisy and giving other birds a bad name, even if they do nothing wrong other than challenge our prejudices and preconceptions and our irrational love of the neat and tidy. It's hard not to think that I'm somehow to blame, that I have the symptoms of the same wider problem. Gulls are ecologically stuck. We pushed them out of their natural areas because we took their food and offered them an easy alternative: gave them areas to nest in, instead, and then wanted to cull them for doing what any human would.

In 2015 the then prime minister, David Cameron, suggested in a radio interview that it was time for a 'big conversation' on gulls, in response to two reports of gulls killing pets (a small dog and a tortoise) in one week. He suggested it was 'dangerous for a prime minister to dive in and come up with an instant answer'. His words sparked a flurry of news articles and lurid headlines from the supposedly sober *Daily Telegraph* about 'murderous seagulls'.

Two years later, Cameron's big conversation happened with a debate in parliament. Alas for him, this was five months after he had resigned as a member of parliament. A parliamentary briefing provided to MPs lacked basic facts. It contained links to seven news articles, of which six were anti-gull: the honourable exception being a comment piece by the nature writer and journalist Patrick Barkham. His was the only ecologically literate argument provided to MPs.[24]

The debate, when it happened in February 2017, was dismal. Kirsty Blackman, SNP MP for Aberdeen North, spoke about that crypto-zoological beast: 'The Aberdeen *seagull* is the size of a large dog . . . They are not like normal seagulls; they are ginormous.'[25] She goes on to use the language of plagues. Others talk about 'blighted lives' and float the prospect of culling when Brexit will destroy the spine of our environmental protections. Nobody spoke on behalf of the gulls. Nobody spoke with anything resembling sound ecological knowledge. Gulls do not have friends in the right places. The parliamentary briefing reported a YouGov survey that 53 per cent of over-60s supported a gull cull, whereas 53 per cent of 18–24-year-olds opposed a cull. Nobody spoke up for the young either.

And that was it. That was Cameron's big conversation. No change, no action, no understanding. And still the anti-gull hysteria continues, stoked by the headlines of local newspapers, in ignorance that gulls moving inland might be a symptom we should not ignore of the depleted state of our environment.

That is why this matters. I hold a debt to Gilbert White, the original birder, parson and observer of wildlife in the eighteenth century.

He was right, I think, when he wrote 'another beautiful link in the chain of beings is wanting' to describe a species exterminated from his parish of Selbourne. A chain without links is broken, defective. Losing wildlife, particularly species that were common, is not just careless. We watch as the world around us becomes defective, as it breaks in slow motion. Each link that becomes broken cannot be fixed. Each broken link undoes not just itself but everything that relies on it too.

I am reminded again of the study linking birds and urban mental health. If we want happier and healthier towns and cities, we could do worse than begin to see gulls as what they are: birds that are resourceful, robust and intelligent, capable of the charisma and beauty we laud in wild rural animals. I wonder, if I had been capable of this, when I needed it, how my time in London would have turned out differently.

Newcastle offers us hope. A counter-example to the prevailing wind of prejudice. The Tyne kittiwakes are a success that shows that the Anthropocene, urban development, people, don't have to be bad for wildlife. That even specialists can adapt and survive, proliferate, if only we let them. A success that seems even more remarkable against the gloomy outlook for the species – and family – as a whole. The adaptability of herring and lesser black-backed gulls is to show that while the Anthropocene might be shrinking the territory of terns, it is opening new opportunities to gulls, new foods and new spaces. That they are still declining is hugely worrying.

On the surface of it, the seabirds that I encounter in the northeast of England seem fine, whether on the zoo-like Farne Islands, begging for chips in harbours, or nestling on ledges in Newcastle's city centre. But appearances can deceive. Our seas are polluted and all of our seabirds are at the mercy of the plastic-bearing currents that wash around the coastline. It is a human tendency to trust eyes over evidence, to ignore the warnings and statistics of declines and to dismiss the perils of plastics and warming oceans that remain so intangible, untouchable, invisible.

To love this landscape and the animals in it is to hate what's underneath the surface, the invisible but detectable symptoms of problems that are entirely our fault.

This may be the new normal.

Rachel Carson first made her name writing books about the sea. We need, more than ever, another Rachel Carson and a new *Silent Spring* for the Anthropocene, for the sea, for the birds that are filling their stomachs with plastics and feeding it to their chicks, and for the warming seas that are pushing our species to the edge of their known range. And while we wait for the conclusive evidence, while we wait for our next Carson, it seems to me to be a matter of responsibility to our neighbours that share our land, our sea and our earth to try to live in ways that don't contribute to the tide of plastics or the fug of carbon emissions.

It is 1 June when I leave Newcastle. Through the train window it is bathed in the golden light of evening, the countryside on the edges of the city rich with vibrant greens. The summer has come early this year.

Summer is a quiet time for birds. From the middle of June to the end of August, the daily business of raising young, moulting feathers, foraging, brooding, providing takes over. And though that sounds frenetic, the activity reaches a stasis, stagnating in the long hours of summer heat. And nature, for the first time in the year, looks tired. I head back to my day job and my regular life, the residual thrill of birds still coursing through my brain.

7

Manx Shearwaters – Skomer

L ate August. After June and the north-east of England, I returned to my work coop and the weather turned sour, the summer fizzling out like a cheap firework in the rain. I feel restless and although I enjoy my job, the pull of the coastal edges and their birds tugs at my imagination again. Seabirds on the brain, squatting on my routine, distracting me from the everyday. It is time I went to Wales, my last long trip of the year, a sort of Lockley pilgrimage. For the week leading up to it, it is all I can think of. I have never been to Skomer Island before. I have no idea what to expect.

I spend time in my town's small natural history museum. It has a North Sea display case, behind a fake ship's porthole, the diorama dressed up with fish nets, strands of seaweed, floating Styrofoam. At the base of the display a model porpoise dives dramatically: tail up, head down, narrowly missing the net full of sprats. Skimming the water line above the porpoise is a taxidermy Manx shearwater, wing tip to the display case, glass eye gazing blankly back. The wings are stiff – in life, as in death, as in a taxidermy specimen – and the body is shaped like a fallen crucifix. It has been tucked into the corner of the case; not, I think, because they're not particularly common in the North Sea, but rather more cruelly because they're not much to look at. The fulmar on the other side of the display gets the same treatment. Neither are as popular as the tabby cat stalking sparrows in the case opposite. Some animals work frozen into taxidermy. Their essence is all in the poise of their pose, like the guillemot, preserved mid-dive with its wings out, water-flying. Or the little auk sitting neatly, head raised ever so slightly, doe-eyed and – awful though the word is – adorable. It is not so with the shearwater, or any of the Procellariiformes. They evolved only with flight in mind. It is their everything.

I take the moment to listen to an unusual song. A digital Manx shearwater loads on my phone. The colony transported into the corner of the museum. The Manx shearwater, similar to the storm petrels of Shetland, has a call that cannot easily be transcribed into words. It is reminiscent of a stifled cackle. It is a throaty, repetitive, gurgled sound: delivered like the braying jeers of a football crowd. Despite the repetition it lacks rhythm. It has no melody. I lack musical ears. I find sounds hard to remember and am left with a paradoxical feeling: that Manx shearwaters sound like nothing else I have ever heard, yet is almost imposs-ible to remember.

Nine days before the end of August. My travels begin again. Last night I watched the sun setting in the south of England and today I watched it rise in the south of Wales, draped with mist in the gently folding valleys beyond Swansea. The haze had burned off by the time I arrived at St Martin's Haven, one of the fingers of rock grasp-ing out into the sea from Pembrokeshire, the south-west hand of Wales. I like my Essex town. But I like an early-morning walk down to a jetty even more, the air fragrant with the sea and the bracken, browning, and the sound of swallows chattering as if nervous, filling the air like a cloud of insects.

It is 9 a.m. The early morning cast of clouds is fraying in the sunlight and the sky and the sea become a delicate duck-egg blue. The mist of tiredness in my mind has dissipated in the freshness of the air, purifying, relaxing. I can't see Skomer Island from here on the jetty, a thin path carved into the rock face on the sheltered side of the inlet. The rest of the curving headland blocks it from view. I am in the middle of a queue of overnight guests, all waiting for the opportunity of an evening with something special. We chatter, excitedly, introductions and, 'Is this your first time here?' The other guests are mostly Welsh and know the island well. I question them for tips and to reground my ears in an unfamiliar accent. We have an easy union. Naturalists, of the non-competitive sort, are generally quick to find common ground and open to learning from each other.

We form a human chain, pass our luggage onto the small blue boat. Fish out the £11 for the journey's ticket – a return – and sit down. We fit comfortably despite the mountain of luggage. There are dire warnings of being stranded here, cut off by foul weather with no food supply on the island other than what we bring. I am laden with spaghetti, packet sauces, a tub of dried parmesan (for luxury), peanut butter, pitta bread, biltong, chocolate: dense energy that will survive in the event of fridge failure. Fuel, not gourmet living. We have all packed with being stranded in mind – one of us at least with a secret longing for this to happen.

The engine splutters into life. The air is suddenly thick with fumes washing over us. We pull out of the inlet, the engine thudding. The sea is rough here, though the wind is mild. Jack Sound is full of water unhappily being forced through the reef-and-wreck-strewn

800 metres between the mainland and Middleholm, with Skomer, Skokholm and Ramsey in a line parallel to shore just beyond. It is the Celtic Sea that races around these islands. It is a vaguely defined sea – best thought of as being the area that is not quite the Irish Sea, the Bristol Channel or the Atlantic. But it is unhemmed by land – there are no barriers between these seas, so the same water that flows around those flows around here, where it meets the resistance of land for the first time. The roiling water it creates is exceptional. Gannets from nearby colonies cluster here, arrowing down into the water. Fulmars sweep along the crests of waves and circle above the cliffs. A small, unseasonable flock of scoter fly out into the bay, a long string of big black seaducks. Fish are a constant unseen presence. Fish-powered wildlife is everywhere and obvious.

A tractor takes our luggage up to the hostel, after we lugged it up the eighty steps from the island jetty to the beginning of the rough track of stone and dirt. The track takes us through the past: beyond a standing stone, evidence of Iron Age walls, roundhouses and ancient farming. The island feels older. The vegetation is mostly bracken, heather, ragwort and grass. What grows does so because it cannot be beaten into submission by the sea breeze or the salt or the sunlight or eaten into submission by the rabbits. The feeling is almost Jurassic. Time preserved. I know this is ludicrous. There are rabbits, after all – a fourteenth-century introduction here. Woody sage lines the path and spring is supposedly a riot of bluebells and other botanical evidence of the woodland that once covered this island, before it was cleared much more recently. It's some trick of bracken and the imagination that makes it feel prehistoric and preserved, untouched by time.

Leighton, the island's Visitor Services Officer, greets our group in the courtyard of the farm, and talks through the island rules. Skomer is special, I'm told, as all small islands are, and needs to be kept that way. The main rule is to keep to the path. It is sometimes hard to fight the urge to make my own way through the bracken. The rule exists because 2,000 pairs of Manx shearwaters breed per hectare in some parts of the island. The soft soil has a subterranean geography of burrows that honeycomb under the turf, sometimes only a few centimetres below the surface. They are prone to crumbling due to careless walkers – a foot falling through and crushing an egg or a chick is a grim, avoidable fate.

We are beckoned into the island's visitor centre. Shearwaters fly well only on dark but clear nights. When it's foggy, as it was last night, they blunder about and get caught out by the darker dawn. They stumble, almost as if groggy, up the steps to the visitor centre where the doors are left open all summer for the swallows that nest on top of an interpretation board. They waddle across the floor and cluster in the shady corners to sleep out the day, avoiding certain death at the bill of a great black-backed gull.

Leighton picks one up and guides us through its anatomy. It nips at his knuckles with a hook-tipped bill.

'They are the ultimate seabird. If they could lay their eggs on the sea, they would.'

Alas. He extends the bird's leg to show us the problem. Shearwater legs are situated far to the back of their bodies. Ideal for swimming but not ideal for a long-bodied bird to walk with. On top of the bill that bites, the 'tube nose', the two small holes that they smell their food on the sea breeze with and expel salt from. It marks them out as a member of the Procellariiformes order, signifying them as distant cousins of the storm petrels of the north and the albatrosses of the south, related by seaworthiness. They don't look it but they are smaller than all British gulls.

He gently extends its long, thin wing. Atlantic black above, white below. The thinness of the wing is deceptive. Shearwaters are capable of scarcely credible feats of flight.

Leighton hides it deep in the vegetation behind the centre, out of sight of gulls or other potential predators. It will drag itself out at nightfall, orient itself into the wind, unfurl its long wings and run until it's not touching land.

A thought crosses my mind: 'I know this sounds weird. But do they smell, like stormies smell?'

Leighton blinks. He looks briefly baffled.

'Erm . . . let's see.'

He picks the next one up from the corner of the visitor centre, bends his neck as if in prayer and sniffs. 'Sort of . . .'

I bend down, my nose to its back, as if in supplication. They smell not as strongly or as oddly pleasant as storm petrels. Not foul like a fishy fulmar. Faintly like damp stale fabric – or maybe that was a case of wishful sniffing.

~

In about a month's time these Manx shearwaters will undertake their own long journey. Unfurling their thin wings, they will sweep down the east Atlantic, crossing to spend our winter on the coastline of South America. Their name evokes a specific, small location in the British Isles, yet they are an Atlantic species, east and west, north and south. Next spring they'll head up the west Atlantic. A handful will stay that side, breeding in Middle Lawn Island, Newfoundland. The rest will cross with the gulf stream and end up back in Wales, Scotland, the Faroes or Iceland. A couple even on the Isle of Man, after years of absence at the paws of shipwrecked rats. Recent attempts to eradicate the rodents have rekindled the original shearwater colony. A colony that Kenneth Williamson suggested can be traced back to a scene in the Icelandic epic, *Njal's Saga*, thought to have occurred around 1014, where a band of soldiers sheltering on ships by the Calf of Man hear a nocturnal 'clamour' and are attacked by 'night ravens'.[1]

Their biology is essentially the same as that of every other bird. Migrate, mate, eat, sleep, raise young, migrate. But they do things to a different timescale. The first are back in the colonies by March and they hang around until September. In those six months they incubate the egg for roughly fifty days before it hatches. The chick then spends another seventy days in its burrow being fed, slowly growing to a third heavier than the weight of an adult, before its parents leave. The chick remains for about a week, starving in its burrow before shuffling out, bumbling seawards, flying for the first time. Flying to Brazil. The sheer length of time it takes to hatch and fledge a young shearwater is extraordinary. But after they have fledged, they fly quickly. Ringed Manx shearwater chicks from Lundy have been found dead 5,600 miles away in Brazil just fifty-six days later.[2] Even more extraordinary is the attachment to their burrow: when they return to the island, which they will begin to do from the age of two, they tend to be found near the burrow they were born in.

They are known by birders as Manxies. Manxies are not the only shearwater. The other species are mostly seen passing our coasts in late summer. The sooty shearwater's passage through our waters begins in July and carries through into September. The North Sea, a shallow, calm cul-de-sac of a sea, doesn't suit these larger, more nomadic species of shearwater. The route back out into the Atlantic takes them past North Ronaldsay's northern end, funnelling them through the 20 miles of rough water between there and Fair Isle, where the North Sea ends and the Atlantic begins. In the early-morning light they come like predators, slipping out, hidden by the glare of the sunlight and lurking between the crashing waves, looking like shadows in the glistening silver sea. They are all dark, except for a slither of silvery feathers running along their underwings. Their wings are swept back, bent, and they fly more leisurely, less hurriedly than Manx shearwaters. They sweep up, down, between the waves, up and out of sight beyond the headland. One every ten minutes some days. One every hour on the slow days. Time and distance is not much to these birds that breed on South Atlantic islands and circle the northern hemisphere in our summer, their winter.

These are British birds. Not that they ever make landfall, not that they ever particularly hang around. They are transient presences on the edges of our edges, but then we are an island nation, a stepping stone to the rest of the ocean, a diversion, a harbour. It is a similar story with the great shearwater (though they breed on Tristan da Cunha, a British Overseas Territory). The great shearwater is one of a few species of bird whose name is both an adjective and an entirely accurate value judgement. They are rarer still, even less likely to find their way into the North Sea, less likely to be affected by the weather. Though sooty shearwaters are regularly seen from North Ronaldsay, great shearwaters are seen once a year on average, a frequency that still makes it one of the best places in Scotland to see them. You're better off in Cornwall when summer storms push them and the similar Cory's shearwater to within sight of the Cornish coast – but then you need to cling to a clifftop in a gale as the rain tries to wash you into the sea and the wind stops you from holding your binoculars steady and the gentle art of birding becomes chilled-to-the-bone masochism.

All shearwaters shun land. Yet landscape – islandscape – seems integral to them as a species. It defines their strength and their absolute vulnerability. Their ability at coping with the wild and the worst of the weather, but their need to live without land-based predators. The last cat on Skomer (called Crusoe) ominously 'left the island' in October 1966.[3] On the Hebridean Isle of Rum red deer have been recorded eating shearwater chicks. More usually it is rats. When rats appear on islands they have previously been absent from, the seabirds of that island will rapidly decline. Their eggs and young eaten in their burrows. It is not just rats. Islands can change the way animals behave and not always for the better: the house mouse, one of the world's most widely spread mammals, was introduced to the islands of Tristan da Cunha in the 1800s. The mice supplement their diet of grains with chicks of the critically endangered Tristan albatross: chicks that are 300 times their weight, and literally eaten alive.[4]

Near land, Manx shearwaters are mostly nocturnal. It is now mid-morning and I have no rush to be anywhere, no urgent desire to do anything other than disperse across the island and immerse

myself in landscape. I pick a direction at random. I head north to
the Garland Stone down the boardwalk, over an Iron Age dyke, then
past thigh-high fields of bracken, their roots the ceiling to thousands
of shearwater burrows. In the languid late morning, there would be
no clue if you didn't know.

Skomer's coastline has a habit of concealing itself, opening out
to a view only when you are by the edge, beyond the lip of contours
running around the coast. The Garland Stone is a sea stack that sits
off the tip of the island like the point of an exclamation mark. The
view here is almost 270 degrees wide. The sea dazzling in three
directions, bordered by the bracken-topped rack of Skomer's cliffs.
Rippled by a breeze that is stronger than on our earlier crossing, the
sea is a vivid green-tinged blue. A white sailing boat looks tiny in the
wide sweep of sea – about the size of a gannet flying at a quarter of
the distance. Distance and scale are hard to judge from up here, in
full view of the disorienting sun with nothing for scale other than
rocks and gannets and other islands.

Due north, on the far side of the bay from here, is Ramsey
Island. Named after the old Norse word for wild garlic, it is an
RSPB-managed island that looks like a lopsided stack of rocks, steep
to the west and sloping to the east. Further out and towards the
open Celtic Sea is Grassholm, where the newly married Ronald and
Doris Lockley first went on their honeymoon tour of surrounding
islands. It looks entirely inhospitable. Grassholm is tiny – even with
the 6 miles of sea separating it from me and the hazes of sunlight
and breeze-blown salt spray. Its sides steep. The main point of interest is the glistening white halo of gannets above its 40-metre cliffs.
Beyond it lies the Smalls lighthouse – the westernmost point of
Wales, further west than parts of Northern Ireland. East, towards

the mainland, I can see St Davids, the smallest city in the UK, across the bay of St Brides, where small boats are gathering.

Porpoises skip out of the wave tops, slipping in–out–in–out of our above-water world. I don't see that many porpoises and I try to study them, though studying is hard when they are always disappearing and reappearing for less than a second, several waves away. Less than a second is enough time for them to slip head and body above the waves then vanish perfectly again, any ripples immediately hidden by the moving of the water. The model in my local museum dives towards the bottom of the display, hiding its snub-nosed face and stumpy beak, like a dolphin shrunken and out of proportion. Its dorsal fin is similarly shrunken and stubby. As models, as illustrations in guides, they look odd, inelegant. Out of their element they don't make sense. In their element they live with the elegance of dolphins, but elusively. They don't seem to hang about, to make the flashy point of leaping out above water as dolphins frequently do.

One Manx shearwater glides past, unusually close to land in the middle of the day, though still distant and small against the sea. It is a rare sight at this time and in this weather, when usually they are safely out of sight of the land. Its stiff wings carve up the breeze, wings as sails, shearing low above the wave tops and swinging up and letting gravity and updraft alternate, propelling them forwards. They adapt their flight to deal with different situations. I remember the first shearwater I saw. It was in an eye-stinging gale that made standing tricky, numbing fingers to the bone and churning the North Sea into the colour and sound of cement being mixed. It flew along the beach, frantically flapping, bafflingly out of place. To my teenage mind it was one of the most exhilarating, unexpected birds I had seen. Nothing extraneous about it – no excess, just a pair of wings and a streamlined body attached.

Back on Skomer I have two impulses. The first is to stay here in this spot and not move for fear that the peace of this moment might slip away. The second impulse, a lust for rock under boot, the idea that the coastline might be even better around the corner, the drive to explore a new island, wins out.

Beyond the Garland Stone the path runs along the clifftop, west to Skomer Head. Skeletons appear, as memento mori left in the short grass of the path. Shearwaters, smashed up, smashed open, by the hatchet bills of gulls twice their size, or perhaps having had their feathers and flesh unzipped by the hooked beaks of peregrines.* Their thin wings, strung out, are still intact. They are comma shaped, I discover, when not stretched open in flight. From the body to the bend of the wing is short – the main bulk of the wing curving away to the long primary feathers that are integral for flight. The wings are attached by a thick bone to the body, but all that exists of that is a mucky beige breastbone, shaped like the keel of a boat. All the matter has been stripped away. Initially by the predator, then by the black-and-red sexton beetles that sense decay and scuttle towards it. It is uncanny that most day visitors here will see the spectacle of the shearwaters only in their corpses littering the coastline.

A chough calls. Then two, skimming the cliff towards me. They land with a bounce and walk with a strut. They call again, the sound like a crow's caw chipped from the rock, ricocheting along the

---

* We are learning currently of their capacity for hunting at night in urban settings. I'm sure it happens away from artificial light, under the brightness of the moon.

clifftop. Then plunge their curved, lipstick-red bills into the earth, probing, strutting, probing. One jumps up to the rock face, shimmies up a crack, legs akimbo, transforming its bill from delicate probe to blunt pickaxe, demolishing clumps of dirt.

Around the next corner, three peregrines rise on a coastal updraft. One adult with two young, one above and one below. They roll about, waving talons, stooping, swiping at each other. All their moves are at half speed, all for show, without intent. Stooping with the stabilisers on – play, in other words. They move along. A buzzard drifts over into the briefly unoccupied airspace, hanging in the breeze where the peregrines played. Another falcon drifts across and stoops and misses the buzzard's wing by mere millimetres. It takes the hint.

I try to follow the peregrines, but my feet are no match for the acceleration of a falcon's quivering wing. They leave me to explore along the path that weaves up and down, along the western coastline. It is a path through the bracken and I am guided by stonechats, perching on the highest plant, calling quietly, flicking to the next highest frond. I am scolded by wrens, scuttling around the stems. I am dazzled by the sea and its repetitions towards a horizon without end. The sea tends to pull me towards it. The interior of Skomer is also crossed with paths and I could have taken any of them but I walk only one (where I find a meadow pipit, lame in its right leg and missing a tail, hobbling around like an omen). The lure of the coast is so intense, I hardly think about walking inland. Around these cliffs and headlands, in this landscape, it doesn't seem to be an option.

On the south side of the island, a track splits off the circular coastal path, offering a shortcut to the southern tip, a sea stack (the Mew Stone) and the view to Skokholm, Lockley's dream island.

From here, looking across Broad Sound to the evocatively named island features: Long Nose, Hard Point, Mad Bay, the Stack; harsh place names stripped of nuance in the same way the light strips the island of relief. It is dark and low, rising gently out of the silver sea like a whale's shallow breaching. The Stack just off the tip like a fluke, flicking up out of the water. Lockley's house is situated where the dorsal would be, just back from his study colony in the Knoll. It is the place where Lockley opened Britain's first bird observatory in 1933, before it languished in relative obscurity, closing in 1976, before re-opening in 2014. Today the boat sails there twice a week and the two islands complement each other well: Skomer the accessible and Skokholm for those living out the Lockley dream for a week.

It is 7 p.m. The spectacle of Skomer comes twice, once in the evening and once at night. We gather at the Garland Stone again, walking over moors darkening in the evening light. Over the westward sea, the last glimmers of peach in the sky are blurring the horizon. Porpoises again – some see dolphins – and the bay is cluttered with tankers dodging harbour fees. Ramsey as a wave of rock, Grassholm tiny and snow-white with gannets.

Then the shearwaters appear. Far out. In the dying of the light they appear as black dots swaying against the grey sea. They drift closer. Against a red tanker a huge drift of several thousand shearwaters, forming a raft, sits on the sea. The sun slips away. The wind picks up. Suddenly they are everywhere. Shearing off from the sea, suddenly independent in the new element, passing in long ribbons off the Garland Stone. Wind is the current that sparks these birds into life. Without it they labour. With it their wings turn into sails. They become effortless and elegant, scarcely a wingbeat needed. The stiff, straight wings lift the body on the current of air and they skim, slipstreaming over waves. As they tilt to maintain their lift, they flash black, white, black, white. They begin to race, around the stone, into the bay, out of sight, towards the North Haven. The suddenness of their appearance is followed by a gradual drift out of sight. We run out of light. The numbers are, to me, uncountable. I'm glad it's not my job. Leighton says the biggest raft he's ever seen was about 50,000, a number I cannot begin to imagine.

I take a break. Refuel with spaghetti and packet sauce. The hostel is comfortable if you expected Spartan living. It is off-grid. The solar panels provide enough electricity for a fridge and to heat the water drawn and filtered from the island well; though that is also limited and the advice is to avoid having a shower if you don't need one. I am happy to oblige. The wardens run a moth trap and a bird log in the evening. The trap is a large wooden box and a light that attracts passing moths, which fly in and nestle among the upturned egg boxes and sleep the night away. The bird log is a way of collecting everyone's bird sightings, to track what's being seen. In practice it degenerates into a reverse bird bingo. The warden names a species – we all shout out differing numbers.

It is 10 p.m. A condition for going out at night is the carrying of a red-filtered torch. Red light protects eyes in the dark. It reduces sight to a third of the human visual spectrum. It lets us look into the light without blinding ourselves. It lets us look into the night without apparently blinding the other animals that see beyond our visual spectrum, although we are told that a shearwater's eyesight in darkness is comparable to a human's. My torch was dug out from the bottom of a cupboard, its batteries failing and its light foggy. Its faltering pool of red light picks out the pale path and the bending bracken curls. My sensory world is shrunk to the stars in the sky and the puddle of light on the path, the brush of bracken on my arms and the sounds, the faint eerie braying of unseen shearwaters. What I can see is pared down to tonal distinctions. The red light picks out dark toads, one every few metres. Some small, some hulking, fat, fist-sized adults, crossing from bracken field to bracken field. They sit in the track, squat and dumpy, apparently unwilling to crawl forwards out of the way of the red-lit giants.

Tonight the night is not truly dark, but lit by the Plough, Cassiopeia, the dull shimmer of the Milky Way and the unfathomable other stars spangling Skomer's sky. If the darkness of some nights can be almost tangible, the lightness of some nights seems the opposite: celestially other and out of reach. To have grown up and mostly lived in parts of the country affected by light pollution, I struggle to comprehend the infinity of a true night sky. The billion stars look almost fake, something I associate with cheap computer graphics, not reality.

But the shearwater activity is quieter than expected. Not the full spectacle. The brighter the night, the riskier it is for shearwaters. The full moon is almost lethal to them, shining like a searchlight onto the clumsy, stumbling Manxies. Tonight it is just a slither of the new moon but the stars are bright enough for birds to see by. And the night is full of gulls that need to eat too.

It is easy, here, to understand Lockley's obsession. The elemental lure of the furthest corner of Wales and the weirdness of the calling shearwaters and the plentiful toads crawling across the path. The urge to make sense of what happens, unseen and unknown in the night. I make my way to the standing stone. I turn my torch off, and enjoy the weird sensation of the lights and wonder what the Iron Age inhabitants, the raisers of this stone, the first inhabitants and dreamers of this island, would have made of it.

I don't sleep well in shared dormitory rooms. I am up with the soft golden dawn of 7 a.m. Fresh air instead of sleep. Early-morning light instead of coffee.

Skomer attracts migrant landbirds too. The gentle sunshine picks out the migrants flicking through the willows, elders and blackthorn bushes. Whitethroats, blackcaps and willow warblers: small songbirds with wings that are the length of your fingers and seemingly so fragile, and yet they fly across the Sahara twice a year on their African migrations. When they migrate they seek out islands as their first or last port of call. First food after flight or last meal before. In this case, Skomer is probably the last of Wales that any of these birds will see until next spring. They make the most of the meagre cover afforded to them. A tiny stream carved into the soil among the bracken gives enough of a roothold for bushes to flourish. It's not just birds either – the moth trap has turned up a convolvulus hawkmoth, a giant of a moth the length of one index finger and the thickness of two, from mainland Europe.

I sometimes wish I could fly; I sometimes wish I had half the bravery, half the intrepidness of these birds and moths heading out towards an ever-receding horizon. From the higher ground behind the hostel, I can see Ramsey to the north and Skokholm to the south in the absolute clarity of early morning, when perspective warps and the contrasting islands are pulled vividly close. Ramsey stands reddish and prominent of the waves, its high peak a volcanic welter on the surface of the sea. Skokholm is low and flat and green, before it turns black in the white glare of sun on sea later in the day. I want to explore both immediately. It's not that there is anything wrong with Skomer – quite the opposite – just the usual island disease, the acute longing for further, remoter, rockier. I want to be flying out over that ever-receding horizon.

～⌣‿

Jessica and James, two PhD students from the University of Oxford take our group and show us some Manx shearwater chicks in their study burrows. Every day they weigh these chicks to track their development over the seventy-day period between hatching and fledging. Some get weighed at night as well in order to work out the gain on being fed by their parent and how much they lose during the day. Each study burrow is marked out by a numbered post or tile. We muck in and help. Put our hands in. Cheeks pressed into turf. Fish with our fingers, feeling damp mud, rough mud, fluff. Grab – gently – thumb to little finger around their back and wings and gently ease them out of the burrow. Downy grey, some sprouting black feathers on wings, backs, necks. Their bills are long, too adult-like for the rest of their baby bodies. We cradle them in Tupperware. Zero the scales. Round the total to the nearest gram. Most are around half a kilo. One is already heavier than an adult. One shares its burrow with a slow worm, as thick as my finger, tunnelling its way down into the dark soil – unlikely roommates, the stuff of a natural history sitcom. One, sad, scrawny chick is half the size of the rest. Its down is looser. Its burrow is apparently almost always wet, the smell fetid. We don't give it much hope. But as we put it back we wish it the best of luck.

The development from a large downy chick to a fledged juvenile bird is extraordinary, but also extremely slow. It takes nearly two months after hatching for them to be ready to leave. The parents abandon them and then, a week later, the suddenly starving young abandon the burrow – and all hope of ever being fed again – and venture out into the night. They won't come back for several years. The metamorphoses of a bird: from egg to chick to flying adult is nowhere as striking as it is with these balls of fluff and the shearwaters they become.

The methods the researchers use are the same as Lockley's. Despite his pioneering efforts, which began in 1929 on Skokholm, it is astonishing how much we still don't know about Manx shearwaters. Nobody really knows what they eat. We have only the sketchiest ideas about where they head to feed and why. No idea why the whole process takes such an excruciatingly long time. And all of this is despite half the world's population breeding between Skomer and Skokholm, less than a mile from mainland Wales. This is despite the chicks being robust enough to be handled daily by researchers, the adults big enough to take GPS locator devices and living to – well, again, nobody really knows, though the record is a bird from Bardsey Island, north Wales, ringed in 1957 as an adult* and found again in 2004 still in the same colony.

It is an irony that many naturalists, like Lockley, started off as egg collectors before the practice was banned. I was a fisherman first, and though the two activities are utterly different, they do provide

---

* Manx shearwaters reach adulthood at five or six years old.

an initiation into nature and the required skills: patience, observation and the reading of signs. But the key, I think, is the contact they provide with the wild. Although I've never robbed a nest of its eggs, and nor would I want to, I imagine the thrill is like catching a fish and the sudden confrontation with the magic, the intricacy, the otherness of a living thing, seemingly far removed from the human world, and all that entails. It is like that with bird ringing or the weighing of the shearwater chicks. It dissolves the distance between us and the wild. Distance is necessary for the majority of animals, which cannot bear the disturbance of too much humanity, but for the robust, this dissolution of distance makes nature real and relevant.

Encounters like this are the kindling that starts the fire in the minds of potential future naturalists. It seems to me that we perhaps need something like a national service for nature, a way of bringing these close encounters, that burn bright in the mind, to the children of our future. I can think of no better way to revive that connection. It is a truism that people want to save only what they love and they love only what they know. Letting people get hands-on with wildlife might just help stem the state of crisis our nature is in. It might just help save the planet.

In July 1934 the eighth International Ornithological Congress came to Oxford. In an article for the American journal, 'Bird-Banding',* Margaret Morse Nice recounts the rarefied scene: E. M. Nicholson, H. F. Witherby, W. B. Alexander, Dr K. Lorenz, Dr W. Ruppell and Julian Huxley (twenty-four years before his knighthood) – all either famous or to become so – sharing papers and debating points in opulent Oxford halls. It was a congress, Nice

---

* Bird-banding is the American term for bird ringing.

writes, that was 'distinguished by the number and brilliancy of the social occasions', a gathering seemingly crowned by an RSPB evening reception at Exeter College, where 'the gardens were flood-lit and where in the Hall ornithologists waltzed to tunes played by the band of His Majesty's Coldstream Guards'. The gathering was 'a very splendid affair'.[5] Meanwhile, the chances are Lockley was lying on the turf of Skokholm, clothes torn and muddy, fishing around in burrows, ringing adults and chicks and puzzling over the monogamy and apparent bigamy in his study colony.

Curiously, the participants in these two contrasting scenes from ornithological history are about to meet. Caroline, Lockley's favourite female shearwater, hatches the chick he calls Hoofti V. Two weeks and a few days later, the HMS *Wolfhound* and HMS *Windsor*, two destroyer-class naval warships, are moored up in a bay just offshore, grey steel on a glistening sea, double-barrelled guns reaching out, chimneys as big as sea stacks. British ships reminding the international crowd aboard of the navy's military muscle, still flexing sixteen years after the First World War. Two hundred of the congress participants take the destroyers out from Tenby, then transfer onto smaller boats to be ferried into Skokholm's jetty. Waiting for them are Lockley's study burrows. Though he writes about showing them only the shearwater, Margaret Morse Nice recounts that he showed them 'puffins, stormy petrels, Manx shearwaters, oyster-catchers, greater and lesser black-backed gulls, razorbills, etc'. She doesn't mention Hoofti V, and glosses over Lockley as merely the 'owner' of the island, as if unaware of the work he does.*

---

* Three years later, Nice would publish a book on the life history of the song sparrow, opening a new path in ornithology that Lockley's work on shearwaters would follow.

To Lockley the most remarkable thing about the occasion was the presence of the abdicated King Ferdinand of Bulgaria – a member of the same Saxe-Coburg and Gotha family that still holds the British and Belgian monarchies – and his niece, Princess Victoria of Leiningen. Lockley brings him Hoofti V. Lockley's focus moves to the hands and a brief meditation on touch. The former king's hands have signed treaties and held control of the powers of the state, but here he is tenderly touching the down of a young shearwater chick. Lockley's prose is customarily earthy, given to the correct rendering of details and the thought processes of an amateur ornithologist working things out. It doesn't often transcend its situation. Yet when he lets go of the earth he writes, 'Look, how happy they are to see Hoofti V on this lovely day; why, a mere bird can smash all petty nationalism; all the world has become one man to pay homage to a fragile morsel of life, a nestling bird!'[6]

An interest in birds is an empathy for the life of another living thing and it doesn't seem too big a leap to turn empathy for animals into empathy for human beings. That sentence is Lockley's way of expressing the same idea that Emily Dickinson famously had: 'Hope is the thing with feathers / that perches in the soul / . . . / Yet, never, in extremity, / it asked a crumb of me.'[7]

It is my second day on Skomer. The afternoons for me are lazy, languorous times. In the sun and out of the wind, the temptation is to bask like one of the lizards that skitter out from the boardwalk and avoid the company of those on the tourist boats. It is part of the small-island spell, the Arcadian magic of a place like Skomer. The other part is when the tourists leave, late afternoon, and I walk out again, another island circuit in golden light and clear air, the heather and ragwort aglow. At the top end of the island a female merlin shoots around the corner of a bluff, flies low towards me and passes within metres, in line with the horizon. Her brown wings flapping furiously, as if trying to part earth from sky. Away from the boom of the waves an almost total silence sets in. A peacefulness almost tangible, as if you could reach out and touch it and try to store it for the journey back.

That evening I read about some experiments that Lockley carried out two years after the world paid a visit to Skokholm. It is June 1936. He is in the company of David Lack, who would become the chair of Oxford's Edward Grey Institute of Field Ornithology, and shape ornithology as a science based on the study of living birds. That is all to come. But in 1936 Lack's second-class degree in zoology doesn't allow him to become an academic. Instead he becomes a science teacher at Dartington Hall School, a place of radical education. The emphasis was on experience, a hands-on grappling with the subject followed by critical thinking. What better location for a biology lesson than Skokholm? Ideal for Lack. Ideal for Lockley. Ideal for the pupils.*

The methodology of the experiment was apparently Lack's. The execution would be the pupils'. Lockley turned enabler, the assistant in the open-air laboratory of the island. The puzzle was migration.

Migration had mystified humans for centuries. Birds were thought to hibernate at the bottom of ponds, fly to the moon or enter a state of torpor. All of these theories were somehow confirmed by what were thought to be empirical observations. Even

---

* Including the children of Bertrand Russell, twentieth-century British philosopher.

the finest early naturalists, from Aristotle to Gilbert White, held these opinions. By the early nineteenth century the first Pfeilstorch – the term for a German white stork with a central African spear through its neck – was discovered, miraculously unharmed, providing material evidence of birds linking north and south. The invention of bird ringing in 1899 helped speed the realisation of the incredible, sense-defying flights birds are capable of. By 1949 Kenneth Allsop could begin his nature-inspired novel, *Adventure Lit Their Star*, with a bird's-eye description of a flock of migrants arriving over the south coast of England.

The question thirteen years earlier was more nuanced. It took as its starting point the young cuckoo, with its lack of contact with its biological parents. That it should make it to Africa and back without a guide, or apparent teaching, was mystifying. It wasn't led by the reed warblers who raised it; it never tried to tough out the winter on an estuary foreshore with its pipit foster parents. So it was deduced that there must be some innate compass, some compulsion towards movement, and some *homing* instinct to bring it back. It was to test whether this applied to the Manx shearwater that Lack, Lockley and the pupils set about their experiments.

They took three shearwaters from nests in Lockley's study colony, including his beloved Caroline. Entrusting them to Lack and the pupils, they were taken by ferry and train and car to Start Point, 125 miles away as the crow flies, an east-facing headland on the south Devon coastline. The aim was to release them from this location and monitor their journeys home, but two of the birds died in transportation – 'unaccountably' – as if a cage on public transport in summer was a perfect analogue for being in an island burrow, brooding an egg.[8] It was 2 p.m. on 18 June that Caroline, the born-survivor shearwater, was released into a humid, windless English Channel, with poor visibility. She was back and brooding in her Skokholm burrow when Lockley checked at 11.45 p.m. that night. He doesn't immediately know how impressive that is, not until the letter from Lack arrives a few days later, detailing the time of release, confirming the location. It would seem to be the perfect evidence for the idea of an innate homing instinct and an inviolable bond between bird and island.

It is hard to see how a man like Lockley, seemingly selflessly devoted to his island and his birds, could stomach the ethics of interrupting a bird's breeding and moving it across the country for an experiment. It seems unforgivably invasive. But Lockley, like a man with a new toy or a point to prove, repeats it. Again and again. Taking the shearwaters of Skokholm outside their then-known range: one to the Isle of May, Fife; one to Le Havre, France; two to the Faroe Islands (and one in reverse), two to Venice, Italy; two to Boston, Massachusetts; eight to South Africa. The long-haul birds all died in transit.

One of the Venice shearwaters made it back to its Skokholm burrow in a fortnight, undoubtedly an impressive feat. But this displays the limitation of the methodology, the primitive nature of their tracking technology. Lockley tries to analyse the distances of the two possible routes it might have taken: 3,700 miles by sea, or 930 miles by cutting across land – if it could cross the high peaks of the Alps. He then decides that the bird took neither of these routes, or rather both: a water-based route involving crossing the inconvenient land between Venice and the Gulfs of Genoa and Lyons and the sardine-rich foraging areas of the Bay of Biscay. An extemporisation that he has no evidence for. A best guess with no basis beyond where the experiment started and finished.

It's hard to escape the idea that Lockley would have loved GPS technology, that his experiments would be more justifiable if they had produced actual data and not just dates. It's hard to understand the role that Lack, the man who helped turned ornithology and amateur natural history into a science, played in encouraging this least scientific of experiments.

Animals weren't different in the 1930s, but our sensibilities were. Canaries were still dying down coal mines in the service of miners' safety (and would until 1986, as they outperformed technology). Real fur coats were still acceptable. Although the first signs of change were apparent: in 1934 the first Wild Birds and Animals Protection Act was passed into law by parliament.

⌣

It is 10 p.m. Darkness smothers Skomer tonight. It falls like something almost tangible. The first shearwaters arrive back on land. Over the light from the moth trap – the only external light on the island – we see shearwaters as white streaks, shearwaters as meteors disappearing through the lit-up square of sky. We hear their calls from inside the hostel, that barely stifled cackle louder this time. This is what we've come for. This is the main spectacle. We pull coats on, locate our red-light torches and slip out under the blanket of darkness and down the toad path, picking our way around the crawlers who slow to a stop, not relinquishing their ground.

My sensory world has changed. Last night vision was split between the torch-lit ground and the bright sky. Tonight there is only the ground. Colours are again stripped back in the red light to just pale and dark. The dark is so much more. The shearwaters are so much louder, braying, as if mocking my slow, cautious steps into their world.

I almost pass the first shearwater. Its dark back on the dark vegetation is not distinct enough in the weak wash of red. I don't spot it until I hear it – its clumsy shuffle, stumble through the bracken, rustle. A walk that relies on resting on its chest, pointing with its bill and bludgeoning its way through barriers. They make their way by force of will. So do I. It takes twice as long as it should to stumble my way through the darkness to the North Haven, picking a route winding past the toads, stumbling on the rocks, my neck bent and eyes fixed on the ground just in front of my feet.

The North Haven is a steep-sided cove, a semicircle of rock that acts like an amphitheatre, amplifying the shearwater's calls. They have another call, one that is unlike the evil cackle. It sounds more like a cockerel gone wrong, as if powered by failing batteries or struck by an asthma attack mid cock-a-doodle-do. The sound is persistent, periodically erupting from different areas of the bracken-clad hillside as the birds return. One is the male's call; the other is the female's. In the darkness these calls are laden with the information that other species get through vision or behaviour.

I turn my torch off. The three tankers in the bay are lit up but not enough to distinguish sea from sky and they appear to be lights floating in a seamless darkness. A distant gas terminal glows. A lighthouse blinks its message from the mainland, a warning of rocks or the welcome of home ground again. The shearwaters flash in front of the lights like apparitions, glimpses of ghosts for my eyes to grasp at in the otherwise absolute dark. The calls, male and female, overlap, forming a single, cackling cacophony, sparking into life across different parts of the cove as the birds return.

It is not often that spectacles in nature are defined by the inability to see them. It is not often in birdwatching that you need to watch with your ears instead. Of all the main avian spectacles – auk cliffs, starling roosts, any great aggregation of life – it is not often a supernatural otherworldliness that comes to mind. It is the elusiveness of these night-dwelling birds, their unusualness, that characterises them, right up until the moment they crash land and blunder up the path towards you. Neither of us are suited to this. Them to land or me to the night.

I turn my torch on. The weak puddle of red light picks out more shuffling shearwaters. I walk back to the farm. This is the shear-water's world. Elusive and transient and hard to get to know. And surreal. As I get back to the farmhouse, I see Manx shearwaters on the front and back steps of the visitor centre, sitting like lords of the island and all that their wings encompass.

8

Vagrants – Lundy, Fastnet, Sole and Fitzroy

Winter follows. A brisk November breeze is creeping into Mount's Bay. It is ruffling the usually placid water, trembling my telescope and sending a skin-seeking chill under my coat, finding my hands, bare forearms, neck. The light is dying behind the peninsula across the bay, the sea turning grey. I am standing in a busy beach car park, watching a sorority of scoter lurking just offshore, waiting for the cover of the night, their pale faces shining out against the water. Great northern divers are strung out, lurking off the harbours, lidos and holiday destinations across the bay. I seek them out. Scope them. Analyse grey flanks, grey back and a dagger-like bill for picking up crabs and removing their pincers with a slap against the steely surface of the sea. I pan across. They're not what I'm searching for.

The far end of Cornwall is a large granite arm, sweeping life in from the corner of the sea where the Atlantic meets the English Channel. The bay is full of fishermen and through my telescope I pick out a cloud of plunging gannets and leaping dolphins, two species defying their native elements in the frenzy for fish. It is a winter destination for seabirds too. The water is rich and sheltered and the living is as easy as it gets, the winter months less bleak, than in the open sea just around the corner.

It's another birder who finds it first. He gives me directions. Off a tall buoy, then off Mousehole, then off the islet at the edge of the bay. Between two fishing boats, then a tanker. It takes me a while to pick out the range and every time I get near it dives – it's what divers do. And then it stops. Preens and hangs around in the shadow of the tanker.

Telescopes amplify things. But there is a trade-off. The closer you zoom, the darker the image, the harder the subject is to find. In the darkness of dusk, it's difficult, the image murky yet unmistakable. A diver – black back, black flanks, no sign of white. A thin chinstrap across the throat. Thin bill. The look is, as the other birder says, almost like a guillemot. But this is no auk – this is a Pacific diver and it is not supposed to be here.

The first Pacific diver to turn up in Europe was found in a Yorkshire gravel pit in 2007 – a fortnight before the second in a Pembrokeshire reservoir, a month before the Mount's Bay bird first appeared: an apparent and inexplicable mass misdirection.

The disorientation of being lost doesn't seem to strike birds as it does us. The first lost Pacific diver sought out water and found it. It didn't seem to matter that it wasn't sea and that it was an ocean and a continent away from where it belonged. Lost birds don't always die, as is usually supposed. These divers in the wrong ocean reappear. The Mount's Bay bird has reappeared every winter since 2007, the Pembrokeshire bird on the same reservoir, at the same time, a year later. Twitching for an exotic vagrant isn't necessarily a morbid act, a premature wake for a waif that won't last out the day, but an act of witness for the lost and lonely and out of place.

Eleven years is not long to a black-browed albatross. Time and distance are different to these birds. They defy scale. They cannot be constrained by metrics or the limits of our imagination. They belong in the southern oceans, no further north than the Pacific coast of Peru, but they are circumpolar – they can be found off southern Africa and the southern half of Australia too.

It was in 1972 that a black-browed albatross first turned up on Hermaness in Shetland, nestling on a ledge, imperiously trying, and failing, to pass as a gannet for the spring and summer. With only three summers spent elsewhere, it then spent twenty further summers perched on that ledge on Hermaness, failing to mate with a gannet. It became a small sensation in the birding world, even earning the predictable nickname 'Albert'.

It is sometimes hard to work out which occurrences are new, which are the same birds in a different place. It seems likely that the albatross that appeared between 2005 and 2007 in the gannetry on Sula Sgeir – a rock in the North Atlantic that makes St Kilda seem a paragon of accessibility – is the same as the Hermaness bird, ten years after it left. If it is, then we can probably assume that the albatross that appeared between 1967 and 1969 on Bass Rock, within sight of Edinburgh, is also the same bird. It was definitely the same bird seen between Hornsea, East Yorkshire, and Hoy, Orkney, in those years. So we know it spent at least twenty years in Britain – and there's a good chance it could be up to forty.

It could also still be around. There has been, at time of writing, an albatross in the gannetry of Heligoland, in the east of the North Sea. On 12 July 2015 it even turned up on a small reedy pool at Minsmere, where I first went birding, though it is more regularly seen at sea between Germany and Denmark. It has turned up on the island of Sylt, off the coast of Germany, where it is reported to be attracted by the presence of swans.[1] It is not a flight of fancy: not defying the gravity of ornithological possibility for it to be a fifty-year veteran of sitting in North Sea or Atlantic gannetries, the ultimate lonely life, looking for love while being adored through the binoculars of birders. It is pure supposition. If this albatross dies on a clifftop somewhere then we can't retrieve the corpse, cut it open and read its growth rings like an oak tree. The mystery is half the satisfaction twitchers derive from the lives that lost birds lead. The excitement of a rare encounter is the other. While 'Albert' was in residence to the north, birders in the southwest were very occasionally seeing different black-browed albatrosses, drifting offshore.

I know just one person who has been thrilled by a British albatross. Mark, the warden while I was on North Ronaldsay, was sitting on a rock at the other end of the country at Gwennap Head, near the village of Porthgwarra, at the windswept, sea-frayed end of Cornwall. He thought it was a joke at first, when the call went up, a tease to see who was still listening. But then other people started seeing it too.

At first there is calm acceptance when there is the possibility of seeing a rare bird: 'I'll see it soon if I keep on looking.' Then excitement decays the directions from the lucky into gibberish, and there are garbled attempts at trying to navigate by waves in an ocean of identical waves. Then panic. Frantic scanning, not wanting to be the only one to miss the almost mythical bird. Mark was in luck. The albatross glided into his telescope view: a disorientatingly massive bird. Panic dissolves into euphoria and then relief. Relief becomes silence, almost as if out of respect for the bird's presence, for the two minutes it takes to fly past. Then there are bear hugs and high fives.

Mark likens it to a sporting occasion, cheering as if your team's just won the cup. A moment he reckons will never be rivalled.

I am riven with envy.

Your life and a bird's life may cross paths for only two minutes, or two seconds, but that is time enough. The bird lives on in memories. The more birds you see, the more meaningful your encounters – for personal reasons, or awe, or rarity – the richer your experience of the natural world becomes, the more intense it feels, the greater the euphoria. Birding can be addictive. It can become all-encompassing.

A wreck, in birding terminology, is when multiple seabirds are driven ashore by a combination of foul weather, bad luck or ill health. Some birds, typically the smaller, weaker species, are more prone to wreck than others. The first British records of the two species of albatross to be seen here were both wrecked inland. In 1897, at the start of July, a black-browed albatross was found exhausted in the unlikely location of Linton, Cambridgeshire. The where and the when are both about as far from normal as conceivable for any seabird. The how is mystifying.

But not as mystifying as the events of 2007, when two juvenile yellow-nosed albatrosses were seen in Europe. One was seen along the Norwegian coastline, like a normal seabird. The other was first found on 29 June in a garden on the way to Brean Down, between Burnham-on-Sea and Weston-Super-Mare, Somerset. A place not known for spectacular birding.* It was taken to a vet, released on 30 June, and next seen on 2 and 3 July on a fishing lake

---

* George, another volunteer on North Ronaldsay, grew up in Burnham-on-Sea and used to swear that he could have seen this bird from his house, if only he had known . . .

in Lincolnshire, 20 miles from the North Sea, where again it managed to give twitchers the slip, showing only to fishermen. It wasn't seen by birders until 8 July, when it was discovered flying along the south Swedish coast, at Malmö. At this point, true to its own bizarre form, it flew inland, apparently between two high-rise buildings, and was never seen again.[2] Some birds, it seems, are determined to wreck themselves.

$$\smile$$

It is perhaps a surprise that seabirds don't get lost more often in the endless glittering sameness of the sea. I have been on small boats beyond the horizon, out of sight of land, and felt the disorienting pull of it. The hypnotism of waves. The desire to head onwards over the horizon again, to feel the awesome scale of the sea. I resisted then, if only because I can't swim. Unlike birds, I had no way of knowing the direction of anything. Our knowledge of how birds navigate began to grow in 1950, with the identification of the sun compass[3] – a method birds have of navigating by cross-referencing the position of the sun with the time of day. Other methods discovered include the pattern of polarisation in light, the alignment of magnetic fields (but not the polarity, which moves) and the pattern of stars in the sky. All of these work in tandem to direct birds from the sea to their nest, or to the destination of their migration.

Recent research is adding to these old ideas. It has been suggested that Procellariiformes, the tube-nosed shearwaters and petrels that are normally nocturnal around land, are actually navigating by smell. A recent study[4] co-authored by Tim Guildford of

Oxford University, experimented with the Scopoli's shearwaters*
breeding on Spain's Balearic Islands. They tested a variety of
navigational methods, attaching magnets to the heads of some
shearwaters to disrupt their magnetic-field navigation and using
a solution of zinc sulphate to temporarily disable the sense of
smell in others. The GPS trackers attached to the birds revealed
some startling results. The differences were most pronounced in
what the scientists termed the 'pelagic orientation home' period of
navigation, when the birds were returning to the colony through
areas of sea more than 25 miles away from a coastline. Out of the
sight of land and devoid of visual clues, they found that the scent-
less shearwaters weren't oriented towards the colony, whereas the
magnet-bearing and control birds tested were. They all made it back
to the colony, reorienting themselves when within the 25-mile distance from the coastline, and visual aids became available to them
again. The suggestion is that in the middle of the sea, when the
seascape is restlessly changing yet forever the same, smell guides
these birds more than magnetism, the sun, the stars or any other
compass.

Though this research is still in its infancy and more studies are
needed, it gives rise to the tantalising prospect of a scent map of the
oceans, where places at sea are not recognised through seamarks
but sensemarks, a map readable to birds and unfathomable to us.

Whether this accounts for the how and why seabirds get lost,
I don't think we'll ever know. But in conjunction with phenom-
ena such as reverse migration – when a bird sets off at exactly

---

* A species almost identical to a Cory's shearwater but limited to the
Mediterranean.

180 degrees from the direction it should be migrating in – and the bad weather that can sweep birds from one side of an ocean to another, it suggests ways for the great disorientation that can afflict seabirds from the largest albatross to the smallest auk.

There are certain places where that seems to happen more regularly than others. The official recording area for Britain's birds extends 200 nautical miles out into the sea, or halfway to the nearest foreign landmass if closer. It produces a distorted outline of Britain, extending far to the southwest and northwest, yet jagged and narrow around the Irish Sea and English Channel. It stands to reason that the further out into the area, the more sea space that surrounds you, the more seabirds you stand a chance of seeing. The Rockall sea area to the northwest of Northern Ireland is too far out, too wild and rough to be accessible. So go anti-clockwise around the British Isles, and you come to the sea areas of Lundy, Fastnet, Sole and Fitzroy. All of these are better bets than Rockall, but Lundy and Fastnet are shadowed by land, and Fitzroy stretches out to the very limits of what can be called British waters, as far south as the tip of Bretagne, as far west as Kerry in Ireland.* Pelagic trips, day boats of birders and shark fishermen, don't reach that far out.

That leaves Sole, the eastern corner of which lies within the 200-nautical-mile line – and also within reach by boat for day-trippers from the Isles of Scilly. This invisible triangle of sea, then, represents a kind of Mecca for British birders, hoping to spot outrageously unusual species – a kind of British Bermuda triangle for lost and wrecked seafaring birds.

* As arbitrarily decided as any border – I'm not convinced 200 nautical miles out is any more British than two or 2,000 miles out.

Underneath the blue surface of Sole is a sandbank, trawled by fishermen. Where fishing boats strike lucky, seabirds follow, the scent of fish thick on the breeze and the tantalising prospect of a free dinner thrown back overboard, snatched from among the flocks of gulls. I have been out into the Sole – but sadly on a windless, blisteringly hot August day when the Bermuda triangle effect wasn't working, when the only pulse-raising bird was my first great shearwater bobbing about behind a French trawler. The lure of Sole is your shot at the big one, the bird you never expected to see, that gets you a certain celebrity among birders. And even if you fail – as the odds overwhelmingly say you will – you still stand a better chance of seeing the next best thing, a great or Cory's shearwater or a minke whale, than you do from land.

Gwennap Head is famous. At the right time, as Mark found out to my great envy, it is the right place. At the right time, birders cling like barnacles to its clifftop, crowding every space. It was like that in 2015 when a red-billed tropicbird flew past the assembled crowds, as if on schedule. Two years earlier, one had done the same thing past a packed Pendeen Watch, another famous location further up the Cornish coast. Only one birder, sitting apart from the crowds, managed to see and photograph the bird. That was the fourth recorded visit to Britain by one of the least likely birds. The nearest colony of the red-billed tropicbirds in the east Atlantic is in the Cape Verde archipelago, off the coast of Senegal; in the west it is the Caribbean. They look tropical too: starkly white, mottled black, scarlet bill and a tail longer than the body. The first and second occurrences (in 2001 and 2002) were in the sea area Sole. The first one flew around a yacht, the occupants of which noticed it was unusual – how could you not? – and took some photos. Thankfully they were curious enough to show them to more experienced birders and ask.

Tropicbird was never expected to turn up once, let alone five times in fifteen years. Neither were any of the frigatebirds. Despite the maritime name, frigatebirds aren't waterproof. Landing on the sea is a death sentence for them. One species of frigatebird – the magnificent – turned up on the tail of an Atlantic hurricane in a Shropshire field, in November 2005, dying. Chester Zoo managed to keep it alive for a few days, after its non-stop flight from (presumably) the Caribbean.* It was wholly unexpected but not, it was thought, without precedent. Or so it was believed until an ornithologist went back to the National Museum of Scotland, where the preserved skin of the first ever frigatebird to turn up in Britain, on the Isle of Tiree in 1953, is kept. It was discovered then that the first example wasn't a magnificent, but was actually an Ascension frigatebird, an endangered bird from the south Atlantic.

That was a remarkable occurrence. A baffling one-off, until 2013, when another juvenile Ascension frigatebird turned up on the Isle of Islay, four days short of sixty years after that first one. Inner Hebridean islands are famous for many things, but not vagrant seabirds.

Both tropicbirds and frigatebirds demonstrate the interconnectedness of our oceans and the staggering unpredictability of birds

---

* A presumption based on the size of the bird, where the hurricane came from and the Caribbean population size being much bigger than that in the east Atlantic.

when they get caught on the wrong winds and ocean currents, with the tenacity to keep going and the stamina to make it somewhere. It is not just birds from the tropics ending up in Scotland that demonstrate this, but birds from the Pacific with an apparently unerring desire to visit Devon.

The murrelets are small auks, found in the North Pacific. Ancient murrelet, a species with grey eyebrow-like markings on its head, breeds mostly off the coast of British Colombia, Canada, and mostly migrates west to the other side of the Pacific in winter. But one individual turned up off the island of Lundy for three springs, from 1990 to 1992. The quiet town of Dawlish, on the south Devon coast, was home for a week to a long-billed murrelet in November 2006, sparking a seafront scrum involving at least 3,000 birders.[5] What was presumably the same bird was seen the following month, getting progressively further lost in a reservoir in Romania.

One theory is that the retreat of ice from the Arctic is ushering birds around new ocean routes, encouraging them to explore. The discovery of the northwest passage, not through Victorian derring-do, or any great hero from the age of exploration, but from global warming melting its way into existence, will surely lead to more of these lost avian explorers of the Anthropocene.

So little is known about the way that birds migrate and become lost that it could almost be called a pseudoscience. A set of rational assumptions, but assumptions all the same, about something we have scarcely any evidence to prove. And I love it. It tests our ability to imagine the progress of birds and piece together some logic out of it. It stretches our appreciation of what birds can be capable of and reminds us that, like people, they don't always follow the guidebook.

~~❥~~

If lightning doesn't strike twice then nobody told the Swinhoe's storm petrel. Robert Swinhoe, a naturalist born in India to a wealthy family originally from Northumberland (where the village of Swinhoe still exists, just inland from Beadnell), was a consul in the British army at the height of the empire. He toured Asia as part of his job and, when not working, indulged in the arch gentlemanly pursuit of collecting animal specimens. He was a part of the vanguard of imperial bureaucrats turned biologists, shooting, describing and naming their way through Asian wildlife for the benefit of eighteen- and nineteenth-century Western science, alongside Edward Blyth (of pipit and warbler), Allan Octavian Hume (of warbler, wheatear and owl) and Peter Simon Pallas (of warbler, eagle and cat). It is part of the dubious legacy of imperialism and science that certain species are lumbered with rather unwieldy, proprietorial names. The Swinhoe's storm petrel is a good case in point.

The counterpart species to a Leach's storm petrel, the Swinhoe's breeds on North Pacific islands. They sing in the night, their song similar to Leach's but distinctive, different to a trained ear, bouncier, a chattering purr with more and higher notes. They have a dark rump and pale shafts at the base of the primary feathers; and although these are proper, significant differences, between crashing waves and salt spray and a jinking flight, they are not at all easy to see. It's not at all easy to convince yourself that you are actually seeing one and not jumping to conclusions on insufficient information.

It is not surprising, therefore, that the first accepted sighting of the species in Britain came when one was trapped in the net of a storm petrel ringer, lured in by the tape of its close relatives.

It is perhaps surprising, though, that this was in the unlikely surroundings of the former Northumbrian town of Tynemouth,* the urban estuary end of the River Tyne, as if it was drawn to the old Swinhoe family region. That would have been unusual enough, or in the sober wording of the paper officially recording for science its presence in Britain, 'considered, at best, fanciful.'[6] But that summer of 1989, under Tynemouth Pier, two were trapped. The next year a third. The most astonishing thing was that the third bird was then retrapped every year thereafter, with its last arrival in the net coming on 25 July 1994.

This was the first such multiple occurrence. But not the only one. On Fair Isle two different males were trapped in 2013. The second bird was trapped again in 2014. None were trapped the following year, but the first bird was retrapped in 2016 and 2017 after two years' absence. What they're doing here is half mystery, half obvious. They are singing, holding territories in the night like the European storm petrels around them are, as they would be doing on Pacific islands. It has been suggested they are breeding. Female Swinhoe's storm petrels trapped elsewhere in the Atlantic have had vascularised** brood patches – the featherless patch of skin that warm blood flows to, for incubating eggs – which is strongly suggestive, but not conclusive evidence of breeding here in the Atlantic. But no nests have been found and they are not reliably seen anywhere in the Atlantic, other than when they repeatedly turn up in trappers' nets. Nonetheless, sightings have been spread throughout the Atlantic, from outlying archipelagos including the

---

* Made part of Tyne and Wear in 1974.
** The term comes from the veiny appearance of the skin.

Selvagens and the Azores, to Portugal, France and Norway. They've even been seen from Eilat in Israel, at the very northern corner of the Red Sea. In Magnus Robb's brilliant book, *Petrels Night and Day* Robb records the delightful anecdote that in 2007 the first Atlantic Swinhoe's storm petrel was rediscovered on the Selvagens after being ringed there twenty-four years earlier – proof that even the smallest of seabirds is capable of albatross-like feats of longevity and survival in the wrong oceans.[7] There are no good ideas about how or why they get here, or what they're doing lurking in the night, the lightning that strikes twice.

Telling one species of bird apart from another is not always easy. During the twentieth century, for example, taxonomists gradually came to realise that two types of petrel – Fea's petrel and Zino's petrel – were not forms of one species (the soft-plumed petrel), but separate species in their own right. Indeed doubts about a third form – the Desertas petrel – persist to this day. All three are essentially identical but for marginal differences in size and the extent of dark on the underwing.

Zino's petrel is perhaps the most elusive, most mysterious bird in the North Atlantic. When it was still considered to be a form of soft-plumed petrel, it was thought to have become extinct until around the middle of the century, when it was rediscovered on its Madeiran mountaintop nesting site. Then, when it was found to be an entirely separate species, it was named in honour of the ornithologist responsible for the discovery: Paul Zino. But for a twist of fate, it could easily have been known as Lockley's petrel. In the months before the Second World War began, Ronald and Doris Lockley were hiking their way up Madeira's Pico do Arieiro and had set up camp in a cave before attempting the final stage of the ascent. Some drunken shepherds attempted to attack and rob them in the night and they were forced to turn back, denying Ronald the chance to become the first ornithologist to see the bird in almost forty years.

Zino's petrel has yet to be seen in Britain. Or perhaps it is more accurate to say that it has never been identified. Neither for certain has the Desertas petrel (if it is indeed a different species).* However, the growing frequency with which summer sightings are reported of Fea's-like petrels – swept close enough on westerly gales to the southwest coastline of Britain – suggests that all three might well make it here. For years these occurrences were vanishingly rare, unpredictable and as shrouded in mystery as the birds themselves were shrouded in rain and fleetingly glimpsed between the waves.

Recently these occurrences have increased hugely so that they are now almost an expected part of the summer sea-watching season. Today the criteria for separating these species from each other are better known, but this isn't recorded in the official record books. They have only six records (as of 2017) – five from the Isles of Scilly, three of which were from sea area Sole – of birds seen and photographed well enough to discern the darkness of the underwing and the size of the hook-tipped bill.

* To briefly return to the heyday of the British Empire – the first known Fea's-type petrel was a Cape Verde petrel, shot and sketched by an artist on board Captain Cook's first expedition to the Pacific: https://britishbirds. co.uk/wp-content/uploads/article_files/V97/V97_N01/V97_N01_P006_015_ A002.pdf.

Sam was another assistant warden with whom I worked, a birder with goals and a relentless drive for self-improvement. He prides himself on being a sharp seawatcher, a finder of rare birds and on his encyclopaedic knowledge of the minutiae of the identification of everything. Sam stayed on North Ronaldsay for a year after I left, and 30 October 2016 is a day he won't forget. His friend Garry spotted the bird first, called it a Manx shearwater and then instantly regretted it. Sam called it more accurately: 'It's a fucking Fea's petrel.' He remembers reaching a state of suppressed euphoria – absorbing the fleeting moment of the bird's passing completely, committing the details to memory, quickly sketching it in his notebook. And when it passed, the euphoria uncorked itself.

For those fortunate enough to see a rare seabird, even at a distance when the identification can't be made certain, the experience is still thrilling enough to dissolve the watcher into a hand-trembling, swearing, over-excited wreck. It doesn't bother Sam that his sighting has entered the record books as an indeterminate Fea's-type petrel, not definitively as a Fea's petrel. He sees this as being honest to his abilities and the realities of the situation. It's why he's a good birder, and he's even better for not being bothered by this. His motivation is the experience, the euphoria of it, not ticking another box on his list. He is guided by birds, not numbers.

Identity is a fluid concept in the birding world. As 2001 ticked over into 2002, two birds thought at first sight to be great skuas were wrecked on British shores and taken into care. DNA samples were sent off for analysis. One had its wings measured; both had their plumage described in fine detail. As these investigations continued, excitement began to grow that the birds might not be great skuas after all, but south polar skuas – a brutal, almost identical, southern cousin of the great skua. This was exciting because no such bird had ever been sighted in Europe before, although they had been known to migrate north of the equator and had been seen from boats far off both North American coastlines. Then the results of the DNA tests brought an even greater surprise.

They were brown skuas – a possibility that hadn't even been considered. After all, these were thought to be sedentary birds – again from the southern hemisphere – most likely to be seen in the background of television documentaries, patrolling penguin colonies and picking off the newborns. They, too, had never been spotted in this part of the world before. A thrill for those lucky enough to have seen them. A new entry on the list of Britain's birds.

However, you won't see 'brown skua' on that list today. Three years of further DNA study revealed that the two birds were definitely from south of the equator but were otherwise indistinguishable from any of the southern-hemisphere skuas. The initial identification of brown skua was withdrawn and debate has continued ever since. The balance of probabilities suggests that they are south polar skuas,[8] but debate is not the same as decision. We cannot, retrospectively, tip the balance of evidence from probable to definite.*

Birders don't take not knowing things well. Unfazed by the difficulty of modern DNA testing techniques, they have set about developing other methods of distinguishing south polar skuas from

---

* If you wish to view the evidence yourself, dose up on headache medication and have a look at the pictures of five potential British south polar skuas: http://www.magikbirds.com/image.asp?title_id=574&show_thumbnails=True.

great. One of these is the moult score – a homespun algorithm, built on the principle that each species moults and replaces its feathers at different times of year. Work out the age of the bird, work out the score (five points for a whole new feather, less for new feathers growing through), and if you come up with a total above the magic threshold, at the right age, the right time of year – you might have a candidate for the south polar skua. It's a work in progress but studies suggest that the method holds true.

You might well ask why all of this matters. Why go to all this trouble? One answer is simply that the pursuit of knowledge – any knowledge – is a valuable activity. But I think there's something else too. We live in an age where to be different is to be bad, where there's a misguided fetishisation of the native. For me, looking at a difficult bird, and taking the time and effort to establish its identity – its what, how, where and why – is an act of attention and empathy.

I remember one December when I was living in London – when I was lost, mired in pre-Christmas misery – I journeyed to Portland in Dorset to try to see a barred warbler. It was a bird that shouldn't have been in Britain at that time of year. Barred warbler breeds in Eastern Europe and spends the winter in the East African Rift Valley. And yet here it was, many thousands of miles north of where it should be, exceptional and hitherto unheard of:* the true definition of lost. It felt as if I was going on a pilgrimage. To the last garden in Dorset, a bird observatory where apples had been strung up in a bare tree to help sustain the bird through the cold. It was a new bird for me and I watched as it defended – and ate – its food with vigour. It would contort its large, bulky body to turn around

* There has been one subsequent wintering record at the time of writing.

and shred the flesh of the fruit from the tip of a flimsy branch. I realised it was simultaneously like and unlike me. We were out of place. Lost and lonely. Surviving but not thriving. The moment of empathy passed and I did what the bird could not: I went home. Two days after Christmas, the barred warbler was reported to have disappeared, presumed dead.

Islands are home for some, but they are also temporary harbours from a hostile sea – offering a kind of asylum for those vagrant birds that end up out of context, in unfamiliar skies, foraging for unfamiliar food. And although I have never found a vagrant seabird, and the chance that I ever will is remote, that will never stop me staring out to sea from a windswept headland. I'll never abandon that hope or my faith in the wondrous, sense-defying, thrilling capacity that birds have of being lost and making that seem . . . OK.

9

Gannets – Orkney

I prevaricated about returning. I can't quite explain why. I had a longing, an almost physical desire to return to the archipelago I first fell for. And when it came to it, I wasted time on route-planning websites, mulled over the four different ferry routes, kicked plans into the long grass of indecision. I find it weird, even now, that those seven months in 2015 should have coloured my perspective so much that it felt a risk to experience it again. As if it would tarnish it, as if memories re-exposed to reality would rust like metal in the rain.

It is May when I make it back. A strange May. The winter had been long and cold, Britain's fields bound repeatedly under a blanket of frost and snow between December and March, and the effects of this lingered, spring limping slowly until May. At 7 a.m., walking through the grey stone and pebbledash town of Kirkwall, what struck me most was the strange sensation of warmth. The sky already the blue of summer. The ferry engines in the harbour were buzzing, sound reverberating around the metal hull and decks. We pull out of Kirkwall, the engines straining, the deck rumbling underfoot with the exertion of moving through the sea. A cacophony of car alarms starts. From the cafeteria on the bottom deck I get acrid black coffee in a Styrofoam cup that I don't want. I drink it on the top deck, flavoured with the exhaust fumes, binoculars in the other hand.

The ferry takes the best part of two hours to thread its way through the firths and sounds between the north isles of Orkney. The archipelago is roughly shaped like an H, two arms of islands reaching north and south from Mainland, stretched out between them. The sea we sail through, between the islands, is sheltered and enclosed, but runs wildly where the different currents around the islands collide. Where they meet, terns dart at the sea, frenziedly. Auks carpet the waves. But the boat tracks up the middle and all the wildlife is ushered to the sides. The lack of open sea makes for a dull ferry ride. The early-morning sun, the lack of decent coffee and the motions of the boat all conspire to drowsiness – until a car alarm from the open deck shrieks and wakes me with a start.

To the Anglo-Saxon author of *Beowulf*, the North Sea, which I can periodically glimpse between the islands to my right, was 'the gannet's bath'.[1] It is, in the context of the poem, an imagined place where people from different lands should meet with love and exchange gifts. A wonderful vision that time has, regretfully, not been kind to. But the kenning captures something of the gannet's mastery of its seascape. The North Sea, small and enclosed, is nothing but a shallow bath to these ocean-goers. Old poems tend not to be particularly biodiverse, so it is notable that the gannet turns up more than once in the Anglo-Saxon canon.

'The Seafarer' is a poem of mysterious provenance. It exists as one of the poems in the *Exeter Book*, a tenth-century anthology of early English poetry. It compelled James Fisher to show off his unusual breadth of scholarship, which extended to Anglo-Saxon literature in the original language. In *The Shell Bird Book* he translates a section from the Old English himself, dates its composition to 'some year before A.D. 685', places it to 'the Bass Rock in what his present heirs call East Lothian', and then suggests the events it describes must have occurred 'between what we would call 20 and 27 April by our calendar. Birds change their distribution but not so much their season'.[2] That phrase is rather damned by the book's association with an oil company and global warming's meddling with the annual calendar of bird movements. However this is not to diminish the quality of the work. It is hard to imagine leading ornithologists nowadays involving themselves with Anglo-Saxon poetry and the deep literary heritage of British birdlife, let alone translating it, and having the hubris to date it to within a week, to a specific place.

What the gannet in 'The Seafarer' is specifically doing depends on your chosen translator. Fisher says they're causing 'pother',[3] Ezra Pound has it as a 'clamour',[4] Charles Harrison Wallace says they're making a 'shanty'.[5] Our suggested seventh-century ornithologist has spent so long at sea the noise of birds becomes as song. The other birds in the poem become as laughter, their singing like a 'mead-drink'. It is authentic. A lived experience of how birds become company in solitude.

We disembark at Rapness at the unspectacular end of the island. Like all ferry terminals, it is a concrete, functional place. On the noticeboard in the waiting room is a poster warning about the threat of rabies from imported animals. The crossed-out silhouettes of kangaroos, pumas and baboons feels optimistic. The community bus takes me from Rapness to Pierowall. The same bus, the same driver as my last trip here during a university holiday five years earlier, but the ticket costs 15p more. It feels good to be back to a land where a bus fare rises only 15p in five years and where the driver takes his vehicle at speed down tight roads, while talking about inter-island football with the only other passenger.

Pierowall is the main village on Westray. It is strung out along the shore of the bay, as azure as a holiday brochure, the only interruption a great northern diver in its chequerboard summer plumage. It just floats. No diving. There's no traffic on the road. I don't see anyone until I walk into the village shop, where they sell cold slices of locally made pizza: as good a breakfast as any when you are travelling.

Despite the small size of Pierowall and despite having done this walk before and having a map, I still manage – in my blissed-out, sun-struck state – to get lost, walking on beyond the turning, towards the ferries for Papa Westray. I am supposed to be walking to Noup Head, the island's northwestern headland. According to the road sign that I should have seen first time around, it is 4 miles. But this feels illusory. It doesn't look that far on the map. From the edge of Pierowall you can see down the straight road to the hill at the back of the headland and the kink the road takes around it. And I don't remember it being that long either. I set off in the right direction at last.

Gannets are the closest thing we have in size to an albatross. They are 6-foot across their thin wings, though their wings bend where an albatross's isn't designed to. Gannets flap and fly directly, where an albatross glides and wheels above the waves. Albatrosses are Procellariiformes like the shearwaters of Skomer and Skokholm.

Gannets are something different: they are Suliformes, which situates them in the same evolutionary branch as the cormorants and shags. It makes some sort of sense. They all dive, grasp and swallow fish, breed in colonies and are rarely seen alone. They all spend some of their time at sea, though the cormorants and shags are not tied to it in the way the gannets are. There is something hard to pin down about the gannet. The old colloquial name in the north of Scotland, 'solan goose', suggests something of this confusion. The 'sol' comes either from the Gaelic word for 'eye' or the old Norse term for the species. 'Gannet' itself has an origin in the Dutch word for 'gander'. The apparent confusion between gannet and goose is clearly more widespread than common sense would suggest. Of all the species they have a likeness to, they are quite unlike a goose.

In the North Atlantic we have nothing else like the northern gannet. We have to head to the southwest coast of Africa for the nearest different species of gannet, the cape gannet, and around to Oceania for the world's only other species – the Australasian gannet. We have to head to tropical latitudes to find the brown and masked boobies: smaller, more colourful examples of the same basic blueprint of gannet.

There is a counter-example for everything. In New Zealand, the Australasian gannet is an almost exact, colony-living replica of our northern gannet. The media reported the story of 'Nigel No Mates', the Australasian gannet that could have come straight from the pages of a Douglas Adams satire.[6] Nigel had been deceived by a fake gannet, a concrete model left on a cliff to attract passing Australasian gannets to nest there. For five years, the reports say, he lived with the replica, alone. In the last few weeks of his life he was joined by a few other gannets. He steadfastly ignored them before dying next to his concrete mate.

It is hard to get close to a living gannet. This is a good thing as gannets are wild and shy. Stranded individuals are capable of lashing out with fear, their dagger-like bills able to strike the eyes and blind would-be helpers. To get close to a dead gannet can be a pungent, deeply unpleasant matter. But it does let you get closer than you ever could while the bird was alive. It reveals unexpected things.

One summer's day, years ago, I was on one of the great shingle banks of the north Norfolk coast. A ladybird swarm had descended on the coastline, draping the shingle in life, which felt at the time surreal, but now seems like a mere incidental detail. High up on the shingle bank, the tide had tossed a dead gannet, leaving it with its wings open and outstretched, like a fallen crucifix. It was an adult. Ladybirds were crawling over its underwings.

Its feet had dried up, curling inwards with the tension of rigor mortis. Gannet feet are webbed with black leathery skin. All birds have feet that work differently to a human's. The viciously curving talons are its toe nails. Its toes are long, almost finger-like and run raised and bony through the leathery skin. What we take to be its leg is the rest of the foot; what looks like a knee is the ankle. Its shin is the upper leg and the knee is hidden, deep inside the body. On top of the toe bones runs a sky-blue line, fading to sickly green at the base of the tarsometatarsus, as vivid as a crack of brilliant light behind a storm cloud. Only adult gannets have these toe stripes. Their purpose is for communication, to draw attention to the feet as they lift their head and body up, point their bills at the sky and slowly raise and lower their feet, flashing the stripes. It is the display one partner uses to communicate to another 'I'm about to fly.' If the dead gannet was a female – there is no way of knowing – it would use the leathery skin between the toes to incubate the eggs in her nest.

The problem with walking on Westray is that Westray is full of distractions. By the side of the road: Noltland Castle, built in the sixteenth century, but never finished, by Gilbert Balfour, a man with a predilection for being caught plotting political murder. It is a historic monument now and a monumental presence in the landscape, where no other building reaches half its height, or the severity of its stark stone walls. It is possible to walk inside it, eyes blinking to adjust to the darkness of its cave-like interior. A spiral staircase takes you all the way up – startling a blackbird in a flurry of alarm calls – to the broken roof, where railings hem you in. Blink to adjust to the light outside again. The view is a panorama of the lower ground back from Pierowall, away from the coast. Loch of Burness nestling in the slack, beyond a barrier of irises waving their golden flowers, buzzing with birds. The map says this is a lie – a trick of perspective and shadows – but from the castle roof the loch looks like it butts up to the distant hills that surround the view to the south, alternating black and green in the shadows of the few racing clouds. In the other direction: a farm, a neatly mown lawn, and the wild grey sea.

I walk on. Past golden fields of dandelions, bursting out as bright as suns. They are ubiquitous on the islands at this time of year. A buzz takes me to a moss carder bee: still regular here, though slowly fading from the rest of Britain. Their thorax the colour of the setting sun; their abdomens the same rich yellow as the pollen they seek. I walk past a wall, from which a starling barks out its impression of a corncrake. A twite flashes its pink rump on a wire fence – they are England's rarest breeding species of finch, but they thrive on the farmlands here. I pass a bungalow with a sheep curled up on its front step bleating, an absurdist guard dog. The morning's early heat gives way to a shower that's over in the time it takes me to wrestle my waterproof out of my bag and put it on. The sun, as if affronted, returns with strength and I'm quickly in my shirt, burning.

The illusion of distance on Westray is that walking to the hill at the back of the headland doesn't take too much time. Following the road as it curves around the hill takes a little longer. The road drops down to 19 metres above sea level, and then rises to 79 metres, straight down the back of the headland. It does not sound like much, but it is a sapping walk where progress becomes a mirage. The heat reflects off the road, broken crab shells by the roadside shine in the sun and the sea dazzles with light all around. Halfway I pause and gaze east, and in the shake of heat haze I can see the tip of North Ronaldsay's candystripe lighthouse. The first time I've seen the island in three years. I feel that as a poke to my gut.

Four miles on an empty road should not be an exhausting walk, but it is here. By the time I reach the end of the headland I slump by the lighthouse wall, exhausted. I have another cold slice of pizza to recover. The sun is rare here, but when it comes it is uncompromising. The clean air and salty atmosphere seem to amplify its effects. On the headland it reflects off the sea in three directions. The lighthouse wall is the only shade, the only respite from the burning bright of it.

There are some majestic cliff edges and there are some that are surprises. By the lighthouse, Noup Head just disappears. The cliff slants inwards as it goes down and it can't be seen from the top. I walk to the edge, look down and see sea instead of rock and my stomach does flips. My palms instantly sweaty, vision blurs at the edges and for a horrible moment I can't pull my eyes away from the drop and the light dancing off the waves. I'm not that scared of heights. But some cliff edges shake me for the way land, solid dependable land, dissolves. For the gap, for the air and space in what should be solid, and the way vertigo strikes and leaves me dumb. I back away. Sit down. Stand up and try again, walking along, back from the edge.

The west-facing cliff zigzags like the teeth of a saw. I sit along one tooth of rock, looking across the cliff: sitting on solid rock, looking at solid rock. Birds are everywhere and the contrast is stark from the barren headland, the short turf blasted and struggling in this spring of extremes. Along the vertiginous sandstone, gannets are sitting sleekly. Kittiwakes and fulmars are flying, flaring in the sunlight, white stars on the edge of vision. There are auks too, ranks of guillemots standing to attention on a ledge. One shattered turquoise guillemot egg lies at the top of the cliff, the yolk and the white taken for food, the victim of a moment's inattention. There's a pair of ravens about and great skuas patrolling the clifftop; either could be the culprit. Around the corner is a similarly broken great black-backed gull egg – large and olive and flecked dark. It takes a bird as brave as a bonxie or as wily as a raven to take on the aggressive bulk of a nesting great black-backed gull.

The solid rock that the gannets sit on is lumpy, like the bark of an oak tree. The sandstone that faces the sea here is a rough rock, not at all like what the gannets nest on at the Noup of Noss on Shetland. It makes lots of rough ledges, but they are small. The birds here are spread out, rather than tightly clustered, and it is hard to get a feel for the fullness of the life they support. In the sunlight the gannetry – white bodies, rocks washed white with guano – burns bright, almost painful to look at through binoculars. So I don't. From my seat of stone, I admire the way the clifftop rises gently like the blue waves that turn white and frothy as they wash into the rock. The Atlantic here is not black, as it was on Shetland, but a shade of rich, royal blue, darker than the azure sky. Offshore to the north, a large flock of kittiwakes is flying in tight formation, almost as one collective body, flickering with the flapping of many wings. Rafts of guillemots float, not doing very much, which feels entirely right, the only thing to do in the lethargy of the heat.

If I turn through 90 degrees and look southwest from here, I could, theoretically, see Sule Skerry and Stack Skerry across 50 miles of sea. These two fragments of Lewisian Gneiss, one low and grassy, the other high and jagged, are the outer reaches of the Orkney archipelago. Sule Skerry literally means 'gannet skerry'. It is therefore a puffin colony, with only a small population of gannets, established within the last twenty years. Stack Skerry is a major gannetry, which the local ringing group struggles to monitor due to 'inclement weather and uncooperative fishermen'.[7] If I looked further, if I could see across to the other edge of Scotland, over 100 miles of sea, it would reveal North Rona, where Robert Atkinson went to look for Leach's storm petrels among the ruins of a lost settlement. If the eye could look 11 miles further southwest it would see Sula Sgeir.

Sula Sgeir also literally means 'gannet skerry'. It is 15 hectares of rocks due north of the Outer Hebrides. It is populated only by gannets, the cairns of past people, and, for two weeks a year, ten men from the community of Ness, the northern tip of the Isle of

Lewis. Sula Sgeir occupies a contested piece of cultural history. The territory where tradition and modern sensibilities collide.

A young gannet is known in the Hebrides as a guga. In midsummer those ten men from Ness set sail north for Sula Sgeir. Those men are guga hunters. Scottish Natural Heritage, a branch of the Scottish government, supplies the guga hunters with a licence to hunt about 2,000 young gannets. There is a short window, where they take the young that are not downy, but not too well feathered. Too young is too fatty; too old is too lean. Those that are killed – by a quick, sharp blow to the head – are plucked, salted and preserved on Sula Sgeir over the two-week period: an intense fortnight of killing and processing that stops only for the sabbath or weather too bad to keep the fire lit. The 2,000 guga are then brought back to Ness and where they once depended on guga meat, it now forms an expensive local delicacy. The great gannet expert Bryan Nelson insists that gannet meat is nicer, more palatable, less fishy than expected, though he also quotes the seventeenth-century explorer, Martin Martin, as saying that eating gannet eggs made his men 'costive and feverish'.[8]

The guga hunt is controversial. It is a secretive hunt. When in Robert Macfarlane's book *The Old Ways* the author sails past the island, disturbing the hunters, he reports, 'They had . . . formed up in a group. They looked out at us unsmiling . . . the implication was clear enough: Keep away, this is our day, our rock.'[9] When the documentary maker Mike Day made his excellent film *The Guga Hunters of Ness*, he was not allowed to film the killing, stay on the island, or travel in the same boat as the hunters. His was the first film made of the hunt since a documentary in the 1950s, footage of which he splices into his film. Little has changed. Even fifty years ago there is talk of the hunt not surviving the future. They still speak

Gaelic when they are on the island. When interviewed they speak of the isolation, the weight of history and the honour of tradition.*

The guga hunt is a relic, one that dates back to the sixteenth century. It harks back to the time of subsistence hunting of wildlife on the islands, not that dissimilar to the bird bones indicating what people were surviving on millennia ago that are found in archaeo-logical digs. Old habits and old fears linger. The Scottish SPCA has been campaigning for the cull to come to an end. The RSPB is, currently, neutral on the issue, while gannet populations are not struggling. Local MP Angus MacNeil is proud of the guga hunt. He once accompanied the hunters on the journey out to Sula Sgier, and has been reported describing the hunt as 'an activity which has attained legendary status in the Outer Hebrides . . . we hope that it will continue for generations to come'.[10] I take the RSPB's position. Between the rock of tradition and the hard winds of modernity, I feel it is important to maintain some sort of link to the past of a place. As long as what the men of Ness take has no impact on the numbers of the species, I don't mind it continuing.

~

A passing cloud takes the edge off the bright gannetry. Gannets sit facing the angles of the rock, the tapering point of their bodies all pointing out to sea. Some pairs stand together, preening each other, stretching out their necks and pointing their bills at the sky, the stripes on their feet glowing. A couple are younger, betrayed by a series of black feathers like piano keys running along their white

* Although, as with all traditions, some things get modernised. They no longer travel to the island by row boat, for example.

wings. When they are young the first plumage they grow is almost entirely dark grey brown, streaked white. As they grow up over the next five years to adulthood, white patches appear in the body and black patches along the wings, until they end up almost all white, with the black found only on the wing tips. From the main mass of the colony a guttural cackling sound wafts upwards. They have a distinctive voice, but not a pleasant one. One for being heard over the breaking waves. Another gannet, pointing at the sky, brings its head down, unfolds its origami wings and takes off into the blue sea air.

Noup Head is a new gannetry: the colony has been here only since 2003. That's living memory for gannet, which are capable of living for up to thirty-seven years, though twenty years is a more usual lifespan. The colony has already reached 600 pairs. This colony lacks the sheer scale of a place such as Bass Rock, the world's largest colony on a lump of rock in the Firth of Forth, just beyond Edinburgh, where 150,000 gannets breed. Their scientific name, *Morus bassanus*, gets the second part from the Bass Rock colony. But the scale is overwhelming. Numbers are ungraspable and abstract to me. The difference between 1,500 and 150,000 is unimaginable.

Offshore to the west, the only thing between me and the sea just south of Greenland's Cape Farewell are diving gannets. They interrupt forward motion to circle, cold, clear eyes down, engaging target. They flip. Beak down, tail up, diving towards the waves. There are certain variables now involved – they can do this from just above the surface of the sea or from 27 metres up. They can slip under or slap the surface of the sea at 60 mph. They can extend their necks or shorten them to protect the bones and muscle. As they approach the water, their wings fold along their body, the inner part pointing directly back, the outer part of the wing (beyond the elbow) flicking out. They hit the water in a Y shape. It is a breath-taking display. And they can do it over and over again. Bryan Nelson kept captive some gannets that were too injured to return to the wild. He found they could eat almost a kilo of fish in one meal.[11]

R. M. Lockley should have picked up an Oscar. Of all the people he met because of his connection with the Welsh islands, Alexander Korda – the Hungarian-born British film director – is perhaps the least expected. It was Sir Julian Huxley who made the introduction. He was one of the leading British scientists of the time, and he was to become the first director general of UNESCO, while leaving behind the dubious legacy of an interest in eugenics and a Wetherspoons pub in Croydon named after him. He was the elder brother of Aldous, author of *Brave New World*, and the grandson of T. H. Huxley, the scientist who pioneered research into the relationship between dinosaurs and birds, going so far as to say in 1863 that birds are 'merely an extremely modified and aberrant Reptilian'.[12]

Together, Lockley, Korda and Huxley would invent the modern natural history documentary in 1934. They did it not far from Skokholm, on Grassholm, that iceberg of gannets that I could see distantly from Skomer. Grassholm is exceptionally difficult to get to. It is a particularly small island in a rough sea. It lacks fresh running water and much in the way of vegetation or anything other than gannets. It is the fourth-largest gannetry in the world.

The documentary they made is almost the type specimen of the species. Although it only lasts for ten minutes, it bears many of the tropes that still, somehow, survive in modern nature documentaries.

The dominant narratives – gannets defending themselves from predators (gulls, of course), and raising young – are still the dominant narratives today, as if they were the only purpose of birds, the only stories palatable for the public. The documentary is almost wholly descriptive of its subject and jarringly anthropomorphic at times – at one point the narrator describes a gannet as 'flapping the laziness out of its system'. When not being descriptive, it is pungently romantic, focusing on the isolation of the location and overegging its subject. It comes swaddled in orchestral music.

Yet – for all its many faults, it is a genuinely incredible, pioneering example of film-making. It is easy to forget this is 1934 and Korda has made a film with aerial footage, slow-motion footage and a sort of time-lapse effect following a chick hatching and growing from the same nest, the sort of footage that is de rigueur in any modern natural history documentary. They even call it *The Private Life of the Gannets*, after Korda's first big success in Britain, *The Private Life of Henry VIII* (itself following on from his films *The Private Life of Helen of Troy* and *The Private Life of Don Juan*). The title became a template: a trope repeated and reused as much as their techniques were. And so it was that the film was nominated for an Academy Award in the category of Best Short Subject (One-Reel).

In Huxley's account of the filming of the documentary, he continually refers to the way that 'we' went about it, but makes it clear that the film is his idea, concluding that he 'had thoroughly enjoyed the making of this film, working with such keen helpers as Lockley'.[13] Lockley remembers it differently, referring in his book *I Know an Island* to 'my long-cherished plan to make a film of the Grassholm gannets'[14] and recording in his diaries his annoyance at being relegated to the role of assistant to Huxley.

Whatever the truth of its genesis, *The Private Life of the Gannets* became the first wildlife film to receive an Academy Award, but it was Huxley who kept the Oscar. In a BBC Radio 3 documentary about the life of his father, Martin Lockley quotes private correspondence between the two men in 1966 – almost thirty years after the awards ceremony. 'Dear Ronald. The Oscar awaits you here. What about coming to tea?' Ronald's reply was: 'No no, you keep it.' Whether through stubbornness or generosity, I don't know.

⌣

Lockley, in 1966, was sixty-three. Two years earlier he had written another 'Private Life' – this time a book, the one that he would end up being best known for. Bizarrely, given his passion for seabirds, it was on a subject entirely tangential to his main interests: *The Private Life of the Rabbit*. Reading it now, it is hard to see why it had such an impact. In fact, the story of how the book came to be written at all is quite shocking.

To survive on Skokholm, Lockley had a plan. He would breed chinchilla rabbits, a domesticated variety of the rabbit with longer, softer fur, and sell their pelts at market for more money than a standard rabbit pelt. To do this, and to stop them interbreeding, he needed to replace the normal rabbits of the island with his new breed, something that proved trickier than he expected. He began in 1927 with gin traps – the rabbit catcher's tool at the time. It snaps steel jaws around the leg of the animal, triggering the trap. It does not kill the animal but tethers it to the trap until it is found and killed by the trapper. Unfamiliar with trapping from his earlier farm, he quickly stops using the device, not because of the suffering inflicted on the rabbits, but because he discovered his beloved shearwaters turning up in them, legs broken by the steel jaws.

Other conventional methods, such as the use of ferrets, snares and nets, also fail to catch and kill rabbits in Lockley's desired quantities, and then the market for rabbit pelts collapses. Lockley then turns to sheep farming as a way of making money, but finds himself again thwarted by the island rabbits, when their grazing – combined with a drought – leads to a shortage of grass for the sheep. Lockley's problems came to the attention of Sir Charles Martin, a physiologist with an interest in toxins and experiments on animals. He called Lockley to propose a simple solution to what he referred to as Lockley's 'rabbit-infested island': myxomatosis.[15]

Setting aside the fact that this so-called 'infestation' dated back hundreds of years to when the Normans first introduced rabbits to Skokholm, the burrows dug by the rabbits provided the shearwaters and puffins with places to nest. There was no problem to solve, as Lockley was to abandon his farming plans and try his hand at writing for money instead.* The myxomatosis experiment, fortunately, failed – the deliberately infected rabbits dying without passing the virus on. Both Martin and Lockley were unaware that the disease was spread by a kind of flea, which the rabbits on Skokholm lacked. It was only by luck, rather than judgement, that the two men avoided triggering the careless, callous, decimation of the whole of Britain's rabbit population.

But Lockley's campaign is not over. Supported by the Universities Federation for Animal Welfare, he attempts to gas his

---

* It is remarkable how frequently Lockley's plans fail. The year he attempted to grow kale was the year of the invasion of 'cabbage white' butterflies: the family of white butterflies that, as larvae, devour brassicas.

rabbit warrens with calcium cyanide. Some welfare. Some success. After both the trial and his life on the island are paused by the Second World War, Lockley returns and finds 'Skokholm had recovered its old pristine beauty. With its rabbits restored in numbers, it was bright with wildflowers again.'[16] He doesn't seem too upset by this.

Of all of Lockley's books, *The Private Life of the Rabbit* is an odd one for him to be remembered by. A commission, instead of the passionate projects that came before, it is neither revolutionary in its approach nor interesting in its conclusions. His book *Shearwaters*, from 1942, is written with the fervour of discovery, the excitement of a pioneer working things out. Twenty years later, the techniques – naming the animals, monitoring them underground, experimenting with them – are as familiar as the title. When Lockley writes, '[The] incessant dozing and sleeping and inactivity of the rabbits was even infectious', we can tell.[17] Where once we could feel his thrill at working things out, Lockley is now so committed to science that he gives us useless information, like a breakdown of the matter in a rabbit pellet and a formula for working out the population of rabbits from the amount of pellets found in any area. Perhaps it is telling that the book is written from his later residence on mainland Pembrokeshire, Orielton. The thrill of the island has gone. But *The Private Life of the Rabbit* is still remembered because the book would later be used by one of Lockley's friends, Richard Adams, to add fur to the bones of the story of *Watership Down*.

Lockley died at the age of ninety-six, having lived through all but three years of the twentieth century. He died, in a sort of self-imposed exile, having emigrated to New Zealand in the 1970s to follow his daughter. On the other side of the world he found more islands to discover, and he explored Antarctica with Richard Adams. His ashes were scattered on Skokholm the summer after his death. A returning, of sorts. A re-becoming of the island. His energy converted, released to the soil his beloved shearwaters burrow through, to the rocks where the lichens grow, to the sea that powers everything. His ashes completing the circle of his life.

The nests that gannets build and raise young in are cups made mostly of seaweed, algae and shit. The gelatine in seaweed sticks the cup together and it lasts for years being built up. Because Noup Head is a new colony the nests are relatively small-sided and easy to see. As seaweed is a precious resource for gannets they will fly for several miles to find the right materials. But the right materials are often the wrong materials. I count thirteen nests out of the 600 there with strands of netting and plastic packaging lurking ominously within their walls.

I have already written about the damage inflicted on seabirds that mistakenly ingest plastic, and it may seem that use of plastics in nest-building is less of a concern. But seabird ecologist Stephen Votier tells a different story – one that takes us back to Grassholm, where Lockley, Huxley and Korda made their documentary some eighty years ago.

The intention of Votier's study was to work out the amount of plastics that Grassholm held preserved in gannet nests. His team took six nests, soaked them in bleach and filtered out what remained after the natural materials had decayed away. From what they found they extrapolated their headline figure: 18.4 metric tonnes of plastics on one 26-acre island, inhabited only by gannets. It is proof of the burden of plastic pollution in the ocean, but it is also proof that birds are interacting with this pollution, that they are actively finding it. On average, 87 per cent of the plastics Votier's team were finding were synthetic ropes, a higher percentage than was being recorded washed ashore on the Pembrokeshire beaches of the mainland. The report speculates, 'The predominance of rope may indicate selectivity by gannets because of its similarity to elongate pieces of marine algae.'

Nature changes intentions. It makes activists of the mildest of people. Votier's team found gannets trapped, entangled in the plastic ropes that they had sought out at sea to make their nests. Beyond the shock of the statistics, Votier found gannets dying 'slow deaths via starvation and constriction'[18] and, shaking off the scientist's detachment, his team attempted to free the trapped and dying, those that would otherwise not survive. Some required amputation. Some required euthanasia. Some young gannets had been entangled from an exceptionally young age, their legs actually growing around the plastic like a tree grows around an impediment rather than pushing through it.

While these materials continue to find their way into the sea, gannets will find them. Gannets will choose to collect them for nesting material and the slow strangulation of their young will carry on: dead without a chance to grow and live out their twenty-year average life expectancy.

What Votier found is proof that plastics are definitively killing seabirds. But what he also found, replicating what other studies have found, is no proof that these deaths are having an impact on the population. His average of 65 entangled gannets a year has had no effect on the colony that grew by 8,604 breeding pairs between 1999 and 2009 to 39,292 pairs. I don't think that this lack of impact means that we can afford to ignore the problem. The issue is not one of conservation – at least not yet – but of ethics. It is about our responsibility for other inhabitants of the planet.

In the time it has taken me to put this book together, the BBC has broadcast its extraordinary series about the Earth's oceans: *Blue Planet II*. The public's consciousness about plastics and the sea has been awoken in a way that at the time of writing has left me feeling unusually optimistic. Corporations are demonstrating the ways that they can lead change, whether it is small acts like J. D. Wetherspoon removing plastic straws from the drinks served in their pubs, cafes offering discounts for people who bring their own reusable take-away coffee cups, or fashion companies recycling ocean plastics into fabrics that the designer label G Star Raw uses for denim. Another company turns ocean plastics into bracelets. Scientists working out of the University of Plymouth have accidentally developed an enzyme that vastly speeds up the process of breaking down plastics, aiding recycling. Public pressure is leading to tea companies cutting out the plastics that help tea bags keep their shape.

Nina O'Hanlon, a seabird ecologist at the University of the Highlands and Islands' Environmental Research Institute, is optimistic too. Her work focuses on the harm that humans have wrought on seabirds, and to that end she is compiling a synthesis of all our current knowledge of the effects of plastics on seabirds. O'Hanlon says:

> The amount of attention marine plastic pollution has received recently, especially post *Blue Planet II*, is incredible. It has really got the attention of organisations and the government

realising that they do need to act. Taking advantage of all this publicity to highlight the issue, we need to use it to lobby companies and governments further to be proactive. The decision to ban unnecessary single-use plastic is great – even if 2042 seems not particularly ambitious.

The difficulty of the task at hand is daunting. O'Hanlon adds:

There will be a time lag before we start seeing declines in marine plastic in the sea but you have to start somewhere! The other point that keeps needing to be highlighted is that we need to tackle plastic pollution at the source, as removing plastic already in the sea is not the answer as so much of it is not floating on the sea surface.

We both agree that compared with the great intractable problem of our time – global warming – plastics seems like an issue that can engage the public on a practical, day-to-day basis. A plastic water bottle discarded is more tangible than carbon emissions, despite the signs of climate change all over the cold winter and the harsh heat of May 2018. Seeing a picture of plastic bags in a dead whale's stomach speaks directly: you don't need to be a specialist to know it's bad; you don't need to interpret a graph to see what the problem is. The solutions seem simpler as well. Reducing and recycling plastics is a more tangible, less ingrained part of our lives than carbon emissions are.

Every species of bird I have focused on in this book is on the official list of birds of conservation concern. Of the sixteen, four (Arctic skua, kittiwake, herring gull, roseate tern) are on the red list of serious concern, the other twelve are on the amber list of milder, watchful concern. Abandoning plastics is not going to solve this. The pressures Britain's seabirds are under are myriad and not easily fixed. Abandoning single-use plastic is not going to take Britain's seabirds back to the days when they could be slaughtered without discernible effects on the population – and nor should it. It's not a shortcut, a portal back to past abundance. But it lessens a pressure that could be with us for as far as we can see into the future.

For the past three hours I've spent on the headland, I've been alone. I haven't seen another human, only their traces in the plastics and the automated lighthouse, and it is not until I return to the road down off the headland, back among the farms, that I see people and cars again. The spell that the peace of Westray casts is a powerful, hypnotic one. I could have forgotten the existence of people. I don't always want to, but the power of being alone in space is the ultimate relaxation. I could not have been further, in those three hours, from my old London life, fleeing from crowds. It is the anti-claustrophobia. But Westray is peopled and has been since the Neolithic. Works on the island have turned up old carved Pictish stones, Bronze Age buildings and 'the Westray Wife', also known as 'the Orkney Venus'. She is the oldest-known depiction of a woman from Scotland and rather charming – a short squat piece of stone, worked into a human form, with a face, breasts and a rough fabric pattern scratched into it.

She was discovered at the Links of Noltland, just around the corner from Noup Head. It's a long corner, the road between there and here that I walk down goes in the wrong direction for much of the distance. I head down a rough track to the sea. The links – a perfect sandy beach lacking footprints – stretched out across the bay. Pale grey sand, azure sea and rain. Rain! I sit out in it, among the beach driftwood, relishing it. Refreshing my burned face, cleansing my salty skin. I count it. On a journey that has been mostly cursed by sunshine and warmth, this is the only fourth time it has rained on me. And it passes after ten minutes, too light, too fleeting to do much good. But I thank it for the momentary relief from the heat.

The rain has brought a Sandwich tern in to explore the sky over the shallows of the bay, while I walk the sand dunes that ripple a short way to the island golf course. This is where the community that worked that piece of sandstone into the Westray Wife lived, five millennia ago. Sand is a fickle thing. For most of the intervening time, the sand has drifted up and hidden their lives, their buildings, their cemeteries, from our view. Elsewhere, the cattle fields, the building of the villages, might have hidden more evidence of the deep past of Westray. Perhaps I should find this troubling. The ease with which island communities can vanish, lives swallowed up by the sand. The ease with which things can be forgotten once out of sight. But it is hard to be troubled for too long in a place so fundamentally enjoyable.

Waiting for the bus back to Rapness, I admire the sperm whale skeleton outside the heritage centre, have a pint in the front garden of the village hotel, hear the winnowing sounds of a snipe in display flight, admire the rusted red anchors, lined up between the bus stop and the bay. I curse the arrival of the bus. I curse the docking of the ferry. I curse having to leave.

10

Fulmars – Orkney

The boatman does not make eye contact with us during the 2.5-mile crossing, his parting words before we step out on to the jetty: 'Once you're off my boat you're not covered by my insurance. Just so you know.'

We watch the boat splutter back into life, and chug slowly back to its mainland dock. The metal struts under our feet are rusting. Black paint flakes off the wooden beams. If you were dazzled by the landscape and not looking, you would go through the gaps where some of the beams have fallen away completely. You would fall the short distance into a sea as clear as tap water, the light dancing through the lapping water to the gravel-and-sand sea floor.

This was part of the appeal.

Copinsay has been uninhabited since the last farming family left in 1958. In 1972 it was bought for the RSPB as a memorial for James Fisher.[1] Some memorial. From the jetty, the island is an almost perfect wedge of rock, a steady ascent to the lighthouse, crowning the 60-metre cliffs at the far end. In between, two fenced fields, piled with hay bales, and one sprawling, mottled, long-grass moor, uncut for who knows how long. That's the extent of Copinsay. One small parcel of rock and grass and birds.

Why is always a good question. Why here? Why fulmars? Fisher, in the introduction to his monumental study on the species, says, 'I have been haunted by the fulmar for half my life; and have needed no spur to explore its history, and uncover its mysteries, save the ghost-grey bird itself, and green islands in grey seas.'[2] I know. It haunts me too, from any clifftop or ferry crossing, wherever the urge to look out to sea exists, my eye is wandering, waiting for a fulmar to fly through. The plainest birds can be the most extraordinary.

The fulmar in Britain and most of Europe is dove grey on the upper wing. It is an average colour, the evening-out of mottled feathers both lighter and darker. Underneath they are as white as wave tops. Their build is architectural. The bill long, curving into a vicious, fish-dismembering hook tip. Pronounced lines like scars run along the side of the bill. Their heads are gently curving, starkly white, the dense layer of feathers never looking ruffled. Eyes as black as flint are set back into niches that are smudged like smoky eyeliner. This is the basic pattern. The further north you head in the Atlantic, the darker, the bluer, fulmars become. I saw one from the top of North Ronaldsay, lurking in a passage of passing shearwaters. It was the dirty grey-blue of a glacier and unexpectedly skua-like, with a flash of white feather shafts revealed by the darker wings. Carry on around the Arctic circle and into the north of the Pacific and they become a dark, dirty grey, the same shade as billowing smoke, like an entirely different species.

The fulmar is a petrel by a process of elimination. A Procellariiform, but easily confused with the more familiar – but actually not more common – gull, if the prominent tubenose on top of the bill isn't seen. If you look more closely, the fulmar's wings are rounder, less pointed; the tail is a diamond shape, not a rectangle, and the body is bulkier. They don't fly like gulls. They are too bulky, too big, for the slenderness of shearwaters – the largest species of which is only slightly bigger than a fulmar.

The only direct relatives of the fulmar are found in the southern hemisphere. The southern fulmar is almost identical, a paler, Antarctica-dwelling version of our northern fulmar. Also found in Antarctica: the Antarctic petrel and the pure white snow petrel. A little further north are the giant petrels: the ultimate scavengers, regularly photographed with a scarlet slick of the blood of other species coating their heads, necks and bills. The fulmarine petrels are an odd bunch of birds.

Fulmars are a blank canvas too. Elusive. It is encoded in their name, literally 'foul gull'. The gull/petrel confusion has long existed. It takes a deeper look to see the truth. Fulmars are constantly moulting their feathers, in the same way that human skin is constantly shed and replaced, and so, aside from the freshly flying young in autumn, it is impossible to tell their age. Any fulmar could be between one and forty years old. Any breeding ones could be between nine and . . . however old. They operate on a timescale that is almost human. They are the antithesis of the Arctic tern: where that species is hyperactive, hypermobile and capable of extraordinary migrations, the fulmar is slower, as if being deliberate about everything. And, like the shearwater, when given wind, they transform: their flight is like that of a kite, playing with the breeze. They are buoyant, coaxing lift from gales, generating speed into headwinds that other birds can't manage. They are elegance in the heaviest weather.

～

For the final leg of my journey I met up with my friends George, Heather and Janie: all of us linked through North Ronaldsay. Copinsay is a place that none of us had been to before. A place apparently not many people have been to. There are no footprints, no worn grooves in the grass to walk in other than the track to the lighthouse and back. We fancied the coast, flipped a coin and set off along the cliffs on the east side. The cliffs here are small, studded with puffins perched on the edge, between burrow and sea, and razorbill pairs on the cliff face, standing tight to each other, shyly away from the rest of the birds. From the clifftop we could see the jetty and the broken buildings at the lowest point of the island. The bay between the island and the mainland is a blue velvet, the water lapping lethargically. Beyond the bay the sea is darker, rippling with running water. The two waters collide as a straight dark line in the sea, stretching all the way to the low green line of the mainland. Under our feet the grass grows long and dense, cushioning us from the soil beneath. The winds that rake these islands have sculpted this clifftop grass into waves, as a stationary sea of green.

Fulmars are not as ubiquitous on Copinsay as they are on other islands. Although the cliffs are low, they are steep and difficult to view down. It's not until the coastline cuts in at a geo* that it reveals a rock face where they nest. The light is harsh and the cliff in shadow and each fulmar dazzles white like snow. They take off into the breeze, stiff-winged, legs dangling, soaring on an updraft. Each tiny wing adjustment changes direction, taking it forwards or up.

It is as if they do it for fun. Launching themselves off the cliff in defiance. As if gravity has been reversed and they plummet upwards, falling away from the sea into sky. Theirs is a mastery of flight that is almost complete. In a group of elegant and powerful fliers, they stand out above all. One slight adjustment cuts them

---

* The term used on the Northern Isles for a steep-sided cleft in the coastline.

away from the updraft. They dip seawards, gravity rediscovered. They slip between waves, tilting one wing tip close to the sea, then the other, twisting like a helix; if you could distil and decode their DNA it would be just pure flight. Gravity discarded again: they kick up, soaring away. And repeat.

It is a shame to leave them, but we must. Our two-hour time limit on the island – a combination of the boatman's schedule and the bus timetable – insists on it. We take a shortcut, cutting inland halfway up, following the point of a geo, along the fence splitting the two fields. The possibility of being stranded without food or shelter is an edge that colours everything on uninhabited islands.

The lighthouse wall is flush to the top of the cliff. We take a break beside it. A 180-degree view of dark sea surrounds us, speckled with auks. To our left the cliff crumples – kicks up and down, as if the edge was wreckage from some old crash. The fractured sandstone blocks clustered with dense guillemot flocks, painted yellow with lichen and white with guano. Behind us, a strip of daffodils still flowering a month after they passed in England. Beyond them, the island falls evenly to the jetty and the three ruins. A small chain of smaller islands offshore, an ellipse of land before Mainland Orkney, the green stripe and dark-shadowed hills of the horizon.

Uninhabited does not mean devoid of people. Two men are working on refurbishing the lighthouse. The hay bales, the recent fences, the planted daffodils are all evidence that the island is still used and worked and cared for, even in the absence of settlement. It feels as if it has a caretaker somewhere, arresting the decline, halting the decay, waiting for someone to take it on. Isolation is relative after all. Between us we discuss islands. Heather, who grew up on North Ronaldsay, is particularly adamant that they are not places for hermits after all. It's harder to be alone in a small community than a busy city. You could not now be St Cuthbert, in self-imposed isolation, a hermit in search of a future cult. Even if you were the solitary resident, you rely on a network of others. Boatmen, suppliers, postmen. Islands compel you into community and being moderate. It is easier, living together, than alone in a place of scarcity. But islands also preserve their own cultures – whether it is dialect or dances or unique animals, like the North Ronaldsay sheep, or traditional crops, like the bere barley of Birsay.

Islands are marked by human activity. They are almost the opposite of wildernesses. The illusion that they are is that they offer a mode of life stripped down to the essence, to the essentials, to the elements. You can season to your own individual taste how much asceticism that comes with.

It was 1911 when Copinsay was first colonised by fulmars. It is difficult to imagine now, but the British population was once restricted to the gabbro and granite spires of the St Kilda archipelago. It was here they were recorded in the seventeenth century by the early Scottish explorer, Martin Martin, who found their presence on land to be 'a sure prognosticator of the west wind'.[3] The fortunes of the fulmar have been the converse of that of the human inhabitants of northern islands. While the numbers of people willing to live on remote islands dwindle, the fulmars have spread, first reaching Foula, off the west coast of mainland Shetland, in 1879, then Hoy, in Orkney, by 1900. The nineteenth and twentieth centuries saw the human abandonment of St Kilda, Copinsay, Handa and the

Monachs, their inhabitants either forced from or voluntarily abandoning their land, the west wind of modernity sweeping outlying
islands, carrying their peoples elsewhere. It took eleven years for
the fulmars to move from Hoy to Copinsay, on the other side of the
archipelago. The twenty-first century stretched their line of distribution from Flamborough Head in Yorkshire, north all the way in
an almost unbroken line around Scotland and the isles. It picks up
again in Wales and Devon, Cornwall and Dorset. Across the rest of
England the absence is explained by flatness. Outliers crop up on
the surprise chalk heights of Hunstanton and the gull-white cliffs
of Kent and Sussex.

Why fulmars? Their spread, which Fisher calls 'probably the
most remarkable change in the numbers and distribution of a wild
animal in Britain that has ever been carefully examined by man', is
a mystery.[4] Fisher and Lockley agree on a likely hypothesis. Of all
the modernising that happened coincident to the fulmar's spread,
the initially fervent whaling, followed by the invention of trawling,
is the best guess. Fulmars may be plankton eaters, but they are
also scavengers of the most unpleasant things. Theirs is a spread
perhaps best explained by fish offal, flensed whales and the scraps
of our messy industries, and coincidentally finding the rest of our
coastline a satisfactory fit. Unusually. No other petrel lives like this
in the North Atlantic.

The boatman was waiting. We had a bus to catch back on the
mainland and a three-hour wait if we missed it. But the impulse
to explore is strong. By the pier is a ruined byre and a cottage.

The stonework of the cottage looks modern, looks habitable, but we are told it dates back to 1880. Rust bleeds down the flaking white paint of the door from the bolt that locks it. Rust radiates out from the nails that hold up the sign, proclaiming, 'RSPB Copinsay Nature Reserve: Managing Habitats for Biodiversity. The European Agricultural Fund for Rural Development: Europe Investing in Rural Areas'. I am writing this under the spectre of a fast-approaching Brexit – the folly of it, the hubris of it – before the reality of it fully hits. The spectre hangs over places like Copinsay. Without European funding, it is hard to see either Scottish or British governments matching that level of financial care for rural and remote communities. It is hard to see what the future is. The fields here are managed for corncrakes, a land bird that has been almost completely obliterated from mainland Britain by modern farming practices. They are a symbol of the care and tradition with which these places need to be maintained.

The bolt on the door sticks but, with a shove, opens. Light floods into one room with two rusting bed frames. Two mouldering armchairs. A noticeboard faded to brown, still bright orange where the posters were once pinned up. A broken range. An empty RSPB leaflet holder. Two paper tags from teabags lying on a table, crisp with age, but looking as if they could have been left there just minutes ago by someone in a hurry. We sign the island guest book. Flicking back a few pages takes you to visitors five years ago. It feels like something apocalyptic. A second exodus from the island. A second death for Copinsay.

White paint flakes from the walls. Algae creeps out from the corners. A bronze plaque slowly oxidises. On it, a single, continuous white line traces the architecture of a fulmar – head, breast and bill. It reads: 'James Fisher (1912–1970), Author and naturalist.' A three-line quote from 'The Seafarer' follows, before: 'This island was purchased by James Fisher's friends to be a nature reserve in his memory.' It is almost grimly ironic. Copinsay feels almost forgotten in favour of islands where the puffins are more plentiful, the guillemots easier to view. Fisher is mostly remembered for being – as most people I talk to about him say he is – forgotten.

~

There are some phrases that leap out of a writer's work. So when Fisher writes of early visitors to St Kilda generally demonstrating a 'healthy inquiring spirit', it feels obvious that he is not just talking about those explorers, but himself, and the mindset he thinks any naturalist should have.[5]

Fisher died in 1970. In the unlovely surroundings of Hendon, his inquiring spirit was extinguished in the wreckage of a car crash. 'If a man can reasonably look forward to three score and ten, he was denied at least a dozen active years and the world at least a dozen great books.'[6] So wrote Roger Tory Peterson, in his obituary for *British Birds*. Peterson, the great American illustrator and obsessive of birds, was Fisher's kindred spirit in ornithological endeavour. It was together they set the benchmark in the mid-twentieth century for what birding could be, both popular hobby and citizen science, on either side of the Atlantic. Peterson described the loss of Fisher as being like that of losing a brother.

If you were casting around for a monument to Fisher, you would have many to choose from: books he wrote, books he published, broadcasts, or the web of organisations and studies he was a part of.

To my mind, it is *The Fulmar*. A New Naturalist book, it is almost 500 pages long, running to twenty chapters and eight appendices. Written when Fisher was just forty, the incredible length of it is a testament to one man's passion for a species, though he would never phrase it quite like that, not in 1952. He says, instead, in the epilogue, 'I have myself written this book not because I have thought it "useful" to do so, but because I like fulmars and everything to do with them.'[7]

A large part of the attraction of fulmars is where they live. For Fisher, as for many people, St Kilda was the ultimate archipelago, the epitome of the point of islands and their allure. In the 1950s, it was not common for natural history writers to talk about themselves. Our clue, then, is the detour, a quarter of the way into the book, that Fisher takes when he talks about St Kilda. The stream of facts and analysis is briefly paused. Impartiality is put on hold. He becomes almost rhapsodic about 'these astonishing islands, which must be seen to be believed', adding in a footnote, 'This cliché sometimes becomes a non sequitur; I have known people, seeing St Kilda for the first time, to be surprised to the extent of incredulity.'[8]

Fisher is hard to track down. His books are out of print and can be difficult to find second-hand. My local library has nothing of his. He is himself often unreachable. We can piece together the breadth of his mind only through his work – and then the subjects he covers as much as how he covers them. I admire his obscurity. I enjoy the way this becomes a paradox: his absolute clarity and elusiveness. The way he and Lockley show the two ways to be a birder and island-fanatic. The way Fisher did not have to live on the islands as Lockley did, to have the birds deeply instilled in his life. The way that Fisher writes about fulmars not because it would be useful to do so, but out of absolute love.

⌄

Nobody goes birdwatching because they want to be remembered. It is a life spent in attention to details, in empathy of small differences and usually one of heightened concern for the rights of wild animals to live unaffected – or at least not to be negatively affected – by our actions.

The irony involved in writing a book about the outdoors is that it keeps me inside. I am recreating and refashioning the world from my kitchen table, from a room with a window blind that's seized up and is kept permanently down since we moved here. It is tiring. When I let myself outside again after a winter in the darkness of work, it is fireworks, ecstasy and relief, and the life outside seems twice as vivid as it did before. It feels like beginning again. That first shot, that first experience, that hook that you know will captivate you again for the rest of your life.

That's what we go birdwatching for. We might go birdwatching because we are sad, and because nature has an effect on that. We might go birdwatching because we are struggling with urban, crowded, busy lives, and it's a reminder of the more important rhythms of life, a reminder of the world that beats more deeply. Because birds exist and birds are beautiful and not everything is – and because birds are present and free (in both senses) and not everything is. Because they give structure to the world outside; they mark the seasons and explain the landscape. Because nature is a language, so the cliché goes, and, as my partner Miranda puts it, birds are the verbs of that language. They give it the structure of purpose and action. That Fisher languishes forgotten is because of all this. We see through him, not onto him. He defines the verbs. He casts clarity on it all. His shadow does not obscure. I am convinced the same impulse drives people to islands now. Not to make a mark, but to be closer to the language of life.

And so I return to the place that left its mark on me.

It is 7.30 a.m. The eight-seater plane is full. I fold myself in. Knees jammed into the back of the seat in front. Elbows tucked in to my sides. The roof of the plane not far from my head. The engine jolts into life and a feeble, lawnmower-like sound fills the cabin. We taxi, accelerate, take off into the grey between sea and sky.

It is my first return to North Ronaldsay after three years away. Nobody there can believe it and neither can I. My seat comes with a sliver of window and I strain my neck to see the familiar shapes of Shapinsay, Stronsay, Sanday. The warped land and silver sea, turning purple and turquoise in the shallow bays. The green fields and headlands unchanging. We bank over North Ronaldsay, coming in across fields instead of the coastline, and memories of birds and walks and air and sheep come rushing back.

Fulmars fly through my memories of North Ronaldsay. It felt as if they were ever present. Frozen in my photographs of the coastline or those living in my mind, skimming the sheep dyke in my first, cold March days on the island, flying into the breeze, making the minute adjustments to pass me by, just out of arm's length. It always felt as if it should be possible to reach out and touch them – the faith of soft, dense feathers against the icy chill. I never tried, yet I know that if I had, a minute flick of a wing tip would have sent them sailing past, untouchable, always out of reach. They left the island in September, a few weeks before I did. They are part of the landscape here.

The most indelible, vivid memory of fulmars on the island involves their young. Ringing young fulmars is a dreaded task. They grow bills like adults quickly, grow adult-sized long before they gain the strength in their wings to fly. They scurry instead. Bob their heads like snakes about to strike, grab with their bills and clamp the sharp tip into your knuckles, kick out at your wrists with their feet. After a day, it feels as if you have been in a fight with a thorn bush. Their feathers are at the opposite extreme: dense and soft to touch. But none of this explains why you have to wear a ragged anorak and a stained pair of walking trousers, two sizes too big, that came out of a rubbish sack, kept deep in the ringing shed.

Fulmars vomit in defence. More threatening to a would-be attacker than claws or a bill, the oily vomit they produce clings, wrecking the feathers of birds of prey or the fur of cats. Regurgitating their last meal and projectile hurling it is one of the most effective deterrents of all the world's birds. Because they nest close to the navigable coast path in parts of the island, you need to watch your step or you'll cop a shoe-full of vomit from a chick you didn't see.

Ringing them involves picking them up. Which involves getting down to their level and getting hold of them before they get you. It mostly works and, for when it doesn't, the old clothes you wear get burned if they become irretrievably stained.

There are electric fences running along some stretches of the stone wall that the fulmars nest under. That is my honest excuse. I was distracted. I crouched awkwardly as I reached out. As I did, the crotch seam of my trousers split open with a loud rip. I paused. One fateful confused half-second. I looked at the fulmar. Jaw widening.

Red jet flying. Hitting me squarely – warmly – in the face and eye. I put my hand out and pushed myself away from the wall. My hand brushed the wire of the electric fence. It wasn't even turned on.

The most disgusting thing about fulmar vomit is how oily it is. It sticks and it does not wash off easily, with anything. It is mostly digested fish – I thought, in this case, butterfish from the vibrant orange-red colour – and has an unmatched pungency. I have not yet met an odour as intensely, stomach-churningly foul than part-digested oily fish.

I ringed forty-three that day. Roughly a third of the young fulmars that will take off from the island in an average year, from the couple of hundred pairs that attempt to breed. I limped back to the observatory, exhausted, hands ragged and foul for days with fulmar stench. It would make sense to dislike them. No bird has caused me so much pain, discomfort or required me to shower so many times. But I can't. I love fulmars as much as I love North Ronaldsay. They are bound up, irrevocably intertwined: place and bird and me.

⌣

The wheels thump into the airstrip. We stop. The doors are opened. I unfold myself. Feel familiar ground under my boots again. Pick up my bag and promptly walk off in the wrong direction. There's a new airfield building. Nobody told me.

'You not seen the new building? Christ, you have been away.'

I return as any prodigal son would – wide-eyed at the window of the observatory van, convincing myself it is real, noticing the changes. The new building, new island cars, old faces and forgotten names. I get out of the van. Bear hugs for the known and handshakes for the new. Memory preserves a place like a glass case around a museum display, but islands are not – should not be – museum pieces, and it is pleasing to see the changes, to feel the continued pulse of the place. I did not know how returning would feel. I did not anticipate it feeling like coming home. But it does. It feels like returning to myself. The landscape here seems to fit me like an old coat. Familiar and perfectly sized. Threadbare perhaps, in need of repair in part, but it feels like mine and I love it.

It's an odd feeling, the sense of being at home in a place that is not really home. It is not one I have a word for. It is not *hiraeth*, the hard-to-define Welsh word for a more than profound longing to return to a homeland. It is not *cynefin*, Welsh for the habitat, or native environment of a thing, as Orkney is not my native land. It is somewhere between *fernweh* and *heimweh*, the German pair of words for wanderlust and homesickness, a longing for the far off and a longing for home. And, being neither Welsh nor German, I could only use them in translation anyway, removed from their linguistic homes and appropriated from their cultures for my own uses, something that goes entirely against my feeling. I don't think I need a word. The feeling is too messy for the neatness of a diction- ary, too personal, too linked to the intensity of those seven months when the wind blew out the dust of my head and my feet took hold among the stones and the sheep. Perhaps the elusiveness of feelings without words to describe them is necessary.

I settle back into the observatory. Varnished dark-wood tables and well-worn sofas. Windows all around framing a view of sheep fields and sea and Sanday. The sheep of North Ronaldsay are unique to the island, adapted to the quirks of it. They are walled out from the fields by the sheep dyke, a unique drystone wall described by

Historical Environment Scotland as 'probably the largest drystone construction conceived of as a single entity in the world'.[9] The ewes are let in only in the spring for the raising of lambs. They are kept out for their own good. Adapted to eat seaweed, a food source low in copper, they die from copper poisoning if given a normal grass diet. They are tidal creatures, eating only when low tide lets them. They are a small, stocky sheep, capable of leaping from rock to rock, and over the sheep dyke, like honorary mountain goats.

The flock around the observatory is semi-wild and self-willed. After coffee I head out with Janie, the observatory housekeeper, to help feed the two caddy lambs. Caddy lambs are orphans hand-raised by the observatory volunteers, who, like me, arrived daft about birds and leave daft about sheep too. Gubbins is the name of one orphan. A late lamb, still small-bodied on long legs, but coursing with enough energy to leap over another lamb on sight of the bottle of lamb milk. Gubbins is white-headed, with black eye-patches, like a panda. I cradle her in my arms to feed her. A sheep runs over – stocky, with a mottled brown coat and a lamb in tow. She pushes her face through the fence up to me. It takes a moment before I recognise her: Plum, one of the lambs I raised three years ago. And though I have no proof for it, other than a deep-lying respect for the capabilities of sheep, I like to think she recognised me too. I recognise in Gubbins the joy of caring, kindling the life in other species that did the same for me.

North Ronaldsay lies somewhere off the Orkney tourist track. Its role in history is marginal. It is not frequently mentioned in the

Orkneyinga Saga, the thirteenth-century Icelandic saga that forms the basis of much of what we know about the Viking past of the northern isles. Not that many notable people have visited. Lockley did in the 1930s,* having had the rare sight of 'the North Ronaldshay [*sic*] lighthouse sticking up like a finger on the horizon'.[10] It is a quirk of perspective, light, land and sea that Fair Isle is visible most days from North Ronaldsay, but not vice versa. The 200-metre lump of Fair Isle's Ward Hill stands out like a black beacon in the grey of the horizon. The 20-metre lump of unnamed hill that is the highest part of North Ronaldsay is completely invisible from Fair Isle. It is only the red and white hoops of the lighthouse, twice as tall as the highest island hill, that sometimes stands out as a blip in the 30-mile haze of distance.

Lockley takes a flight – at the cost of 15 shillings – and lands on the island that he knows as 'the garden of Orkney', an epithet that I have not heard, would not recognise and one that seems to have fallen so far out of use as to be untraceable.[11] He tries to walk the circumference of the island: he expects it to take a not unreasonable eight hours. Instead he finds so much to explore that, 'It took us three days . . . to complete our peregrination of the island'.[12] The geographical bones of the island that he saw then remain much the same now, minus some eroded parts of the shoreline, minus some crofts later abandoned and left to disintegrate. He likens it to the Fens in flatness and dampness, and I agree. Everything else is almost unrecognisable. He saw an island with a population of just under 300 (298 in 1931), but one that was already in the grip of

* He doesn't specify when, though I suspect it was in 1937. The book suggests, but doesn't state, that it was the year after he visited Heligoland, which was in 1936.

decline.[13] The population would halve in the next thirty years.[14] A population that, according to Orkney Council's own report, had the second steepest decline in the archipelago between 1981 and 2001.[15] When Lockley says, 'There is a Danish neatness about the farms',[16] he might be labouring the Viking heritage too far, or it might once have genuinely looked like that. There is little that remains neat and tidy now about the island, where broken cars are left to decay in fields, crumbled walls go unrepaired and plastics wash ashore.

It is hard to tell if, under his stiff lip, he likes it. I suspect he does. Particularly compared to later islands, such as the Westmann's, where he complains to the consul, 'I came here because I thought the people lived simply, as primitively as the St Kildans used to, on fish and sea-birds and sheep. I see nothing to lead me to suppose that I am not in a thriving English fishing port, even to the huddle of concrete and corrugated iron.'[17] The search for a simple life can be a complicated one, even for Lockley. He is usually a well-mannered traveller – but then he usually lacks a diplomat to harangue.

$\smile$

I headed over the fields to the coast. Retracing my first steps around the Twingness headland that very first full day three years ago. Discarding clothing. I had no recollection of the island as muggy in May. Despite Westray, despite the forecast, the heat is still entirely unexpected. We tend to take our first experience of a thing or place as the average, the baseline. I saw it with visitors who would visit and think of it as a sunny paradise or a cold, wet hell depending on the weather. It is a normal way of thinking. I remember May as cold and wet and dressed for my memories. Now I'm in just a shirt, my face fluorescent with sunburn, the stark sun beating down and the island devoid of shade, the glare sparkling off the sea.

I see things I remember doing. Digging the hole in the stony ground for the concrete gate strainer posts. Planting a windbreak of flaxes, now mostly a metre high. The stile by the Heligoland trap still there, still bearing the bodyweight of exhausted birders. My previously unexplored construction and gardening skills still keeping up. I make it to the hide overlooking Loch Gretchen, a shallow pool in a boggy field. I fall upon the bannock – a local flat bread I bought in Kirkwall the night before – for breakfast. Gretchen is a hotspot for migrant birds and two red-necked phalaropes drop in, next to a garganey. The latter off to the bogs of Scandinavia. The phalaropes on their long, incredible journey from winter on the coastline of Peru to breed on the lochs of Shetland. They're watched not just by me but also by a bustle of nesting Arctic terns, the shrieking common gulls of the colony, electric lapwings chasing off the fulmars taking a shortcut, innocent but gull-like enough to require a frantic noisy escort as they drift over the field. The island is alive with birds again.

It was here, where the Twingness headland meets the main bulk of the island, that I first fell in love with fulmars. At this corner of the west coast, the wind and the waves seem stronger, as if it faces exactly into the angle of the prevailing gales. It is here where the fulmars sweep along the wall, into the breeze, curve up and head out across the small bay. It is their ideal theatre for flight and, when it gets too much, they drift over and onto the loch, to run freshwater through their feathers.

Today they are present but reluctant to fly. I walk up the west coast, on the thin path between the airfield wall and the waves washing into the rocks. I walk past the cleft geos and boulder beaches near where the fulmars nest. They are strewn with discarded tyres, wellies, strapping, fragments of fishing net. Walking with the distant shadows of Papay and Westray, hazed by the heat. The fulmars are ever present.

In the unseasonably good and still weather, they are calmed. The effortless bird requires effort. It is instructive to see them like this. Out of their native element, without the wind that coaxes them into incredible powers of flight. The humdrum fulmar on an ordinary day, if on the ground, needs to run with wings out to achieve take-off. If on a coastal rock, they leap, feet slapping the sea, straining, creaking for air under wings to achieve lift.

The west coast is the wild coast, the Atlantic end of the island. The sheep dyke runs parallel inland and the grassy heaths along the coast are cropped close by the sheep's teeth. It should, by now, be spangled with spring squill and tormentil and the other stunted, dwarf plants of the maritime heath. But the winter was long, spring was a week's interlude, before what now feels like summer. A weird, bare summer. But birds are still with me wherever I walk here. Nesting terns ratchet bark at me, plunging if I stray too close. Ringed plovers whistle and shuffle, feigning injury to lead me away from their nests in the plover-sized, plover-coloured stones.

The wild path takes me around another curving headland to Westness. A croft, one of the loneliest on the island, is perched on the side of a bay between two headlands, facing due north. It is sheltered from the land by a maze of sheep walls and a low rolling hummock of marram grass. It is unprotected from the other side. In the stillness of today, the azure sea laps gently onto the stony beach by a concrete seawall. Where the seawall ends, the ground has been bitten by waves, eroded out from under the long grass. Earth and stones crumbling back into the sea. It has been abandoned. The roof has caved in. The rooms full of junk. The walled garden deep in weeds.

In the sundial shadow of the lighthouse – the tallest onshore in Britain – lies an older, much smaller lighthouse. The old beacon is clad in scaffolding, preserving it. The hole where the light once was is plugged with a stone stopper, like a bottle. It was built in 1789 and actually caused more accidents on the reefs surrounding the island than it prevented. It was too low, too dim; its existence – or rather the knowledge of its existence – lulled sailors into a false, lethal, sense of security as they sailed around the island. It is morbidly appropriate: the shimmering light of North Ronaldsay can lure you in like a siren.

North Ronaldsay is haunted by the idea that it might be no more. Thanatophobia courses through the nervous system of small islands. Its primary school, on the leaving of its last pupil, has been mothballed, at the time of writing. The ferry, the only way for freight to reach the island, comes only twice a week in summer, once a week in winter. Its population is dwindling, and the official 2011 census result of seventy is too high. It was estimated by islanders at fifty-two when I arrived and forty-nine when I left seven months later. Crofts are abandoned and left to fall apart. The flagstone roofs fall apart. Rot sets in. And the cost of refurbishing and renovating them often exceeds what is practical.

It has almost happened before. The islands are haloed by kelp beds, the shoreline often deep in tangle, as it is known, fragrantly decaying in the sun. In spring, the beaches shake with crazed clouds of kelp fly, food for the myriad waders that pass along the shoreline heading for the far north. There was a kelp craze here between 1770 and 1830. Evidence of it can still be seen. Machinery – winches and cables – left to rust in the corners of the island where the banks of tangle would be brought ashore by men and women. The work was tidal. Breaks dictated by high tide when the seaweed was taken out of reach again. Hours dictated by low tide, whenever that began. It was a job in tune with the rhythms of the island, the beat of the earth, and it was, as all jobs of its kind are, brutal, exhausting labour that is hard to imagine in the current calm of the island. The kelp would be dried, then burned in what they called a kiln; in reality, a shallow depression in the soil surrounded by stones. Acrid smoke would fill the air. The end product would be hacked up, sold and taken by ship to the great ports of Glasgow, Leith and Newcastle, where it would find itself used in the production of glass and soap. Kelp brought prosperity. Kelp brought people. The population of North Ronaldsay reached ten times its current level.

It could not last. As all bubbles must burst, so the kelp price crashed. The market disappeared. New materials were found to take the place of kelp. Thirty-two families were removed in an 'organised emigration' and taken either to Eday or out of the archipelago.[18] Kelp was a fever for the island. It consumed all. And though on North Ronaldsay you can feel completely unconnected to the rest of Britain, the shockwaves from a collapsing economy are often more keenly felt here, amplifying as they travel through Britain to its deprived edges. The island was burned out and hasn't been the same since. It was the last point of growth for North Ronaldsay.

The Scottish Island Federation reports European research stating that an island needs to have a population of 4–5,000 to achieve a net population growth and sustainability of services.[19] It seems that people are like seabirds. People like to live among people, as one pair of seabirds will attract others. North Ronaldsay could not support 5,000 people. It is simply too small. There are only six Scottish islands that, in the 2011 census, had a population over that growth threshold. However, those six islands include Mainland Orkney and Mainland Shetland: perhaps North Ronaldsay and Unst will survive by proximity. I know of at least two islanders who work jobs on both Mainland Orkney and North Ronaldsay, commuting by plane.

This might be what the future holds for the Scottish islands. They look different from the nature reserve islands of England and Wales, and that is entirely a good thing. Skomer and Skokholm are lovely, but we can't all be like Lockley and live there. Living on the Farnes would be purgatory – so many birds and so little space to move in. Shetland and Orkney manage the balance that makes me feel like Goldilocks, demanding a life on an island that is wild but liveable and just right.

I was nervous about returning to Orkney because I didn't want to tarnish memories. The mistake I had made – so easy to slip into – is thinking that islands are one-off experiences. Places that you have only one shot at, places that are as ephemeral as mayflies. Which is nonsense. The Orkney archipelago has been populated for at least 5,000 years. Barring apocalypse, Armageddon or other extreme disasters, it will be populated for another 5,000 at least. Islands are not one-offs, but real, lived experiences, often stretching to the deepest past, the most mysterious of lives, like the inhabitants of Skara Brae in 3,000 BC, making beads from bone, or those of the Tomb of the

Eagles, buried with eagle's talons, or those that turned the stones around them into highly polished tools.

⌣

From the old beacon you can look down the concave eastern coastline of the island, to the Brides peninsular where the island broch lurks low, a round drystone ring stuck in the turf. The beach by the golf course in between, glistening, an alluring strip of sand in the sunlight. The eastern, North Sea coastline of the island is tamer. The contrast between seas and coastlines on North Ronaldsay is striking. It is lower and more fertile and the fields between me and the track to the golf course are golden, thick with dandelion suns. On the golf course the sheep dyke curves inland, the sheep given the work of greenkeeper. I have never seen anyone play golf on the island. It is left to the wildlife and at various times of the year runs wild with forget-me-nots, grass of Parnassus and migrant waders dropping in for respite and dodging the sheep's use of the flat and firm of it as a racing track.

All golf courses have their hazards. Here, sides of the green are studded with fulmars. Walking down the golf course flushes them out one by one, feet slapping into the grass to get the lift under their stiff wings. The course broadens out and I keep enough distance to avoid disturbing them. I follow the line of the beach below the wave of grass, where the sand has been eaten out from under it by the sea. The dog faces of common seals stare back at me offshore. Sanderling sprint along the tideline, leaving faint footprints in wet sand. A 50-gram bird doesn't make much of a mark. The sheep leave a different mark: a track of ruffled sand down the middle of the beach where they run in each other's steps. It is erased by the tides and remade each day.

Like all seabirds in the Anthropocene, fulmars have to face the deadly hazard of plastic pollution in the world's oceans. In fact, because fulmars are surface eaters, they are particularly vulnerable to ingesting floating plastics, and the fact that they scavenge on dead fish and marine mammals also exposes them to any plastics that those animals have eaten. But fulmars also play a key role in helping us to understand, measure and deal with the problem.

This is thanks to OSPAR – a pan-European organisation set up in 1972 to reduce and prevent pollution in the Atlantic, from the Azores to the Arctic, via the North, Celtic and Irish Seas. To quantify the challenge and monitor the success of its programme, OSPAR decided to use the fulmars of the North Sea as a yardstick and a target. The yardstick: 60 per cent of fulmars have ingested at least 0.1 grams of plastics. The target: to lower that to less than 10 per cent of fulmars.

The work carried out by OSPAR has been conducted with rigour. There have been a number of studies identifying the prevalence of plastic ingestion among seabirds but, according to Nina O'Hanlon, writing in a synthesis of research on plastics and seabirds, 'The majority of information currently collected is ad hoc and opportunistic.' In contrast, she says that OSPAR's study of fulmar in the North Sea is 'the only example of a coordinated effort to monitor marine plastic in seabirds.'[20]

OSPAR's yardstick figure of 60 per cent has been more or less stable since 2000, which, in itself, has been a source of some positivity given, as OSPAR points out, 'the growth in marine activity and the increasing proportion of plastics in wastes.'[21] But stability is not reduction, and the target of 0.1 per cent remains as far away as ever. For that, we need to tackle the issue of plastic pollution: it is no coincidence that the fulmars in the English Channel – with its busy ports and highly populated coastlines – were the most contaminated by plastics. Nor that the fulmars here, around the Scottish islands, were found to be the least. And it is sobering that every geo, every bay and every beach up here on these remote islands has been found to have some level of plastic pollution. It is to be hoped that the fulmars can continue to help us find a solution.

I have only a couple of hours left on the island. Time enough for more wonders. Cutting inland, I head past the shallow waters of Hooking Loch, its banks a dense tangle of irises. There, among the irises – a foot or two too tall for its environment – is what I'm looking for. A great white egret, found earlier that day, only the fourth ever to have been seen on the island. It is stark. A freshly laundered white, in the brilliance of the sunlight. Its neck curves elegantly, an elegance that hides a muscular neck that springs forwards, driving its bill down to feast on the frogs that were introduced to the island a few years back. I have no way of knowing, but I suspect it is the most northerly great white egret in the world.

Back to the observatory to pack my bags, I'm told there's been a call about killer whales back up at the lighthouse. The bags can wait. We jump into the van, go full throttle up the island, arrive in a hectic rush of anticipation and excitement. And then . . . nothing. The headland gives a view of sea in three directions and height to see out for distance. But there are no interruptions to the waves, no thick black dorsal fins raised with intent above the water like the periscopes of submarines. An extraordinary great white egret, and some elusive killer whales. That's North Ronaldsay. Unexpected and contrary. Always the right place to be, if you are prepared to wait for the right time.

But my time is done. I pack my rucksack, shoulder it and walk back to the airfield as clouds colour the sky fulmar grey again. The plane is busy, the flight full with people from another island on their way to Kirkwall via North Ronaldsay. 'Looks a bit flat,' says a voice from several seats in front, laden with disdain.

It's true, I suppose, but the remark reveals less about the island than it does about the speaker. We are culturally conditioned to view certain landscapes in certain ways. My ferry over to Orkney from the mainland passed close by the coast of Hoy, its dramatic, richly toned sandstone cliffs Mars-red in the evening light. The entire right side of the ferry was lined with passengers taking photos, experiencing the awe of it. It would be unusual or churlish if people did not feel this way – did not experience the cliffs and beaches without the twin awes of scale and isolation.

Writing in 1935, the poet Edwin Muir – Orkney's second most famous literary son after George Mackay Brown – suggested that the islands offered the tourist something dream-like:

If he goes there in the middle of June, the long light, which never fades at that time of the year but ebbs and ebbs until, before one can tell how, morning is there again, will charm and tease him; he will lose his sleep for a few nights and be discontented during the day, and feel that he is not quite in the real world. If he has an eye for such things, he will be delighted by the spectacle of the quickly changing skies and the clearness and brightness of all the colours . . . Orkney is full of fine scenery, but that has to be looked for, and of historical interest, but that requires acquaintance with a history in which even experts are uncertain.[22]

North Ronaldsay offers neither scale nor isolation. No great hills or sea-cleaved cliffs. You could not go more than half an hour without evidence of people. Yet for me it still feels as dream-like as the other, more famed isles of Orkney. I spent my time there walking in a waking dream, where things might not be real, where distraction and curiosity and wonder abound, where knowledge of things can take you only so far.

There are some landscapes that keep time and event. Wooded landscapes keep a record of the seasons of growth and decay. They literally encode years of boom and bust in their growth rings, integral to their flesh. North Ronaldsay is not one of those landscapes. Things do not linger. After the harvest, there is no record of the year – whether it was cold, wet, dry, fecund or famine. It has no record of my growth and recovery, my personal fecundity and flood of 2015. It is a blank canvas. A landscape like this is what you make of it. It is what you dream of it.

North Ronaldsay is the place that brought me back to the language of life. Like all languages, it is a living, used thing. Not a precious wilderness, but a worked landscape, a place working to the rhythms of the seasons, for both birds and people. A language is a relationship. Words exist only because they are written, spoken, shared. It is through use that they remain valid and charged with meaning. Nature is the same. It is a two-way street. But when I was living in London, I took a wrong turn and became lost down a soulless cul-de-sac. It was the fulmars of North Ronaldsay that guided me back on track. It took being hands-on with these seabirds, covered in their bite marks and vomit, to reorient myself. But then I was always a dramatic young man. You might not need to go so far or be so extreme.

The plane taxis. Takes off into the air above the west coast – my first arrival route in reverse – and turns to fly over Gretchen and the bird observatory. From above, the light gone from the day, the land looks dark and the sea silver. Loch Gretchen looks like a hole, a gap where the land has worn thin. To me, the heart-shaped Twingness headland where the observatory sits is filled with significance, but I imagine that for everyone else on the plane it is barely worth a second look. Easily passed over or passed off. Just like the plain dull-grey fulmars are so easily overlooked – their incredible spirit so easily missed.

But if it wasn't for that observatory and those fulmars, if it wasn't for all seabirds, I don't know where I would be or who I would be. I might be leaving the island, but it will never leave me.

Epilogue

The sting in the tail of any journey out is the return back. In the days leading to my first departure from North Ronaldsay, I developed anxious tics. Idle itches became repeated. I scratched nervously until I bled. I stared blankly at the sea. Found new wrinkles and a scattering of grey hairs at twenty-three. The place had grown into me as if it was emotional scar tissue. If I hadn't left then, I might never have.

I get a 75p ticket for the last bus out of Kirkwall. The night ferry from Shetland to Aberdeen calls in at the out-of-town ferry terminal. The night boat is an unusual experience. It carries enough people when fully occupied to be the twentieth most-populated Scottish island. It would take twelve North Ronaldsays to fill. It leaves Kirkwall at midnight, having left Lerwick, Shetland at 5.30 p.m. Two different sets of islanders and their tourists, intermingling.

I opt for a 'sleeping pod', which amounts to an eye-mask and a padded chair on which I fitfully sleep until 5 a.m., when I give up. Through the salt-hazed window, the world is split into three parts: the horizon grows pink, the sky bright blue, the sea darker. The sea is calm, the ferry rumbling rather than rocking through waves. It docks into the grey granite of Aberdeen before 7 a.m. Three hours to kill until the cheap, cramped, crowded trains south, which I take for eight and a half hours, with the bright glare of day dazing me, before I reach my front door. The mainland has its ways of bringing any island journey back down to earth. It reminds me of the first time I made this journey back from North Ronaldsay. I wanted a Twix from the vending machine at Peterborough station, but found its array of buttons so confusing that I went hungry.

This time. No tics. No baffled hunger. Just the tired daze of a long, long journey by bus, ferry and train.

A week on Orkney doesn't quite detach you from the rest of the world in the way that seven months will.

I cannot claim to be an islander, but I love islands. And perhaps it takes the fresh eyes of the traveller to see things that others do not. Similarities, echoes, rhymes across island coastlines. The hidden quirks, the necessary eccentricities that islands breed: the Unst bus stop, the Faroese storm petrels used as candles, the repacked history of Lindisfarne, the corpse-littered coastline of Skomer, or North Ronaldsay's seaweed-eating sheep.

John Donne famously wrote that 'No man is an island, entire of itself.'[1] I'm not sure whether any man can be an island, but I'm not sure either that an island is entire of itself. Donne, of course, was writing in the seventeenth century and had his own meaning to convey, but we have an ecological awareness in the twenty-first century that was lacking back then. And so, to me, just because water rings rock, it does not make an island remote or apart or self-contained. One thing I have noticed – especially through my study of island birds – is that things are connected and physical distances can be elided. Birds are bridges. I found fulmars everywhere on my journey, ghosting along shorelines in effortless flight. They make me feel at home, regardless of how distant the ground under my feet is. I seem to seek out these similarities. They feel as important to me as the differences that make each island unique.

If nature unites each island, then so too does culture: the defining influence of humans (or the lack of them); what they need and how they go about it. Robert Burns once wrote about disturbing the nest of a mouse: 'I'm truly sorry man's dominion / Has broken Nature's social union.'[2] And though this is true in many places across the world,* I'm not so sure that it is here on the islands of Britain. To me, the culture of British islands seems to be interwoven with nature. Perhaps, due to the often harsh conditions, there is no way that it can't be. Less dominion, more union. But I understand why Burns capitalises 'Nature'. There are times and places where nature is no mere abstract concept, but a living embodied thing. That's certainly what I found on North Ronaldsay.

My island journeys have been transformative – but writing about them has also made me feel insignificant. I was drawn to travel among seabirds, and the outlook for them and for the wild places I visited is as bleak as ever. Donne also wrote, 'Any man's death diminishes me, / because I am involved in mankind.' I am involved in bird-kind, climate-kind, sea-kind too. It feels as if every time I go online I find another story, sticking in my craw, of another terrible prediction of our plastic future, or another species killed by something unrecycled or unrecyclable. My story doesn't matter, but these stories do.

One more journey. While writing this book, I decide to move back to Scotland, for my third time, for good. Another upheaval, a

---

* New Zealand, I'm sorry for every species lost.

re-rooting of life. Autumn is the time for change, for migrations, for the necessary movements of animals. As most of our seabirds head south or far out into open ocean, away from land, I move northwards, into the cold, and from east to west, out of the dry and into the wet edge of the country. Away from the flat and into hill country.

Then comes winter. The cliffs and islands of Britain fall almost silent. Wardens pack up for the year. Wind and rain scrubs the guano from the cliffs. Frost scorches the well-burrowed turf. The cliffs echo only to the sound of the hardiest gulls, the occasional fulmar and the slapping of waves into sandstone, dolerite, granite.

The seabirds will return. One night in late March, the first shearwater will bludgeon a path back to its burrow through the bracken. Later that same month, the first murmurs of auks will be heard from the cliffs, and the gannets will fearlessly spear into the water again. The coastline will come back to life. These are the rhythms to which my mind beats.

North Ronaldsay – the island as idea and memory – is lodged within me, splinter-like. Dormant mostly, yet prone to occasional eruptions of painful longing. But so too, now, are other islands: Skomer, Unst, Inner Farne – I carry them all with me. But at my journey's end, I am at home and I am happy – privileged to be around loved ones and our elderly cat. No island is entire of itself; and neither are we. This man closes his eyes and sees waves and rocks, edges and seabirds.

Acknowledgements

A writer's first book never appears fully fledged first time. Like a tern chick, it needs perfect conditions and plenty of support from others. Support needs thanking.

Thanks to Jennie Condell and Pippa Crane at Elliott & Thompson for taking a chance on me and letting me spend twenty-one months of my life indulging in birds and writing and for making it feel like proper work. Thanks also to Jon Asbury and Jill Burrows for their exceptional editing.

Special thanks are due to the Society of Authors for giving me the Roger Deakin award, which was invaluable for allowing me to spend three months without employment, fully focused on finishing the book.

My sense of self-confidence works like the tides, so I cannot thank enough my partner Miranda Cichy for her patience, wise advice and ability to turn an ebbing tide of confidence. Miranda was also an incredible, uncompromising and inexhaustible proofreader, as was her mother, Victoria Cichy, who never knew she was so interested in birds. Thanks also to George Cichy for promising to buy two copies.

Chapter 5 is based around an essay that *Zoomorphic* magazine first published. My thanks to James Roberts and Susan Richardson, the editors who put time and effort into helping improve the original essay.

I have no qualifications in science and do not have access to a university library, so I must acknowledge the ornithological guidance and research help of Nina O'Hanlon, Stephen Menzie and Sjúrður Hammer. Any inaccuracies in the text are absolutely my own fault.

The library I do have access to is Dumfries's delightful Ewart Library. In a time where access to community services such as libraries and museums is underfunded and being cut further or closed, I feel it is important to acknowledge these places and the staff, who were always willing to get books out of their basement for me. The natural history museum I mention in Chapter 7 is Colchester's Natural History Museum, a lovely gem of a building. Local libraries and museums empower us.

North Ronaldsay bird observatory, as I hope I've made clear, occupies a large part of my heart. For that I must thank Kevin Woodbridge and Alison Duncan for seeing my application form and taking a punt on a washed-up wannabe writer and for extending my two months to four, then six, then seven. I must also thank Mark and Fleur Warren, Heather Woodbridge, Gavin Woodbridge, George Gay, Samuel Perfect and Molly Laban for the help and company and making my time there truly exceptional.

Despite the relative proximity of Shetland and Orkney, the two archipelagos are completely different. So I must also thank Sally Huband and her family for putting me up (and putting up with me) and being an incredible source of knowledge of the islands and the island experience.

Thanks to David Borthwick, Julian Hoffman, David Knowles and Richard Smyth for invaluable encouragement as I first began to write. Thanks to anyone who ever tweeted me to say something nice – your support has been essential for giving me a sense of belief in what I do.

Thanks also to Sophie Green, Emily Hasler, Jake Hearn, Chris Larkin, Christian Leppich, Sarah Thomas, Emyr Young and Chris Rutt.

And last but not least: thanks to my dad for introducing me to an interest that went rogue and took over my life, and for willingly doing a lot of driving, and thanks to my mum for the never failing support. I would be nothing without either of you.

Bibliography

Allsop, Kenneth, *Adventure Lit Their Star* (Middlesex: Penguin, 1972)

Amélineau, F., et al., 'Microplastic pollution in the Greenland sea: background levels and selective contamination of planktivorous diving seabirds', *Environmental Pollution* (2016), 219, 1131–9

Ardamatskaya, Tetyana B., 'The expansion of the common eider *Somateria mollissima* at Ukrainian coast of the Black Sea', *Acta Ornithologica* (2001), 36.1, 53–4

Atkinson, Robert, *Island Going* (Edinburgh: Birlinn, 2008)

Bakolis, Ioannis, et al., 'Urban mind: using smartphone technologies to investigate the impact of nature on mental well-being in real time', *BioScience* (2018), 68.2, 134–45

Bede, the Venerable, *Bede's Ecclesiastical History of England: a revised translation*, trans. A. M. Sellar (London: George Bell & Sons, 1907)

Birkhead, Tim, *Bird Sense* (London: Bloomsbury, 2013)

Birkhead, Tim, Jamie E. Thompson, et al., 'The point of a guillemot's egg', *Ibis* (2017), 159, 255–65

Blackburn, Jez, et al., 'The breeding birds of Sule Skerry and Stack Skerry', *British Birds* (2007), 100, 300–304

Bonadonna, Francesco, and Ana Sanz-Aguilar, 'Kin recognition and inbreeding avoidance in wild birds: the first evidence for individual kin-related odour recognition', *Animal Behaviour* (2012), 84, 509–13

Burns, Robert, 'To a Mouse', in Alice Oswald (ed.), *The Thunder Mutters: 101 poems for the planet*

Buxton, John, *The Redstart* (London: Collins, 1950)

Cabot, David, *Wildfowl* (London: Collins, 2009)

Carson, Rachel, *Silent Spring* (London: Penguin, 2000)

Cocker, Mark, *Birds and People* (London: Jonathan Cape, 2013)

Cocker, Mark, and Richard Mabey, *Birds Britannica* (London: Chatto & Windus, 2005)

Collins Bird Guide, *see* Mullarney, Svensson, et al.

Coulson, J. C., 'Productivity of black-legged kittiwake *Rissa tridactyla* required to maintain numbers', *Bird Study* (2017), 64, 84–9

Courtene-Jones, W., et al., 'Consistent microplastic ingestion by deep-sea invertebrates over the last four decades (1976–2015), a study from the north-east Atlantic', *Environmental Pollution* (2019), 503–12

Cubitt, Mark G., 'Swinhoe's storm petrel at Tynemouth: new to Britain and Ireland', *British Birds* (1995), 88, 342–8

Den Rooijen, Huub, 'Offshore wind operational report: January–December 2017', *The Crown Estate*; https://www.thecrownestate.co.uk/media/2400/offshore-wind-operational-report_digital.pdf

Denlinger, Lynn, Kenton Wohl, et al., 'Seabird Harvest Regimes in the Circumpolar Nations' CAFF Technical Reports, Arctic Council; https://oaarchive.arctic-council.org/bitstream/handle/11374/171/Seabird_Harvest_Regimes_Circumpolar_Nations_CBird_2001.pdf?sequence=1&isAllowed=y

Dickinson, Emily, *Selected Poems* (New York: Dover Publications, 1990)

Donne, John, 'Meditation XVII', *Devotions Upon Emergent Occasions*; https://web.cs.dal.ca/~johnston/poetry/island.html

Eaton, Mark, et al., 'Birds of conservation concern 4: the population status of birds in the UK, Channel Islands, and Isle of Man', *British Birds* (2015), 108, 708–46

Fisher, James, *The Fulmar* (London: Collins, 1952)

Fisher, James, *Bird Recognition I* (London: Penguin, 1954)

Fisher, James, *The Shell Bird Book* (London: Ebury Press, 1966)

Fisher, James, and Jim Flegg, *Watching Birds* (Middlesex: Penguin, 1978)

Fisher, James, and R. M. Lockley, *Seabirds* (London: Bloomsbury, 1989)

Fraser Darling, Frank, *Island Years, Island Farm* (Dorset: Little Toller, 2011)

Gantlett, Steve, and Tony Pym, 'The Atlantic yellow-nosed albatross from Somerset to Lincolnshire – a new British Bird', *Birding World* (2007), 20.7, 1–17

Garner, Martin, and Killian Mullarney, 'A critical look at the evidence relating to "the chalice petrel"', *British Birds* (2004), 97, 336–45

Gaskell, Jeremy, *Who Killed the Great Auk* (Oxford: Oxford University Press, 2000)

Gaston, Anthony J., *Seabirds: A Natural History* (London: Helm, 2004)

Gilg, Olivier, Alexandre Andreev, et al., 'Satellite tracking of Ross's gull (*Rhodostethia rosea*) in the Arctic ocean', *Journal of Ornithology* (2015)

Gorky, Maxim, 'The Song of the Stormy Petrel', trans. Albert C. Todd, in
  Twentieth Century Russian Poetry selected by Yevgeny Yevtushenko,
  edited by Albert C. Todd and Max Hayward (London: Fourth Estate,
  1993), pp. 19–20

Halle, Louis J., *The Storm Petrel and the Owl of Athena* (New Jersey:
  Princeton University Press, 1970)

Harrop, Andrew H. J., 'The "soft-plumaged petrel" complex: a review of
  the literature on taxonomy, identification and distribution' *British Birds*
  (2004), 97, 6–15

Haswell-Smith, Hamish, *The Scottish Islands: A Comprehensive Guide*
  (Edinburgh: Canongate, 1996)

Heaney, Seamus, *Beowulf: A New Translation* (London: Faber and Faber,
  1999)

Herzke, Dorte, et al., 'Negligible impact of ingested microplastics on tissue
  concentrations of persistent organic pollutants in northern fulmars
  off coastal Norway', *Environmental Science and Technology* (2016), 50,
  1924–33

Holloway, Simon, *The Historical Atlas of Breeding Birds in Britain and
  Ireland 1875–1900* (London: Poyser, 1996)

Hull, Robin, *Scottish Birds: Culture and Tradition* (Edinburgh: Mercat Press,
  2001)

Hume, R. A., 'Common, Arctic and roseate terns: an identification review',
  British Birds (1993), 86, 210–17

Hume, Rob, *Seabirds* (London: Hamlyn, 1993)

Huxley, Julian, *Memories* (London: George Allan and Unwin, 1970)

Huxley, Julian, *Memories II* (London: George Allan and Unwin, 1973)

Huxley, Thomas Henry, *Lectures on the Elements of Comparative Anatomy*
  (London: John Churchill & Sons, 1864)

Jones, Josh, 'A Curious Infatuation with Swans', https://www.birdguides
  .com/articles/a-curious-infatuation-with-swans/

Lewis-Stempel, John, *Where the Poppies Blow: Nature and the Great War*
  (London: Weidenfeld & Nicolson, 2017)

Lockley, R. M., *The Way to an Island* (London: J. M. Dent & Sons, 1941)

Lockley, R. M., *Shearwaters* (London: J. M. Dent & Sons, 1942)

Lockley, R. M., *I Know an Island* (London: George G. Harrap and Co., 1947)

Lockley, R. M., *The Island* (London: André Deutsch, 1969)

Lockley, R. M., *The Private Life of the Rabbit* (Newton Abbot: Readers
  Union, 1976)

Lockley, R. M., *Flight of the Storm Petrel* (Newton Abbot: David & Charles, 1983)

Lockley, R. M., *Letters from Skokholm* (Dorset: Little Toller, 2010)

Lockley, R. M., *Dream Island* (Dorset: Little Toller, 2016)

Lockwood, W. B., 'The philology of "auk", and related matters', *Neuphilologische Mitteilungen* (1978), 79.4, 391–7

Macfarlane, Robert, *The Old Ways* (London: Penguin, 2012)

Maftei, Mark, Shanti E. Davis, et al., 'Quantifying the fall migration of Ross's gulls (*Rhodostethia rosea*) past Point Barrow, Alaska', *Polar Biology* (2014)

'Martin, Sir James Charles', *Oxford Dictionary National Biography*; http://www.oxforddnb.com/view/10.1093/ref:odnb/9780198614128.001 .0001/odnb-9780198614128-e-34903?rskey=ZGi18h&result=3

Mearns, Barbara, and Richard Mearns, *Biographies for Birdwatchers* (London: Academic Press, 1988)

Minard, Antone, 'The mystery of St Cuthbert's duck: an adventure in hagiography', *Folklore* (2016), 127.3, 325–43

Moss, Stephen, *A Bird in the Bush: A Social History of Birdwatching* (London: Aurum Press, 2004)

Muir, Edwin, *Scottish Journey* (Edinburgh: Mainstream Publishing, 1979)

Mullarney, Killian, Lars Svensson, et al., *Collins Bird Guide* (London: Harper Collins, 1999)

Murray, Donald S., *The Guga Hunters* (Edinburgh: Birlinn, 2008)

Nelson, Bryan, *The Gannet* (Berkhampstead, T. & A. D. Poyser, 1978)

Newell, Dick, 'Recent records of southern skuas in Britain', *British Birds* (2008), 101, 439–41

Nice, Margaret Morse, 'The Eighth International Ornithological Congress', *Bird-Banding* (1935) 6.1, 29–31

O'Hanlon, Nina J., et al., 'Seabirds and marine plastic debris in the northeast Atlantic: a synthesis and recommendations for monitoring and research', *Environmental Pollution* (2017), 1–11

Orkneyinga Saga: The History of the Earls of Orkney, trans. Hermann Palsson and Paul Edwards (Middlesex: Penguin, 1981)

Oswald, Alice (ed.), *The Thunder Mutters: 101 poems for the planet* (London: Faber, 2005)

Padget, O., et al., 'Anosmia impairs homing orientation but not foraging behaviour in free-ranging shearwaters', *Scientific Reports* (2017), 7.9668, 1–11

Bibliography

Pennington, Mike, Paul Harvey, et al., *The Birds of Shetland* (London: Christopher Helm, 2004)

Perkins, Allan, Norman Ratcliff, et al., 'Combined bottom-up and top-down pressures drive catastrophic population declines of Arctic skuas in Scotland', *Journal of Animal Ecology* (2018), 1–14

Perrow, Martin, et al., 'The foraging ecology of Sandwich Terns in north Norfolk', *British Birds* (2017), 110, 257–77

Perrow, Martin, James J. Gilroy, et al., 'Quantifying the relative use of coastal waters by breeding terns: towards effective tools for planning and assessing the ornithological impacts of offshore wind farms', ECON Ecological Consultancy Ltd, Report to COWRIE Ltd

Peterson, Roger Tory, 'Obituary: James Maxwell McConnell Fisher', *British Birds* (1971) 64.5, 223–7

Pontoppidan, Erik, *The Natural History of Norway* (London: A Linde, 1755)

Rankin, Niall, *Haunts of British Divers* (London: Collins, 1947)

Robb, Magnus, Killian Mullarney and the Sound Approach, *Petrels Night and Day: A Sound Approach Guide* (Poole: The Sound Approach, 2008)

Rochman, Chelsea M., et al., 'The ecological impacts of marine debris: unraveling the demonstrated evidence from what is perceived', *Ecology* (2016), 97.2, 302–12

Rylands, Kevin, 'Long-billed murrelet in Devon: new to Britain', *British Birds* (2008), 101, 131–6

Saunders, David, and Stephen Sutcliffe, 'Great Bird Reserves: Skomer Island', *British Birds* (2017), 110, 278–95

'The Seafarer', trans. Ezra Pound, in Alice Oswald (ed.), *The Thunder Mutters: 101 poems for the planet*

Shell Bird Book, The, see Fisher, James

Sibley, David, et al., *The Sibley Guide to Bird Life & Behaviour* (London: Christopher Helm, 2001)

Tennyson, Alfred, Lord, *In Memoriam* (New York: W. W. Norton, 2004)

Tesson, Sylvain, *Consolations of the Forest: alone in a cabin in the middle taiga*, trans. Linda Coverdale (London: Penguin, 2013)

Thompson, William P. L., *The New History of Orkney* (Edinburgh: Mercat Press, 2001)

Thoreau, Henry David, *Walden; or, Life in the Woods* (New York: Dover Publications, 1995)

Van Donk, Susanne, et al., 'The most common diet results in low reproduction in a generalist seabird', *Ecology and Evolution* (2017), 1–10

Vevers, Gwynne, and Clemency Thorne Fisher, 'Fisher, James Maxwell McConnell', *Oxford Dictionary of National Biography*; http://www.oxforddnb.com/view/10.1093/ref:odnb/9780198614128.001.0001/odnb-9780198614128-e-33142?rskey=VdCsaD&result=2

Votier, Stephen C., et al., 'The use of plastic debris as nesting material by a colonial seabird and associated entanglement mortality', *Marine Pollution Bulletin* (2011), 62, 168–72

Wanless, Ross M., et al., 'Can predation by invasive mice drive seabird extinctions?', *Biology Letters* (2007) 3.3, 241–4

Williamson, Kenneth, *The Atlantic Islands: A Study of the Faeroe Life and Scene* (London: Routledge & Kegan Paul, 1970)

Williamson, Kenneth, 'The antiquity of the Calf of Man Manx shearwater colony', *Bird Study* (1973), 20.4, 310–11

Wiltschko, Roswitha, and Wolfgang Wiltschko, 'Avian Navigation', *The Auk* (2009), 126.4, 717–43

Yarrell, William, *A History of British Birds*, vol. iv (London: John Van Voorst, 1885)

INTERNET RESOURCES

1 Storm Petrels – Shetland

https://www.bbc.co.uk/sounds/play/p009mvtj (R. M. Lockley, *Desert Island Discs*)

2 Skuas – Shetland

http://www.energy-oil-gas.com/2014/01/07/sullom-voe-terminal/
http://www.gov.scot/Uploads/Documents/AE17Braer.pdf
https://www.bbc.co.uk/programmes/p009y8lp (James Fisher, *Desert Island Discs*)
https://canmore.org.uk/search/site?SIMPLE_KEYWORD=skua

3 Auks – Northumberland

http://chrisjordan.com/gallery/midway

4 Eiders – Northumberland

http://datazone.birdlife.org/species/factsheet/common-eider-somateria-mollissima
http://farnephoto.blogspot.co.uk/2012/09/eider-down.html

http://geographical.co.uk/places/mapping/item/1165-uk-land-becoming
-more-urban

http://icelandeider.is/?p=3056

http://www.birdlife.org/europe-and-central-asia/news/criticism-finlands
-spring-hunting-common-eider

https://app.bto.org/birdfacts/results/bob2060.htm

https://twitter.com/SteelySeabirder/status/867033102526402562

https://www.ons.gov.uk/peoplepopulationandcommunity/
populationandmigration/populationprojections

5 Terns – Northumberland

http://archive.spectator.co.uk/article/7th-december-1895/29/mr-henry
-seebohm

http://ntnorthumberlandcoast.blogspot.com/2017/08/a-quick-tern
-around.html

http://rbbp.org.uk/

http://www.bbc.co.uk/news/uk-england-tees-40326587

http://www.dailypost.co.uk/news/local-news/fox-goes-rampage-wales
-only-13177543

http://www.itv.com/news/anglia/2017-06-23/10-rare-bird-eggs-stolen
-off-the-suffolk-coast/

http://www.ncl.ac.uk/press/news/2016/06/arcticterns/

http://www.rspb.org.uk/reserves-and-events/find-a-reserve/reserves-a-z/
reserves-by-name/c/coquetisland/webcam.aspx

https://blx1.bto.org/birdfacts/results/bob6160.htm

https://ww2.rspb.org.uk/our-work/our-positions-and-casework/
our-positions/climate-change/action-to-tackle-climate-change/uk
-energy-policy/wind-farms

https://www.rspb.org.uk/about-the-rspb/about-us/our-history/

6 Gulls – Newcastle

http://jncc.defra.gov.uk/page-2889

http://nhsn.ncl.ac.uk/wp-content/uploads/2015/12/DMTurner-River
-Tyne-Kittiwake-breeding-data-2017-ver5.pdf

http://nhsn.ncl.ac.uk/wp-content/uploads/2016/01/DMTurner-River
-Tyne-Kittiwake-breeding-data-2001-to-2009-ver3.pdf

http://researchbriefings.files.parliament.uk/documents/CDP-2017-0044/
CDP-2017-0044.pdf

http://www.bbc.co.uk/news/uk-scotland-north-east-orkney-shetland
-36600404

https://www.birdguides.com/news/illegal-egging-devastates-poole
-harbour-gull-colony

http://www.chroniclelive.co.uk/news/north-east-news/council-call
-move-birds-tyne-1395566#ixzz1Ez8Gl9rA

https://britishbirds.co.uk/article/gull-decline-scottish-island-linked
-decline-fishing-discards/

https://hansard.parliament.uk/Commons/2017-02-07/debates/AE1CEE4F
-5DF9-467C-9F36-657C51315D1C/Seagulls?highlight=seagull

https://www.theguardian.com/environment/2016/jun/09/seagull-turns
-orange-after-falling-into-vat-of-chicken-tikka-masala

https://www.youtube.com/watch?v=Kqy9hxhUxK0

7 Manx Shearwaters – Skomer

http://www.birdsoflundy.org.uk/index.php/species-updates/swans-to
-grebes/35-manx-shearwater

8 Vagrants – Lundy, Fastnet, Sole and Fitzroy

http://www.magikbirds.com/image.asp?title_id=574&show_thumbnails
=True

https://britishbirds.co.uk/wp-content/uploads/article_files/V97/V97_N01/
V97_N01_P006_015_A002.pdf

9 Gannets – Orkney

http://www.alliteration.net/poetry/seafarer.htm

https://www.bbc.co.uk/news/uk-scotland-highlands-islands-14561486

https://www.theguardian.com/world/2018/feb/02/nigel-lonely-new
-zealand-gannet-dies-concrete-replica-birds

10 Fulmars – Orkney

http://portal.historicenvironment.scot/designation/LB46400

http://www.orkney.gov.uk/Files/Council/Publications/2009/Orkney_
Population_Change_Study_April_09.pdf

http://www.scottish-islands-federation.co.uk/island-statistics/

https://www.ospar.org/work-areas/eiha/marine-litter/
plastic-particles-in-fulmars

Notes

Introduction
1. Known as a Heligoland trap, after the German island and seabird colony where they were invented.

1 Storm Petrels – Shetland
1. Robin Hull, *Scottish Birds: Culture and Tradition*, p. 92.
2. Francesco Bonadonna and Ana Sanz-Aguilar, 'Kin recognition and inbreeding avoidance in wild birds: the first evidence for individual kin-related odour recognition'.
3. https://www.bbc.co.uk/sounds/play/p009mvtj (R. M. Lockley, *Desert Island Discs*).
4. R. M. Lockley, *The Way to an Island*, p. 13.
5. Ibid., p. 13.
6. Ibid., p. 81.
7. R. M. Lockley, *The Island*, p. 21.
8. R. M. Lockley, *Flight of the Storm Petrel*, p. 7.
9. Ibid., p. 35.
10. Ibid., p. 32.
11. Mark Cocker, *Birds and People*, p. 110.
12. Barbara Mearns and Richard Mearns, *Biographies for Birdwatchers*, p. 224.
13. Robert Atkinson, *Island Going*, p. 9.
14. Ibid., p. xvii.
15. Ibid., p. 35.

2 Skuas – Shetland
1. Allan Perkins, Norman Ratcliff, et al., 'Combined bottom-up and top-down pressures drive catastrophic population declines of Arctic skuas in Scotland', pp. 8–9.
2. Ibid., p. 5.
3. http://www.energy-oil-gas.com/2014/01/07/sullom-voe-terminal/.

4. Figures from FRS PDF: http://www.gov.scot/Uploads/Documents/AE17Braer.pdf.
5. Gwynne Vevers and Clemency Thorne Fisher, 'Fisher, James Maxwell McConnell'.
6. https://www.bbc.co.uk/programmes/p009y8lp.
7. https://canmore.org.uk/search/site?SIMPLE_KEYWORD=skua.
8. Niall Rankin, *Haunts of British Divers*, p. 72.

3 Auks – Northumberland

1. Robin Hull, *Scottish Birds: Culture and Tradition*, p. 196.
2. Mark Cocker and Richard Mabey, *Birds Britannica*, p. 257.
3. Hull, p. 196.
4. Mark Cocker, *Birds and People*, p. 225.
5. Kenneth Williamson, *The Atlantic Islands: A Study of the Faeroe Life and Scene*, p. 84.
6. Hull, p. 193.
7. Cocker and Mabey, p. 252.
8. Simon Holloway, *The Historical Atlas of Breeding Birds in Britain and Ireland 1875–1900*, p. 230.
9. William Yarrell, *A History of British Birds*, vol. iv, p. 71.
10. Tim R. Birkhead, Jamie E. Thompson, et al., 'The point of a guillemot's egg', p. 261.
11. Ibid., p. 262.
12. Tim Birkhead, *Bird Sense*, p. 10.
13. W. B. Lockwood, 'The philology of "auk", and related matters', p. 395.
14. Cocker and Mabey, p. 257.
15. Dorte Herzke et al., 'Negligible impact of ingested microplastics on tissue concentrations of persistent organic pollutants in northern fulmars off coastal Norway', p. 1924.
16. F. Amélineau, et al., 'Microplastic pollution in the Greenland sea: background levels and selective contamination of planktivorous diving seabirds', *Environmental Pollution*, p. 1131.
17. http://chrisjordan.com/gallery/midway.
18. W. Courtene-Jones et al., 'Consistent microplastic ingestion by deep-sea invertebrates over the last four decades (1976–2015), a study from the north-east Atlantic'.
19. Chelsea M. Rochman et al., 'The ecological impacts of marine debris: unraveling the demonstrated evidence from what is perceived', p. 309.
20. Yarrell, p. 62.
21. Ibid., p. 63.
22. Ibid., p. 65.

23. Jeremy Gaskell, *Who Killed the Great Auk*, p. 142.
24. Lynn Denlinger, Kenton Wohl, et al., 'Seabird Harvest Regimes in the Circumpolar Nations', p. v.
25. Ibid., p. vi.
26. Ibid., p. 90.
27. R. M. Lockley, *The Island*, pp. 103–4.

4 Eiders – Northumberland

1. David Cabot, *Wildfowl*, p. 208.
2. Ibid., p. 209.
3. BTO birdfacts: https://app.bto.org/birdfacts/results/bob2060.htm.
4. Tetyana B. Ardamatskaya, 'The expansion of the common eider *Somateria mollissima* at Ukrainian coast of the Black Sea'.
5. Louis J. Halle, *The Storm Petrel and the Owl of Athena*, p. 109.
6. Cabot, p. 204.
7. http://icelandeider.is/?p=3056.
8. http://datazone.birdlife.org/species/factsheet/common-eider-somateria -mollissima.
9. Erik Pontoppidan, *The Natural History of Norway*, section 2, p. 72
10. Pontoppidan, *The Natural History of Norway*, p. v.
11. Ibid., section 2, p. 70.
12. Ibid.
13. Lynn Denlinger, Kenton Wohl, et al., 'Seabird Harvest Regimes in the Circumpolar Nations', p. 19.
14. http://www.birdlife.org/europe-and-central-asia/news/criticism-finlands -spring-hunting-common-eider.
15. Pontoppidan, section 2, p. 71.
16. Sylvain Tesson, *Consolations of the Forest: alone in a cabin in the middle taiga*, p. 29.
17. http://farnephoto.blogspot.co.uk/2012/09/eider-down.html.
18. https://twitter.com/SteelySeabirder/status/867033102526402562.
19. Halle, p. 109.
20. Robin Hull, *Scottish Birds: Culture and Tradition*, p. 124.
21. James Fisher, *The Shell Bird Book*, p. 49.
22. Antone Minard, 'The mystery of St Cuthbert's duck: an adventure in hagiography', p. 328.
23. Ibid., p. 339.
24. Harry Walter Shellard.
25. R. M. Lockley, *Dream Island*, p. 16.
26. Ibid., p. 13.
27. Ibid., p. 26.

28. http://geographical.co.uk/places/mapping/item/1165-uk-land-becoming-more-urban
29. https://www.ons.gov.uk/peoplepopulationandcommunity/population andmigration/populationprojections

5 Terns – Northumberland
 1. Killian Mullarney, Lars Svensson, et al., *Collins Bird Guide*, p. 184.
 2. James Fisher, *Bird Recognition I*, p. 126.
 3. http://www.dailypost.co.uk/news/local-news/fox-goes-rampage-wales-only-13177543.
 4. http://www.bbc.co.uk/news/uk-england-tees-40326587.
 5. http://www.itv.com/news/anglia/2017-06-23/10-rare-bird-eggs-stolen-off-the-suffolk-coast/.
 6. Erik Pontoppidan, *The Natural History of Norway*, p. 93.
 7. http://archive.spectator.co.uk/article/7th-december-1895/29/mr-henry-seebohm.
 8. R. A. Hume, 'Common, Arctic and roseate terns: an identification review', p. 210.
 9. Ibid.
10. Ibid., p. 212.
11. https://blx1.bto.org/birdfacts/results/bob6160.htm.
12. http://www.ncl.ac.uk/press/news/2016/06/arcticterns/.
13. Alfred, Lord Tennyson, *In Memoriam*, lv, lines 5–8.
14. R. M. Lockley, *I Know An Island*, p. 139.
15. James Fisher and Jim Flegg, *Watching Birds*, p. 9.
16. Ibid.
17. https://www.rspb.org.uk/about-the-rspb/about-us/our-history/.
18. Stephen Moss, *A Bird in the Bush: A Social History of Birdwatching*, p. 170.
19. Ibid., p. 168.
20. John Buxton, *The Redstart*, p. 1.
21. http://www.rspb.org.uk/reserves-and-events/find-a-reserve/reserves-a-z/reserves-by-name/c/coquetisland/webcam.aspx.
22. Martin Perrow, et al., 'The foraging ecology of Sandwich terns in north Norfolk', p. 257.
23. Rob Hume, *Seabirds*, p. 119.
24. Huub den Rooijen, 'Offshore wind operational report: January–December 2017'.
25. https://ww2.rspb.org.uk/our-work/our-positions-and-casework/our-positions/climate-change/action-to-tackle-climate-change/uk-energy-policy/wind-farms.

26. Martin Perrow, James J. Gilroy, et al., 'Quantifying the relative use of coastal waters by breeding terns: towards effective tools for planning and assessing the ornithological impacts of offshore wind farms', p. 4.
27. http://ntnorthumberlandcoast.blogspot.com/2017/08/a-quick-tern-around.html.
28. http://rbbp.org.uk/.

6 Gulls – Newcastle
1. Mark Eaton, et al., 'Birds of conservation concern 4: the population status of birds in the UK, Channel Islands, and Isle of Man'.
2. http://jncc.defra.gov.uk/page-2889.
3. J. C. Coulson, 'Productivity of black-legged kittiwake *Rissa tridactyla* required to maintain numbers'.
4. http://nhsn.ncl.ac.uk/wp-content/uploads/2015/12/DMTurner-River-Tyne-Kittiwake-breeding-data-2017-ver5.pdf.
5. http://nhsn.ncl.ac.uk/wp-content/uploads/2016/01/DMTurner-River-Tyne-Kittiwake-breeding-data-2001-to-2009-ver3.pdf.
6. http://www.chroniclelive.co.uk/news/north-east-news/council-call-move-birds-tyne-1395566#ixzz1Ez8Gl9rA.
7. Ioannis Bakolis, et al., 'Urban mind: using smartphone technologies to investigate the impact of nature on mental well-being in real time', p. 134.
8. Ibid., p. 142.
9. R. M. Lockley, *I Know An Island*, p. 230.
10. Henry David Thoreau, *Walden; or, Life in the Woods*, p. 4.
11. R. M. Lockley, *Dream Island*, p. 70.
12. Ibid.
13. Ibid., p. 25.
14. https://www.birdguides.com/news/illegal-egging-devastates-poole-harbour-gull-colony/.
15. Olivier Gilg, Alexandre Andreev, et al., 'Satellite tracking of Ross's gull (*Rhodostethia rosea*) in the Arctic ocean'.
16. Mark Maftei, Shanti E. Davis, et al., 'Quantifying the fall migration of Ross's gulls (*Rhodostethia rosea*) past Point Barrow, Alaska'.
17. Mark Cocker and Richard Mabey, *Birds Britannica*, p. 239.
18. https://britishbirds.co.uk/article/gull-decline-scottish-island-linked-decline-fishing-discards/.
19. Susanne Van Donk, et al., 'The most common diet results in low reproduction in a generalist seabird', p. 7.
20. https://www.theguardian.com/environment/2016/jun/09/seagull-turns-orange-after-falling-into-vat-of-chicken-tikka-masala.
21. Louis J. Halle, *The Storm Petrel and the Owl of Athena*, p. 44.

22. https://www.youtube.com/watch?v=Kqy9hxhUxK0.
23. http://www.bbc.co.uk/news/uk-scotland-north-east-orkney-shetland
-36600404.
24. Brief yourself here: http://researchbriefings.files.parliament.uk/
documents/CDP-2017-0044/CDP-2017-0044.pdf.
25. https://hansard.parliament.uk/Commons/2017-02-07/debates/
AE1CEE4F-5DF9-467C-9F36-657C51315D1C/Seagulls?highlight
=seagull.

7 Manx Shearwaters – Skomer

1. Kenneth Williamson, 'The antiquity of the Calf of Man Manx shearwater colony'.
2. http://www.birdsoflundy.org.uk/index.php/species-updates/swans-to
-grebes/35-manx-shearwater.
3. David Saunders and Stephen Sutcliffe, 'Great Bird Reserves: Skomer Island', p. 279.
4. Ross M. Wanless, et al., 'Can predation by invasive mice drive seabird extinctions?'
5. Margaret Morse Nice, 'The Eighth International Ornithological Congress', p. 30.
6. R. M. Lockley, *Shearwaters*, p. 94.
7. Emily Dickinson, 'Hope', in *Selected Poems*, p. 5, lines 1–2, 11–12.
8. Lockley, p. 151.

8 Vagrants – Lundy, Fastnet, Sole and Fitzroy

1. Josh Jones, 'A Curious Infatuation with Swans'.
2. Steve Gantlett and Tony Pym, 'The Atlantic yellow-nosed albatross from Somerset to Lincolnshire – a new British Bird'.
3. Roswitha Wiltschko and Wolfgang Wiltschko, 'Avian Navigation', p. 717.
4. O. Padget, et al., 'Anosmia impairs homing orientation but not foraging behaviour in free-ranging shearwaters'.
5. Kevin Rylands, 'Long-billed murrelet in Devon: new to Britain', p. 132.
6. Mark G. Cubitt, 'Swinhoe's storm petrel at Tynemouth: new to Britain and Ireland', p. 342.
7. Magnus Robb, Killian Mullarney and the Sound Approach, *Petrels Night and Day: A Sound Approach Guide*, p. 266.
8. Dick Newell, 'Recent records of southern skuas in Britain'.

9 Gannets – Orkney

1. Seamus Heaney, *Beowulf: A New Translation*, p. 60, line 1862.
2. James Fisher, *The Shell Bird Book*, pp. 43–4.

3. Ibid., p. 43.
4. Anonymous, 'The Seafarer', trans. Ezra Pound, in Alice Oswald (ed.) *The Thunder Mutters: 101 poems for the planet*, pp. 39–42.
5. http://www.alliteration.net/poetry/seafarer.htm.
6. https://www.theguardian.com/world/2018/feb/02/nigel-lonely-new-zealand-gannet-dies-concrete-replica-birds.
7. Jez Blackburn, et al., 'The breeding birds of Sule Skerry and Stack Skerry', p. 301.
8. Bryan Nelson, *The Gannet*, p. 281.
9. Robert Macfarlane, *The Old Ways*, p. 136.
10. https://www.bbc.co.uk/news/uk-scotland-highlands-islands-14561486.
11. Nelson, p. 289.
12. Thomas Henry Huxley, *Lectures on the Elements of Comparative Anatomy*, p. 69.
13. Julian Huxley, *Memories* (London: George Allen and Unwin, 1970), p. 220.
14. R. M. Lockley, *I Know an Island*, p. 63.
15. Anonymous, 'Sir James Charles Martin', *Oxford Dictionary National Biography*: http://www.oxforddnb.com/view/10.1093/ref:odnb/9780198614128.001.0001/odnb-9780198614128-e-34903?rskey=ZGi18h&result=3.
16. R. M. Lockley, *The Island*, p. 130.
17. R. M. Lockley, *The Private Life of the Rabbit*, p. 101.
18. Stephen C. Votier, et al., 'The use of plastic debris as nesting material by a colonial seabird and associated entanglement mortality', p. 171.

10 Fulmars – Orkney

1. Hamish Haswell-Smith, *The Scottish Islands: A Comprehensive Guide*, p. 289.
2. James Fisher, *The Fulmar*, p. xiii.
3. Ibid., p. 122.
4. Ibid., p. 145.
5. Ibid., p. 140.
6. Roger Tory Peterson, 'Obituary: James Maxwell McConnell Fisher', p. 223.
7. Fisher, p. 467.
8. Ibid., p. 119.
9. http://portal.historicenvironment.scot/designation/LB46400.
10. Lockley, *I Know an Island*, p. 168.
11. Ibid., p. 170.
12. Ibid., p. 174.
13. Hamish Haswell-Smith, *The Scottish Islands: A Comprehensive Guide*, p. 331.

14. Ibid.
15. http://www.orkney.gov.uk/Files/Council/Publications/2009/Orkney_
    Population_Change_Study_April_09.pdf.
16. Lockley, p. 174.
17. Ibid., p. 208.
18. William P. L. Thompson, *The New History of Orkney*, p. 360.
19. http://www.scottish-islands-federation.co.uk/island-statistics/.
20. Nina J. O'Hanlon, et al., 'Seabirds and marine plastic debris in the north-
    east Atlantic: a synthesis and recommendations for monitoring and
    research', p. 2.
21. https://www.ospar.org/work-areas/eiha/marine-litter/plastic-particles
    -in-fulmars.
22. Edwin Muir, *Scottish Journey*, p. 237.

Epilogue
1. John Donne, 'Meditation XVII', *Devotions Upon Emergent Occasions*.
2. Robert Burns, 'To a Mouse', in Alice Oswald (ed.), *The Thunder Mutters:
   101 poems for the planet*, pp. 58–9, lines 7–8.

Index

A

Aberdeen, gulls in 143–4, 145
Adams, Richard 214
Ainslie, John 34
Åland archipelago 89–90
albatrosses 11, 74–5, 154, 157,
    179–82
allopreening 64–5
Amble puffin festival 71
ancient murrelets 187
Antarctic petrels 223
Anthropocene epoch 72, 146–7
archaeology 17–18, 45, 55, 80, 219–20
Arctic skuas 39–40, 42–3, 46, 49,
    51, 54
Arctic terns 103, 104, 106, 108–14,
    115–16, 119, 124, 223, 239
Ascension frigatebirds 186
Atkinson, Robert 34–5, 206
auks 12, 26, 43, 51, 57, 61–81, 143,
    198, 205, 254
Australasian gannets 201–2

B

Baltasound, Unst 53–4
Baltic Centre for Contemporary
    Art, Gateshead 126–7
Barkham, Patrick 145
barred warblers 194–5
Bass Rock, Firth of Forth 62–3, 209
Bede 99
Bevan, Dr Richard 115
Birkhead, Tim 67
black-backed gulls 68, 131, 135–6,
    140–1, 142, 146, 205

black-browed albatrosses 179–81
black guillemots ('tysties') 11, 13–15
Blackburn Skua aircraft 51–2
blackcaps 165
Blackman, Kirsty 145
Blue Planet II BBC documentary
    217–18
boobies 201
Braer oil disaster 44
Bronze Age Jarlshof, Shetland 46
brown skuas 193
Brownsman, Northumberland 69
Brünnich, Morten Thrane 109
Burns, Robert 253
burrows, Manx shearwater 166–7
burrows, puffin 70–1, 80–1
Buxton, John 118
buzzards 161

C

Cameron, David 145
Canada 78, 93–4
Canna, Inner Hebrides 142
cape gannets 201
Carson, Rachel 74, 147
cave paintings, France 80
Celtic Christianity 55
Cetti's warblers 2
choughs 160–1
city bird populations 132–4
common eiders 86–7
common terns 103, 108–10
Conservation of Arctic Flora and
    Fauna (CAFF) 78, 79
Copinsay, Orkney 221, 223–9

Coquet Island, Northumberland 71, 119–21, 124
cormorants 201
corncrakes 229
Cory's shearwaters 157, 185
Cosquer Cave, France 80
Cree 93–4
cuckoos 172

D
Darwin, Charles 88, 89
DDT 74
Desertas petrels 190, 191
dolphins 159, 177
Donne, John 252, 253

E
East Anglia 122–3
egg collecting 26, 135–6
eggs, guillemot 66–7
eggs, gull 135–6
eggs, razorbill 67
eider down 87–8, 90
eiders ('St Cuthbert's duck'/'Cuddy's duck') 12, 62, 68, 83–8, 89, 93–5, 119–20
Eshaness volcano, Mainland Shetland 35–6
extinctions 77–8, 79–80, 81, 119

F
Fair Isle, Shetland 5, 59, 189, 237
Fairey Fulmar aircraft 52
'falls', bird 5
Farne Islands 61–6, 68–72, 98
Faroe Islands 40, 51, 60, 87
Fea's petrels 190, 192
Ferdinand of Bulgaria, King 170
Finland 89–90
fish catches, declining 142–3

Fisher, James 45–6, 94, 117–18, 134, 198–9, 221–2, 229–32
fishing industry 63, 142–3
Flamborough Head, Yorkshire 66
frigatebirds 186–7
fulmars 11, 110, 149, 152, 154, 205, 221–5, 226, 227, 230, 232, 239, 244–6, 249, 252–3

G
gannets 12, 37–8, 57, 62–3, 152, 162, 177, 198–9, 200–3, 205–12, 215–17
Garland Stone, Skomer Island 158–60, 162–3
giant petrels 223
goldcrests 5
goosanders 120
Gorky, Maxim 30–1
goshawks 9
Grassholm, Wales 81, 158, 162, 210–12, 215–18
great auks 46, 77–8, 79–80
great black-backed gulls 140–1
great northern divers 177
great shearwaters 156–7, 185
great skuas ('bonxies') 39, 40–1, 43, 47, 48, 50, 54, 56–8, 193–4, 205
Green, Sophie 49–50, 56
Greenland 73, 75, 116, 137
guga hunters of Ness 206–8
Guildford, Tim 182–3
guillemots 11, 13–15, 26, 59, 64, 65, 66–8, 80, 205, 206, 225
gulls 6, 12, 40, 41–2, 43, 49, 62, 66, 124, 125–47, 154, 160, 211, 222
Gwennap Head, Cornwall 180–1, 185

H

Halle, Louis J. 87, 93–4, 143
Hammer, Sjúrður 51
Heligoland, Germany 116
Hermaness, Unst 50, 56–8, 63, 179
herring gulls 66, 131, 132, 136, 140,
141–4, 146
Hewitson, William Chapman 66–7
Hickling, Grace 95
Holy Island of Lindisfarne,
Northumberland 90, 91–2,
95, 98, 99
Hooking Loch, North Ronaldsay 246
Hume, Rob 122
hunting, seabird 78–9, 89–90,
93–4, 207–8
Huxley, Sir Julian 210–12

I

Icelandic Eider Association 88
Inner Farne Island 83–5, 92–3, 99,
101–2, 106, 115
International Ornithological
Congress, Oxford (1934)
168–9
Inuits 93–4
Isle of Islay, Inner Hebrides 186
Isle of Noss, Shetland 37–8, 41, 46
ivory gulls 139–40

J

Jarlshof, Shetland 45–6, 47
Jefferson, Thomas 79–80
Jordan, Chris 75

K

Keen of Hamar, Unst 54
kelp, North Ronaldsay 242
Kerr, Ian 94
king eiders 86

kittiwakes 11, 26, 125, 126–31,
132–4, 144, 146, 205, 206
Korda, Alexander 210–12

L

Labrador seabird hunts 79
Lack, David 171–4
lapwings 239
Laysan albatrosses 74–5
Leach, William Elford 32–3
Leach's storm petrels 32–5, 188, 206
lesser black-backed gulls 140
Lewisian Gneiss 47–8, 63, 206
Lindisfarne, Northumberland 90,
91–2, 95, 98, 99
Linnaeus, Carl 110
little auks 73, 75
little terns 103–4, 106–8, 115
Loch Gretchen, North Ronaldsay
239, 249
Loch of Spiggie, Mainland Shetland
47
Lockley, Ronald M. 23–8, 81, 96–7,
116, 118, 134–6, 158, 161–2,
169–70, 171–4, 190–1,
210–12, 214–15, 230, 237–8
London 6–9, 10, 134–5
long-billed murrelet 187
Long Nanny bay, Northumberland
105–7, 123–4
long-tailed skuas 38–9
Lundy Island 26–7, 66, 187

M

Macfarlane, Robert 207–8
MacGillivray, William 110
magnificent frigatebirds 186
Mainland Shetland 35–6, 41–8,
49–51, 59–60, 243
Manual of British Birds
(H. Saunders) 25

Manx shearwaters 11, 25, 27, 60,
    149–50, 153–6, 157, 159, 160,
    162–3, 164, 166–7, 172–6
Martin, Martin 207, 226
Martin, Sir Charles 213
McKibben, Bill 72
meadow pipits 161
Mediterranean gulls 136, 142
mental health, urban 133–4, 146
Mersey Estuary 34
Mew Stone, Skomer Island 161–2
microplastics 75
Midway Atoll, North Pacific 74–5
migration experiment, Lockley's
    171–4
Minard, Antone 95
Minsmere, Suffolk 2
Mount's Bay, Cornwall 177–8
Mousa Broch, Shetland 17–21, 22
Mousa, Shetland 17–22, 31–2
Muir, Edwin 247–8
murrelets 187

N
navigation studies, bird 182–4
Nelson, Bryan 207, 210
Neolithic Scotland 46, 219–20
Newcastle-upon-Tyne 125–34,
    136–7, 146
Newfoundland seabird hunts 79
Nice, Margaret Morse 168–9
Noltland Castle, Westray 203
Norfolk coast 5, 122–3, 202
North Haven, Skomer Island 175–6
North Rona, Scotland 34–5
North Ronaldsay, Orkney 2, 4–6,
    9–15, 29–30, 33, 48, 80, 85–6,
    87, 98–9, 104, 110–14, 124,
    127–8, 140–1, 156, 157, 192,
    232–49, 254

North Sea Oil 43–4
North Uist, Outer Hebrides 33
Noup Head, Westray 200, 204–6,
    208–10, 215, 219–20

O
O'Hanlon, Nina 245
oil spills 44
Old Scatness, Neolithic village 46
Orkney Islands 1–2, 4–6, 9–15,
    29–30, 33, 65, 77–8, 87, 104,
    110–14, 124, 127–8, 140–1,
    156, 157, 197–8, 199–200,
    203–6, 208–10, 215, 219–20,
    221, 223–6, 227, 228–9,
    232–49, 254
OSPAR study 245–6
Oswald of Northumbria, King 92

P
Pacific divers 178
paleo-ornithology 45–6
parakeets 132–3
peregrine falcons 74, 132, 160, 161
Peterson, Roger Tory 229
petrels 11, 18–19, 27–36, 154, 182,
    188–92, 206, 222–3, 227
    see also fulmars
pigeons 132
Pitt Rivers Museum, Oxford 28–9
plastic pollution 73–7, 146–7,
    215–19
pomarine 'pom' skuas 39
Pontoppidan, Erik 88–9, 90, 109
population growth/expansion, UK
    97–8
porpoises 159, 162
predators, animal 106, 107, 113, 157
Private Life of Gannets documentary
    211–12

Procellariiformes 11–12, 150, 154, 182–3, 200, 222
   see also albatrosses; petrels; shearwaters
puffins ('Tammie Nories') 35, 53, 59–62, 69–71, 80, 83, 224

R
rabbits, Skokholm 212–14
Ramsey Island, Pembrokeshire 158, 165–6
Rankin, Niall 52
Ratcliffe, Derek 74
ravens 205
Ray, John 65, 88
razorbills 59, 64–5, 67–8, 69, 80, 224
red-billed tropicbirds 185–6
red-necked phalaropes 239
Redfern, Dr Chris 115
redshanks 9
redstarts 118
Reginald of Durham 93, 95
reverse migration 183–4
ringed plovers 105, 240
ringing, bird 14, 22, 29–30, 33, 113, 168, 172, 233–4
Robb, Magnus 190
Rochman, Chelsea 76–7
rooks 117
roseate terns 104, 119–21, 124
Ross, Admiral John 137, 138
Ross, James Clark 138–9
Ross's gulls 138–9
Royal Society for the Protection of Birds (RSPB) 25–6, 117, 119, 169, 208, 221, 228

S
Sabine, Edward 137
Sabine, Joseph 137–8

Sabine's gulls 137
sanderlings 244
sandwich terns 103–5, 121–3, 220
Scopoli's shearwaters 183
scoters 152
Scottish SPCA 208
Sea Skua missiles 52
seabird 'cities' 72
seabird harvesting/hunting 78–9, 89–90, 93–4, 207–8
'The Seafarer' poem 198–9, 229
seagulls *see* gulls
Seahouses, Northumberland 61–2
seals 41
Second World War 51–2, 116–17
Seebohm, Henry 109–10
shags 64, 201
shearwaters 11, 25, 27, 60, 149–50, 153–76, 182–3, 185, 222, 254
sheep dyke, North Ronaldsay 235–6, 240
sheep, North Ronaldsay 235–6, 244–5
Shetland Islands 17–23, 31–2, 35–6, 37–8, 41–8, 49–51, 53–8, 59–60, 65, 87, 94
Skokholm, Pembrokeshire 23, 27–8, 96–7, 116–17, 135–6, 161–2, 165–6, 169–70, 171–4, 212–15
Skomer Island, Pembrokeshire 149–54, 157–67, 170–1, 174–6
skuas 12, 33, 37–43, 46, 48–51, 52–3, 56–8, 193
Skúvoy, Faroe Islands 40
snipes 7, 56
snow petrels 223
Sole 184, 186

'The Song of the Stormy Petrel'
    (M. Gorky) 30–1
sooty shearwaters 11, 156–7
south polar skuas 193–4
spectacled eiders 86
spotted flycatcher 26
St Cuthbert 92–3, 94–5, 102
St Cuthbert's Island,
    Northumberland 90–1, 92,
    95
St Davids, Pembrokeshire 159
St Kilda, Outer Hebrides 226, 229,
    230
St Ninian's Isle, Shetland 47
Stack Skerry, Orkney Islands 206
Staple Island, Northumberland 62,
    63–6, 68–72, 84
Steller's eiders 86
storm petrels 11, 18–19, 27–36,
    154, 188–90, 206
Stout, Margaret B. 88
Sula Sgeir 206–8
Sule Skerry, Orkney Islands 206
Sumburgh Head, Mainland
    Shetland 59, 60
Swinhoe, Robert 188
Swinhoe's storm petrel 188–90

T
Temminck, Coenraad Jacob 32
Tennyson, Lord 115
terns 11, 12, 42, 43, 44, 61, 62, 83,
    101–16, 118–24, 220, 240
Tesson, Sylvain 92–3
thanatophobia 241
Thoreau, Henry David 135
Tristan da Cunha 156, 157
tropicbirds 185–7
tubenoses 12, 153–4, 182–3
twites 204

U
Unst, Shetland Island 53–8, 243

V
Vikings 55, 93, 94, 99
Votier, Stephen 215–16
vomiting defence, fulmar 233–4

W
Wallace, Charles Harrison 199
warblers 2, 3, 25, 165, 194–5
Watching Birds (J. Fisher) 117–18
webcams 120–1
Westmann Islands, Iceland 238
Westray, Orkney Islands 199–200,
    203–6, 208–10, 215,
    219–20
'Westray Wife', Bronze Age artefact
    219–20
wheatears 56
white egret 246
White, Gilbert 88, 145–6
white-tailed eagles 50–1
whitethroats 165
Williamson, Emily 25–6
Williamson, Kenneth 60, 155
willow warblers 165
wind turbines 114, 116, 122–3
Wisdom (Laysan albatross) 74–5
woodcocks 5
wrens 47, 161
wrynecks 5

Y
Yarrell, William 66, 77–8
yellow-nosed albatrosses 181–2

Z
Zino, Paul 190
Zino's petrel 190–1